A BEGINNER'S GUIDE
TO SAVING AND INVESTING

A BEGINNER'S GUIDE TO SAVING AND INVESTING

10 STEPS TO FINANCIAL SUCCESS

W. Patrick Naylor

edition q, inc.
Chicago, Berlin, Tokyo, and Moscow

© 1994 W. Patrick Naylor

Published by edition q, inc.
551 N. Kimberly Dr.
Carol Steam, IL 60188

Library of Congress Cataloging-In-Publication Data

Naylor, W. Patrick.
  A beginner's guide to saving and investing: 10 steps to financial success / W. Patrick Naylor.
     p. cm.
  Includes bibliographical references and index.
  ISBN 1-883695-04-X
  1. Finance, Personal. 2. Investments. 3. Saving and thrift.
  I. Title.
  HG179.N385 1994
  332.024—dc20   94-6692
                                                            CIP

Manufactured in the United States of America

CONTENTS

To my wife Pennie for her love,
encouragement and hours of research.

PREFACE

Are you unhappy with the low rate of return on your bank passbook savings account and certificates of deposit? Are you overwhelmed by the complexity of the financial world but feel inadequate to do anything about it? Do you lack a financial direction or plan for yourself or your family? If you answered yes to any one of these three questions, then *A Beginner's Guide to Saving and Investing: 10 Steps to Financial Success* can help you develop a better understanding of the investment opportunities that are available just for the asking. These services are either free or involve a nominal charge, at best. And you don't need to pay a financial advisor or stockbroker to set up your financial program. You can do it entirely by yourself and without much difficulty.

For example, did you know that you can buy some of America's leading mutual funds for just $25 per month and have the large, lump-sum initial investment waived? And are you aware you can purchase high quality, dividend-paying "Blue Chip" stocks for as little as $10 or $25 a month? Such investment programs exist, and they are not gimmicks or scams. Far from it, they were created especially to attract *your* investment dollars. Unfortunately most people are not aware these opportunities are even available, let alone how to take advantage of them. Yet the globalization of world financial markets allows Americans to invest domestically and overseas while affording foreign investors equal opportunities to purchase shares in U.S. mutual funds and stocks.

The 10 steps in this investment strategy have something to offer most everyone from the beginner to the more seasoned investor. With the 10-step strategy you'll learn about establishing a budget, organizing and automating your banking, creating an emergency fund and setting financial goals. Then you'll see how a 3-tiered investment strategy based on mutual funds, dividend reinvestment programs and individual growth stocks gives diversification to your investment portfolio.

More importantly, the investment strategy is one that you mold to *your* income level, financial goals and risk tolerance. And you'll see it is one you can actually manage on your own. In fact, once you've read all 10 steps, you'll probably be surprised how easy it is to get started.

Note: Many of the examples used in this book are based on personal knowledge. As a matter of ethics, I have highlighted in **bold** typeface any investment in which I retain a financial interest. These investments are not to be taken as specific recommendations and are cited for purposes of illustration only.

I would like to extend a special thanks to Mr. Mark Dirlam, Indianapolis, Indiana, for his assistance in preparing the illustrations.

Get Started *Today!*

If a book such as this were published several years ago, it would have been appropriate to consider it better suited to U.S. citizens and the American financial markets. But times have changed. The passage of the North American Free Trade Agreement (NAFTA) in 1993 signaled yet another step toward global economic cooperation and growth. While U.S. investors seek new opportunities in Canada, Mexico and around the world, NAFTA signaled to Canadian and Mexican investors that they may want to look for equally attractive financial opportunities just over the border. In fact, they may even wish to invest their money in U.S. mutual funds and stocks. So understanding money management and investing is not something unique to Americans. Quite the contrary; the desire to attain financial security is one that crosses national boundaries. Simply bear in mind that the examples and discussions in this book will focus on the American scene, but hopefully readers outside the U.S. will learn just as much as their American counterparts.

Regardless of your national origin, if you're like most people, you want to start a savings and investing program, but simply don't know where to begin. You read the newspaper, watch television and realize the financial world of stocks, bonds and mutual funds is not only complex but highly technical. Just to communicate intelligently with stockbrokers and financial planners you have to use an entirely new language.

So, the idea of learning to make investment decisions for yourself may appear intimidating initially. You'll soon see, however, that with an understanding of sound money management and investing, you too can set financial goals and create a strategy to meet those goals. Armed with this new-found knowledge, you can then implement your strategy by selecting investments that are appropriate for you and by learning the best ways to put money aside on a regular basis. As those assets grow, you can then see tangible results of your efforts, which will motivate you to continue investing. But you have to take that first step. You've got to get started and you might as well begin today.

HERE'S AN INCENTIVE TO GET YOU MOTIVATED

We all have our own reasons for wanting to save money. It may be a desire to purchase a home, to pay for a child's college education or, more long range, to create a nest egg for retirement. If you think social security and your company's pension (if you have one) will meet those needs in your twilight years, you are most mistaken. In 1993, Financial Accounting Standard 106 went into effect, forcing employers to subtract from profits the cost of providing future health benefits to retirees. Prior to this 1993 change, employers deducted only those costs actually paid. The impact of this requirement could be perceived as a reduction in company profits (on paper at least), which would, in turn, influence the way in which potential investors view corporations and the value of their stock. As a counter measure, more and more companies have begun searching for means to restore profitability and one obvious approach is to reduce retiree benefits.

Such benefit reductions would require retirees to divert more of their fixed income to pay for the health care expenses previously provided by their former employer's retirement program. As these costs continue to rise, the portion of one's retirement income devoted to health care is certain to increase as well. This shift in responsibility from employer to employee will require retirees to set aside more retirement dollars for these expenses than were previously planned. Individuals still working must recognize the need to plan for this eventuality *before* reaching retirement.

The situation is compounded by the fact that consideration is also being given to raising the Medicare eligibility age from 65 to 67.[1] Should that change go into effect, everyone would have to work two years longer than anticipated or retire as planned at age 65 and use savings to cover the years until Medicare coverage begins.

YOUR PENSION PLAN MAY NOT PAY OFF

Nationally syndicated personal finance writer Jane Bryant Quinn once wrote that "a good deal of personal retirement money is invested poorly."[2] Ms. Quinn went on to add that individual investors left to make financial decisions on their own tend to be too cautious. An estimated 60% of money placed in 401(k) retirement accounts is either invested in slow-growth bonds or fixed-payment guaranteed investment contracts (GICs).[2] When comparing long-term growth performance, investing in stocks provided a return of 7% above inflation compared to 1.6% for bonds. As a result, the pension plans of such conservative investors may not blossom into hundreds of thousands of dollars 10 or 20 years from now because of some poor decisions made today.

Why is this cautious approach to saving and investing taken by so many people? It might very well be that most workers simply do not understand *how* to invest their money wisely. They know their money is safe buying certificates of deposit and keeping cash in government-insured bank accounts. They simply aren't aware of other suitable alternative investments. In other words, there's an "information gap" between the services they actually use and the full range of investment options that are available to them. Bridging that information gap is no simple task.

And How Safe Is That Pension, Anyway?

If you want to learn first hand about the safety of a pension, find a former employee of Pan American World Airways. According to a *Wall Street Journal* report, some workers who retired from Pan Am saw their entitlements nearly cut in half as a result of the company going bankrupt.[3] And those cuts were not made by Pan Am, per se, but by the federal Pension Benefit Guaranty Corporation (PBGC) which was obliged to oversee the operation of the plan. One retiree who believed he would receive more than $1,000 a month from his pension saw that actual payout drop to $595 under PBGC's management. That's a hard dose of reality for anyone who did not have personal investments to supplement a retirement program. For the poor individual mentioned in the story, the difference between what he thought he would receive and what he was actually paid meant he couldn't meet expenses. So he went back to work at less than one-half his former salary.[3]

Only 85% of PBGC-insured pension plans are fully funded, and those are set at a maximum guaranteed payout of $29,250 per year.[3] A subsequent *Wall Street Journal* article reported that the results of a Congressional Budget Office (CBO) study of the Pension Benefit Guaranty Corporation suggested not attempting to raise employer premiums to make up for underfunding of pensions and mounting losses.[4] Instead, the CBO report advised going right to taxpayers to find the money needed to rescue failing pensions. Now that's reassuring.

Fortunately, the news is not all gloomy, and most retirement funds are protected. But the fact remains that workers must recognize the need to protect themselves against this possibility or face the consequence that befell that former Pan Am worker. The best protection is creating your own personal savings and investment program separate from your employer's retirement plan.

AMERICANS ARE POOR SAVERS

Unfortunately, Americans are not good savers. It's one thing to put a little money aside and not get the best return on your investment because you're not a financial expert. You're saving money, and at least you're heading in the right direction. But as a nation, Americans don't do a good job when it comes to saving money. In his Street Talk column in *USA Today*, columnist Daniel Kadlec discussed the results of a Princeton University study commissioned by the Merrill Lynch brokerage firm.[5] The study found that baby boomers are only putting away 34% of the money they should to support themselves in retirement at age 65. Looking at it from the other end, that means they're short by a whopping 66%. According to Mr. Kadlec, the baby boomers are not alone. It seems the savings rate for the U.S. as a whole is less than 5% compared to 20% for the average Japanese and an unbelievable 42% for the citizens of Singapore.

SO HOW IS *YOUR* CASH INVESTED?

Perhaps you already recognized the need to put money away for the future to supplement your company's pension. But do yourself a favor and take a second look at the health of that retirement plan. First, find out how your money is doing in that plan. Do you have investment options? If you do, are you using the best ones and getting the most from them? Second, are you also setting aside some of your money in other investments? If you are, good. But do you think you've got matters well in hand because your "savings" consists of a passbook saving account, plus a few CDs and maybe even some Series EE U.S. Savings Bonds? Yes, your money is safe and producing a small amount of income but with fixed rates of return there is no growth potential in any of these assets. In order to simply keep your "head above water" financially, you will have to create a financial strategy and begin a savings and investment program to maximize the *growth* potential of your investments.

How about a reality check right now? There was a part of the story on the Princeton study that I didn't mention. The report not only looked at the savings rate of baby boomers but also indicated how much cash individuals should have saved by now. In other words, folks who plan to retire at age 65 and wish to maintain their present standard of living should already have some money invested toward retirement. The exact amount of money socked away is based on factors such as income, age and gender.[5] You had better sit down before you read these numbers.

COUPLES

The future looks brightest for couples, at least in this survey. Apparently a couple with a combined income of $30,000 only needs to have $600 in the bank at age 35. If they are age 45, then their savings should amount to $15,000. Couples age 55 must have at least $52,000 accumulated, but if they are 65 years old, then those savings should total $88,000.

Couples with an income of $50,000 should have $9,600 amassed if they're age 35, $33,000 if they're 45, $94,000 if they're 55, and if they are age 65 they are expected to have $183,000 in their combined accounts.

The very fortunate who together make $100,000 a year are advised to have $36,000 in savings by the time they are 35 years old. Couples presently age 45 should have $118,000 set aside, $288,000 for folks who are now 55, and those already age 65 are expected to have amassed $521,000 in savings. The rules are you can't include the house, the car or any expected inheritance as part of the $521,000.

SINGLE MEN

If you're a single male, age 35 and making $30,000 a year, you get away easy. You only need to have $3,000 in the bank. If you make that same amount of money but are 45 years old, your savings should be no less than $27,000. Those of you who are 55 or 65 should have $65,000 and $96,000 in the bank, respectively.

Men making $50,000 are supposed to have a lot more cash as well: age 35 ($6,000), age 45 ($36,000), age 55 ($96,000) and age 65 ($172,000).

High flyers who reach the $100,000 salary level are expected to have stashed away $29,000 if they're age 35, $129,000 if they're 45, $299,000 for those 55, and a cool $511,000 for single men already age 65.

SINGLE WOMEN

The financial forecast hits single women harder than either couples or their single male counterparts for at least two reasons. First, historically women's income does not grow as fast as that of men. And second, women live longer than men, so they'll need more money to support that longevity. The numbers make this information all the more sobering. A single woman making $30,000 a year is expected to have a savings of $26,000 if she's 35, $51,000 if she's age 45, $82,000 if she is 55 years old and $108,000 in the bank if she is already 65 years of age. Even at age 35 the difference in the amount of savings between single women ($26,000) and single men ($3,000) is striking.

Women making a salary of $50,000 per year are expected to do a whole lot better than men at the same age. Those now age 35 should have $36,000 in the bank, with $73,000 for women who are 45 and $127,000 for single women age 55. Women who are 65 and choose to retire are expected to have current savings of $190,000. Looking at the comparison in the 35-year-old bracket again, women need far more of a savings ($36,000) than their male contemporaries ($6,000) at this particular income level.

Those single women who command an income of $100,000 a year should have put aside $90,000 if they are age 35, at least $203,000 if they are 45, $361,000 for those already 55 years old and a whopping $539,000 if they have reached the age of 65. Again, the gap between the 35-year-old single man ($29,000) at this level and a comparable single female ($90,000) is huge.

Actually, that was the *good* news. The bad news is that these figures assume that you are *covered by a pension plan* at work and you are also making contributions to that plan. If your employer doesn't offer a retirement program, the numbers are strikingly different. Take the couple age 35 who make $50,000 a year. Their current savings should be $9,000, but only if they participate in a retirement program. Without a pension, those folks should have saved not $9,000, but $20,000 as of right now. And the couple who are 45 and make $50,000 a year may need $33,000 (if covered by a pension), but twice that amount, or $64,000, if they are not enrolled in a retirement program. Instead of socking away 5% of their income, they'd have to start saving 10% each and every year from now on.[5]

These figures represent guidelines against which you can compare your present savings with the salaries and age criteria for these data. But if the other part of the study is indeed correct, there are millions of baby boomers with only about one third (34%) of the money they should have in their savings.[5] If you haven't attained these levels of savings, you probably have a lot of company.

TAKING THAT FIRST STEP

More importantly, if you don't know how or where to begin a savings and investing program, then the investment strategy presented in the following steps can help you get started. The fact that you are reading this book is, in itself, a *first step*. Now all you have to do is make the commitment to familiarize yourself with each of the remaining nine steps. Once you've done that, you'll be in a better position to select a course of action to implement the strategy you will create for yourself.

DON'T DELAY YOUR DECISION TO START SAVING AND INVESTING

Time is one of the most important factors in investing. For example, if you have $500 that you would like to invest, but you know you will need the money in six months, that leaves little time for that $500 to grow. So you would be better off selecting an investment that will protect your principal (the $500) yet produce a respectable income. Because the $500 will be needed in the near future, safety is of the utmost importance. On the other hand, if that same $500 could be invested for five or more years, then time is no longer a *liability* but an *asset*. This money can be used to purchase any number of mutual funds or stocks in well-known companies and increase in value. In fact, the greater the length of time you have to invest those dollars, the more investment options are available to you.

Let's use some more examples. This one comes from Peter Lynch's book *One Up on Wall Street*.[6] Mr. Lynch, the former manager of Fidelity's Magellan Fund, is well known within financial circles for his skill in selecting stocks and managing a large portfolio. In fact, during the 12-year period he ran Magellan (he retired in 1990), Mr. Lynch was able to generate an *average* annual return of 28%. Compare that yield to your bank certificates of deposit! In his book, Mr. Lynch gives a wonderful illustration of how money grows or doesn't grow over time. To make his point, he compares the performance of a $1,000 investment made in 1927 over a 60-year period using four different financial strategies. In other words, the $1,000 was put away in 1927 and left untouched until 1987. The four investments selected were U.S. treasury bills, government bonds, corporate bonds and common stocks. Guess which choice was the best and which the worst?

If you thought U.S. treasury bills were the winner, you lost and you lost big. As it turns out, common stocks outperformed the remaining three investments and by a large margin. According to Mr. Lynch's figures, that $1,000 would have grown to only $7,400 if simply put into treasury bills, $13,200 if government bonds were purchased and $17,600 if that same $1,000 had been invested entirely in corporate bonds. But $1,000 worth of common stocks bought in 1927 would have grown to a staggering $272,000 by 1987. Granted, $1,000 was indeed a great deal of money back in 1927, but over a long period of time (60 years in this case) that same amount of money performed so differently in the four types of investments.

If you're thinking you're not a financial wizard like Peter Lynch, and that is a reasonable response, you should hear what Mr. Lynch says about the skill one needs to select stocks. In the introduction to his book, he goes on record to say "Twenty years in this business convinces me that any normal person using the customary three percent of the brain can pick stocks just as well, if not better, than the average Wall Street expert."[6] Investors who have followed Mr. Lynch since his retirement know he has repeated that view on more than one occasion. If we can believe Mr. Lynch when he makes statements like this, and there is no reason not to, then stock picking is something the average investor can certainly consider including in a personal investment strategy. You may not see returns the likes of $272,000 simply because not everyone, including this author, has 60 years left on this planet. That's an exceptionally long period over which to watch any investment grow. But we should at least start to develop confidence knowing that potential exists, even for the small investor.

Another obvious lesson is that the sooner you begin investing the better. If you're fortunate enough to have money left over each month after meeting all your financial obligations, you are in a position to make investments, if you haven't already done so. Just where do you put your cash so it is safe and has an opportunity to grow? Bank passbook savings accounts and competitive money market accounts have been paying only single digit returns. Despite the relative safety of this cash, how can these dollars keep pace with inflation (3.1%)? Where's the growth potential to meet your financial needs in 5, 10 or 20 years? Let's assume your average annual return is 5% per year. Even if that 5% yield remains ahead of inflation, there are still state and federal taxes to pay with the remaining 1.9% (5% minus 3.1%). Yes, you have some savings, but what is left for growth? The answer is *virtually nothing*. For those of you approaching retirement, there is no way a nest egg maintained in a passbook savings account will keep pace with the rising cost of living, exceed your tax liabilities and generate an income to maintain a secure lifestyle. As inflation and taxes erode your principal, your standard of living is apt to be affected adversely. If you are young and only now venturing into the world of investing, then time is your ally. But you need to think and act smart as well as find ways to take advantage of those years of potential growth you have ahead of you.

Even if you have no appreciable cash in the bank, only the prospect of a steady income and a few dollars left over every month, you still have something to invest. Did you know you can develop an investment strategy with as little as $25 a month going into a mutual fund and $10 a month to purchase stocks? We'll get into the actual mechanics of buying mutual funds and stocks later in the book, but suffice it to say that *you do not need a lot of money to get started.* What you do need is the motivation and a plan, a financial strategy, if you will.

DON'T THINK YOU CAN'T AFFORD TO BEGIN INVESTING NOW

It is important that you not let the present state of the economy or the fact that you have bills to pay deter you from planning for your future. You have rent due, a car payment to make or perhaps a school loan to repay. Each of these obligations exerts a certain amount of pressure on your monthly budget. Maybe you feel there is no way you can escape the burden of these bills, let alone think about investing, right now.

Just remember that everybody has bills to pay. The challenge is to put balance in your life and direct your money so it works to your benefit.

Today's rent will probably become tomorrow's mortgage, car payments do eventually end if you opt to hold on to your car rather than trade it in every three or four years and school loans don't go on forever. They may seem to, but they don't.

If you are single, you may be looking forward to marriage and children. In other words, your life changes with a normal progression in time. Those changes are often accompanied by new financial demands that must be balanced with existing ones. In all likelihood, you will never free yourself entirely of all financial obligations (unless you win the lottery or inherit a fortune), so you'll eventually have to address the need for a financial plan and investment strategy. The longer the delay in beginning a savings and investment program, the fewer years there are for growth of those invested dollars. Remember, it is the long-term investor who reaps the greatest financial rewards and maximum gains.

What if You Don't Know Anything About Financial Matters?

Don't feel as though you are alone in the belief that the world of high finance can be complex and intimidating. There is nothing wrong with admitting that beyond putting money in the local bank or savings and loan you know absolutely nothing about other financial matters, particularly investing. Perhaps you've heard of mutual funds and know people can buy stock in many different companies, but you're not familiar with the processes involved in undertaking such transactions. After all, you've been focusing all your energy on *making* money, leaving you little time to understanding how to *invest* money. That's perfectly okay and one of the principal reasons this book was written.

However, it's also important for you to have another perspective on managing your money, one which you may not have thought of before. Let's assume you have a good job, and after meeting all your financial obligations each month you have money remaining that could be placed

$ 10,00,000 = million dollars

in a long-term investment for retirement. If you are young, prudent in your savings efforts and place the money in a good growth-oriented investment, you could amass a large sum of cash by the time retirement actually rolls around. Remember that earlier example from Peter Lynch! For the sake of illustration, let's say you're looking at amassing $500,000 by the time you retire at age 65. Say you attain that goal, so at age 65 your assets amount to half a million dollars. The logical question to ask is who will manage that $500,000 portfolio? We'll define "manage" as making the decisions on where and when to invest the principal (assets) you accumulated to ensure there's enough income to meet your expenses once you've quit working. In retirement you will have at least three, and possibly four, objectives:

1. To have enough current income to meet expenses.

2. To preserve your assets so you don't lose money you can't readily replace.

3. To have your holdings grow to support you in those latter years of retirement. If you don't know how to manage money yourself, then you'll have to pay someone to make those financial decisions for you. In that case, add a fourth objective:

4. To make enough money to pay the costs of a financial advisor.

Managing other people's money is big business. Literally thousands of individuals make a living providing advice and managing assets that belong to so-called "average investors." You can obtain the services of a financial planner, stockbroker or have a mutual fund manager to make those daily decisions so your assets increase in value faster than inflation and your taxes. But remember, those folks don't work for free. Like you, they have families and financial goals of their own, and naturally they expect to be paid for their services.

So unless you take an interest and active role in the management and decision making of how your money is invested, you can expect to direct some of those resources to pay for financial advice. Obviously, the more active you become in managing those assets, the lower the costs and the more of your own money can work for you. Don't misunderstand. The expenses incurred to secure the services of a stockbroker and a financial planner generally are well worth the money. Looked at this way, if all investment decisions are made *for* you rather than *by* you, the cost of managing your assets will be higher than if you played a more active role and implemented your own strategy.

Take heart. For those of you who don't have a burning desire to be a financial guru and don't like the idea of giving away any more of your hard-earned money than you have to, you can find salvation in no-load mutual funds (Step 7). For the stouthearted, Steps 8 and 9 offer more adventuresome approaches. But before going into these details, you need to examine your personal finances and get these matters in order.

In Review

1. Make the decision to learn more about saving and investing today.
2. You will always have financial obligations and debt to manage, so your investment strategy must take this into consideration.
3. Don't rely exclusively on your employer's retirement program to support you after you've stopped working.
4. Americans typically are poor savers, putting away only 34% of what they'll need to have by retirement. So try to beat the averages and save as much as you can.
5. Couples appear to need less savings than single men or women of comparable age.
6. Single women will need to save far more money than their male counterparts.
7. If *you* don't make the decisions on where to invest your money, you are going to have to pay someone to make them for you.

8. The greater your knowledge of saving and investing, the more you will become an active participant in your financial success.

WHAT'S NEXT?

It's important to remember that success in any venture, be it your career or your financial future, is attainable if you work hard and have realistic expectations or goals. Congratulations! You've just completed Step 1, now turn to **Step 2: Establish a Budget.**

NOTES

1. AP wire story. "Report: Medicare Needs Aid." *Dayton Daily News,* 10 January 1993: 12A.

2. Quinn, Jane Bryant. "Get Smart: It's Your Money." Smart Investor, *Dayton Daily News,* 28 December 1992.

3. Karr, Albert R. "Imperiled Promises: Risk to Retirees Rises as Firms Fail to Fund Pension They Offer." *The Wall Street Journal,* 4 February 1993: A1.

4. Karr, Albert R. "Report Says Taxpayers May Pay Price of Bailing Out Federal Pension Insurer." *The Wall Street Journal,* 5 February 1993: A5.

5. Kadlec, Daniel. Street Talk, "Baby Boomers Are a Bust on Saving." *USA Today,* 28 January 1993: 3B

6. Lynch, Peter with John Rothchild. *One Up on Wall Street.* New York: Simon and Schuster, 1989.

ESTABLISH A BUDGET

Once you've made the commitment to develop a financial strategy, the next step is to determine how much of your income can be set aside for investing each month. You cannot arbitrarily decide to invest any amount of money until you are sure you can pay your current and future bills. Those obligations must be met month in and month out. The portion of your income left over after the bills are paid is what you want to identify. Those are the funds you can consider investing.

The cash accumulating in the bank represents only the *past* performance of your money management. By establishing a budget, you are taking a major step to identify untapped resources that can be directed to new investments. In other words, no matter how much cash you've put away in the past or what savings techniques you've used, those arrangements can probably be improved to enhance your money's *future* performance.

WHY DO YOU NEED A BUDGET?

Before even thinking about which specific types of investment opportunities suit your needs and desires, first determine how much money you actually have available to invest. Then and only then can you structure a framework to implement a financial strategy.

The best place to begin is with a monthly budget. Simply write down every expenditure you make each month for a period of two to three months. If your spending habits are relatively simple and few in number, then a two-month period can represent typical monthly spending levels. Should you prefer to maintain a more dynamic lifestyle, it may be better to extend the monitoring period to as many as four months, particularly if you have an active social life and travel a great deal. The bottom line is that at the end of this exercise you should be able to accurately predict how much you spend each and every month (your expenditures). That's it, pure and simple. You'll know what portion of your income actually leaves the household and how much remains with you.

The difference between your income and expenditures, and hopefully, there will be a positive difference, we will call your disposable income. I prefer the designation "disposable income" and consider it an accurate description because any money remaining after all bills have been paid is left at your "disposal." In other words, it can be spent as you see fit without impairing your ability to meet your financial responsibilities. But first, you'll need to know how to establish a budget before determining the amount of that "disposable income."

How to Establish a Budget

To start things off, obtain a notebook to record all monthly expenditures for the two- to three-month trial period (four months if you think it necessary). Couples may find it helpful to set aside a time each evening to review the day's activities and update the expenditures in the notebook. If you're single, keep the notebook in your briefcase or carry it on your person. Then simply record your spending as it occurs rather than waiting and having to jar your memory at the end of the day.

Proposed items for a monthly budget.					
Expenses	**Estimated**	**Actual**	**Expenses**	**Estimated**	**Actual**
Auto loan	_____	_____	Insurance		
Auto maintenance (routine)	_____	_____	Automobile	_____	_____
			Disability	_____	_____
Auto repairs	_____	_____	Health (medical and dental)	_____	_____
Babysitter	_____	_____			
Cable television	_____	_____	Life	_____	_____
Charitable donations	_____	_____	Renters/Homeowners	_____	_____
Church	_____	_____	Medical expenses	_____	_____
Other	_____	_____	Mortgage	_____	_____
Child care	_____	_____	Home maintenance	_____	_____
Clothes	_____	_____	Home improvements	_____	_____
Credit card payments	_____	_____	Other (you specify)	_____	_____
Daycare	_____	_____	Professional dues	_____	_____
Entertainment	_____	_____	Rent	_____	_____
Food	_____	_____	Subscriptions		
Groceries, including nonfood items	_____	_____	Newspapers	_____	_____
Dining out, including workdays	_____	_____	Magazines	_____	_____
			Other	_____	_____
Gasoline	_____	_____	Telephone	_____	_____
Hobbies	_____	_____	Travel	_____	_____
Holiday gifts (religious, birthdays, etc.)	_____	_____	Utilities		
			Gas	_____	_____
Home or office miscellaneous items	_____	_____	Electric	_____	_____
			Water/sewer	_____	_____
			Sanitation	_____	_____
			Veterinary bills	_____	_____

Your master budget should list all fixed and variable expenses and be flexible enough to include a monthly estimate of irregular or annual lump sum expenditures. These last two categories would include such items as: vacations, holiday gifts, travel and spending, estimated income taxes, veterinary bills, individual retirement account (IRA) payments, annual dues to organizations, auto registration renewals, summer camp for the kids, hobby-related expenditures (new golf clubs, camper maintenance, etc.) and so on.

AVERAGE YOUR BUDGET

If you recorded every expenditure for the month and considered the estimated expenses, you can pretty well get an idea of where money goes. Next, calculate the average of these monthly totals. Hopefully the amount of money going out is less than your income. If not, then this is not the only book you need to read. You should find a publication that deals with living within your means. But that's another story.

Let's assume you are fortunate enough to have more money coming in than going out. We would all like for that difference to be hundreds or thousands of dollars, but that is not always possible. Besides, the strategy you'll learn in this book will work with $10, $25, $50, $100 as well as with thousands of dollars. Of course, it's a whole lot more fun when the numbers are $100, $500 and $1,000, but we have to be realistic. Not everyone has $1,000 to invest each and every month. More important, the strategy you will learn is not influenced by how *much* or how *little* money you have to invest. As a so-called individual or "average" investor, the approach is still the same, but obviously the more money there is to work with, the greater the number of choices. Remember the old saying, "money begets money."

DETERMINING YOUR DISPOSABLE INCOME

Let's assume we've already established that more money comes in each month (income) than goes out (expenditures). For the sake of realism, we'll say that the difference amounts to $200. That's $200 that can be put aside each and every month, or $2,400 annually. You can take that vacation to Hawaii, get that new muffler for your car, buy some nice Christmas presents for the family and still have an average of $200 left over at the end of the month. That $200 will be referred to as your *monthly* disposable income and the $2,400 is your *annual* disposable income.

If after two or three months of monitoring expenditures you are not pleased with the level of your disposable income, you should aim to make changes in your budget or try to increase your income. Let's assume you wanted to reach the $200 a month level but only managed to clear $100 on a regular basis. Obviously, you need to reassess spending habits first. A budget is a written history of expenditures that can be studied to determine where those dollars went and if cuts can be made to raise the level of disposable income. Do you spend too much on entertainment or food purchased on the job? If so, cut back in these less critical areas. Rent more videos and take a brown bag lunch to work. Perhaps you are too extravagant in your gift giving. Spend more time being creative rather than lavish. You'll be able to have the same effect, but at a reduced cost.

The decisions of where and how much to cut back are entirely *yours*. If you've already cut expenses to the bare bone and still can't reach the $200 a month target, then consider obtaining a part-time job if you are that determined. Otherwise, adjust the monthly target for your disposable income to a more realistic and obtainable goal. This exercise is not designed to put stress into your life; quite the contrary, it is simply intended to help you be more productive through improved organization.

Save Those Budget Records

With a written budget, you have precise records of actual levels of spending and saving. So keep those budgets on hand. Refer to them periodically and monitor your ability to spend within these estimates. If expenses increase, review your budget and decide where adjustments can be made without affecting either the amount of disposable income or your investment strategy.

IN REVIEW

1. You should know how to prepare a budget and determine your average monthly expenditures.

2. The positive difference between your average monthly expenditures and your monthly income(s) will be referred to as your **disposable income.**

3. Regardless of whether the amount of your disposable income is $100, $50, $25 or even $10 per month, you can still use this investment strategy.

4. One of the quickest ways to increase the amount of your disposable income is to adjust your budget (reduce your spending level in one or more less critical areas).

WHAT'S NEXT?

Now that you know how much money you have to invest each month (your disposable income), you may find it helpful to organize and automate your banking. How you keep track of your money need not be costly or complicated. In fact, as you will see, it can actually be made quite simple as explained in **Step 3: Organize and Automate Your Banking.**

ORGANIZE AND AUTOMATE YOUR BANKING

You might consider yourself a beginning investor, yet you probably have already started some type of savings plan. It may be that you met with an account representative at a local bank and opened a checking account, a savings account or both. For the sake of convenience, you may be allowing your cash to build up in these accounts, because you know the money is not only safe, but accessible. Or perhaps you were a little more aggressive in your money management and established a competitive, higher yielding money market account. Maybe you went as far as to put extra cash in a certificate of deposit for an even better return. Regardless of which types of accounts you own, you already have a business relationship with a financial institution. The larger question is, are you getting the most for your money in terms of yield and service? Chances are the answer to that question is a resounding *no*.

You may not know it, but there are services available through banks, savings and loans or credit unions that enable you to better organize and automate your banking. And these services generally are provided to customers at no charge.

Organize Your Banking

The easier you make the transfer and availability of money, and the simpler your investment strategy, the more likely you are to continue on a course of regular investing. But the automation process has to begin somewhere, and the foundation for that approach rests with a sound footing in your banking arrangements.

How to Handle Your Paycheck

One simple way to ensure your pay reaches the bank is to take advantage of *direct deposit* to an account in your name. Unfortunately, not all employers offer this service, but if yours does, sign up! With direct deposit, your pay is electronically moved each pay period to an account you specify and the service is generally *free*. No need to worry about drives to the bank, lost checks or late deposits. Rain or shine, night or day, that money finds its way into your account.

How Many and What Types of Bank Accounts Do You Need?

It's advisable to have at least two bank accounts. Consult the financial institutions in your area for details on the account services they offer. Ask what the prevailing interest rates are, how they calculate interest, what minimum balance is required and what charges, if any, pertain to each type of account. Don't be afraid to shop around and be a consumer. Ideally, you would like to establish two interest-bearing accounts that have no accompanying service charges in *federally insured* financial institutions.

Consider opening two, no-minimum or low-minimum *checking* accounts so you have check writing privileges and ready access to your cash. Put just enough money in each account initially to accrue interest and avoid service charges. When selecting checks, order a different color for each account to avoid possible confusion later on.

WHY THE NEED FOR TWO BANK ACCOUNTS?

Establishing two separate bank accounts will make it easier to track your monthly income and expenditures, both personal and financial. And it is important to keep the two activities as separate as possible so you don't create an administrative monster. If you think it's tough balancing your present checkbook, imagine what would happen if you tried to manage all your personal expenses and investments in a *single* account?

Designate one account for investments and the other for personal money management. For example, let's make the first checking account for investment use only and call that account 1. The second account, or account 2, can serve as your personal checking account. If you already have a personal checking account, then you can think of it as your checking account 2. And you can continue to pay your monthly bills with checks drawn from this account.

When the bank statements arrive for the two accounts, go through the checks and balance each one separately. You will soon find that the bookkeeping is straightforward because your investment transactions in account 1 are few and easy to identify. As a result, the monthly account statement can be reconciled literally in a matter of minutes. Account 2 is a regular personal checking account, and if you make accurate entries and do your addition and subtraction correctly, it too can be balanced without much difficulty.

While the two-checking account banking method may appear cumbersome at first glance, it will actually make your money management easier, particularly as your portfolio and investments grow in number. But now you're on your way to getting your banking *organized*. The next thing to do is *automate* your banking, and that's done principally through the use of automatic transfers to link the accounts.

WHAT'S AN AUTOMATIC TRANSFER?

One of the nice features of this type of banking arrangement is that you can move money between accounts electronically each month using what are called automatic transfers. An **automatic transfer** is simply an account to account movement of funds by wire. It is termed "automatic" because the conditions of the transfer (date and amount of money) have been prearranged by *you*, so the transaction occurs regularly without any subsequent action on your part. Instead of writing a check and having it mailed to your savings account or an investment account outside your bank (mutual fund or brokerage account), you arrange to have the money sent each month by wire on the day you specify. Like direct deposit services, there is no need to worry about lost checks or possible delays in mail distribution.

You can also move funds between accounts within the same institution (bank) or between institutions (bank to mutual fund or brokerage account). As the number of your investments increases you may find that you'll want to own several mutual funds as well as a brokerage account. To move money to these accounts might require three, five or ten automatic transfers. You will learn later that mutual funds not only encourage the use of automatic transfers, but they also make it easy for you to change the amount and day of the transfers when necessary. These changes, like the service itself, should be made free of charge. Can you begin to see how this service directly benefits you, the individual investor?

USE A CREDIT CARD FOR OVERDRAFT PROTECTION

If you are self employed or direct deposit is not available at your place of employment, ask your bank if you can obtain a bank credit card and use it for overdraft protection on your accounts. This protection is needed if you ever have a problem with a check clearing or being returned. The "overdraft protection" allows the automatic transfers to take place on schedule each and every month. If you have to use this service, you pay only a small fee for the use of any funds drawn on your credit card, but at least you have this protection should a problem arise.

Link Your Two Bank Accounts

Now that you know what the automatic transfers are, how do you take advantage of them? More importantly, how do you go about setting up these transfers, and what is the best way to do it? To answer these and other related questions, you have to organize your bank accounts so this automation works to your advantage.

Automatic Transfers Between Accounts

Let's assume you opted to open two checking accounts at your local bank. If you can arrange direct deposit, have your paycheck sent to account 1. If you do not have the direct deposit option, then simply plan on depositing your paychecks into account 1 each pay period. In Step 2 we chose to use the example of a disposable income of $200 per month. To continue with that example, let's further assume that you are paid every two weeks and your net pay each pay period is $800. Have the entire $800 deposited into account 1 through direct deposit on the 1st and 15th of each month, or the next business day if those dates fall on a weekend or holiday.

Next, call your bank and ask if they have a form to complete for automatic transfer requests. If they do not, write a letter of instruction in which you ask that $700 be transferred to account 2 *each* payday. If you don't have direct deposit services ask the bank to make the transfers to account 2 a day or two after payday, giving you time to deposit those paychecks. And be sure to ask the bank how soon after a deposit you can actually write a check. Use that date or one soon thereafter for any subsequent automatic transfers. If your pay varies from paycheck to paycheck, then instruct the bank to transfer a lesser amount of money that you are certain to receive every month. When your pay is above that minimum, ask the bank to transfer the added money to account 2 as well. Use common sense to work out what works best for you. But remember, your sal-

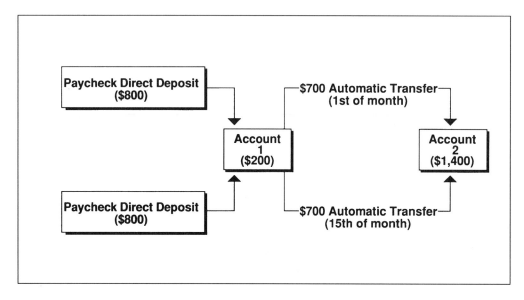

Paycheck Direct Deposit ($800)

$700 Automatic Transfer (1st of month)

Account 1 ($200)

Account 2 ($1,400)

Paycheck Direct Deposit ($800)

$700 Automatic Transfer (15th of month)

Have your pay directly deposited to account 1 and transfer most of your pay to account 2.

vation is that you can write checks from both account 1 or account 2, so your money is accessible regardless of which account it is in.

For the time being the number of transactions is limited to two $800 paychecks going into account 1 followed by two $700 automatic transfers to account 2. After you read Steps 6 and 7, you'll appreciate the value of separating investment checking from personal checking. Be sure to transfer enough money to account 2 to pay your rent/mortgage, make your car payment and pay all those other customary monthly bills. By sending a fixed amount of money to account 2 you are encouraged to live within your established budget.

In this example, $1,400 a month is going into account 2 each month with $200 remaining in account 1. If you don't need the entire $1,400 to cover your monthly expenses, you can keep a larger portion of your income in account 1, so that balance increases each month. Once you establish your accounts and determine how much money is to go where, the transfers will be made month after month, automatically. That's how this service got its name.

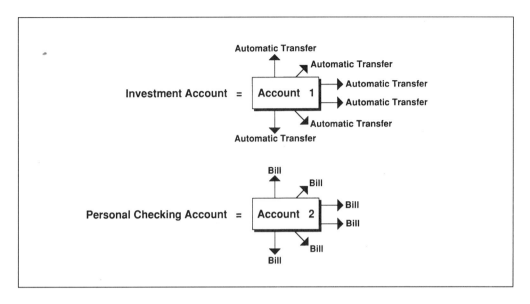

Arrange to have all automatic transfers come out of account 1, leaving account 2 to serve solely as your personal checking account to pay your monthly bills.

AUTOMATIC TRANSFERS TO INVESTMENT ACCOUNTS

You know what to do with the money in account 2, your personal checking account. That's right, you pay all those bills that come in every month. The next logical question is, "What do you do with the cash that's building up in account 1?"

At this point in time suffice it to say that eventually the money in account 1 will be automatically transferred to an investment account, and money can be drawn from that account by check to purchase other types of investments. After reading Steps 7, 8 and 9 this will make a lot more sense, I promise. But for now, you merely have to understand that how you use account 1 will depend to a large extent on the type of investment you select—mutual funds (Step 7), dividend reinvestment programs, (DRIPs, Step 8) or individual growth stocks (Step 9). You can use automatic transfers for these strategies with the exception of the vast majority of DRIP accounts, where you'll have to make payments by check.

Now Your Banking Is Organized and Automated

To see how far you've gone with this strategy, take a moment to look back and see where you've been. For starters, all you have to do is look at your present banking arrangements:

Organization

How have you arranged your bank account(s)? Are you paying service charges? Do your accounts have no- or low-minimum balances or at least pay some interest?

Automation

Have you linked your accounts using automatic transfers or do you have to go to the bank in person and move money from one account to another? If you opened a mutual fund account today do you know if you can have money withdrawn from your savings account? Or would you have to write a check from your checking account and mail that money to the mutual fund?

Hopefully it is now apparent how advantageous it is to have at least two bank accounts that require no- or low-minimum balance, don't have service charges and pay some interest on your account balance. You also understand that you can move money between accounts within your bank and from your accounts to certain types of investments (mutual funds and money market funds) that will be explained later.

If you already have a checking account for paying bills and your pay is deposited there automatically through direct deposit, do you have to change things? Of course not. Instead, keep checking account 1 as your personal account, but do open a second checking account for investments (account 2) and order different colored checks. Then have the bank make automatic transfers to that account each pay period.

These recommendations are intended to help you organize and automate your banking within the limits of the services offered in your community. Remember, the whole idea is to make your life easier, not more complex and difficult. So talk with your bank to arrange a plan that works best for you.

A NOTE TO FOREIGN INVESTORS

Foreign nationals residing in America can avail themselves of these same services. However, if you are a citizen of a country other than the United States and live outside the continental U.S., you too may want to use this model to organize and automate your banking. Check with your local financial institutions for details.

IN REVIEW

1. Establish two checking accounts; account 1 can be for your investments and account 2 should be for your personal expenses.

2. Sign up for direct deposit (if that service is available) and have your pay deposited into account 1.

3. Use automatic transfers to move money between accounts whenever possible.

4. Ask for credit card overdraft protection for your accounts.

5. Have most of your pay transferred to checking account 2, leaving enough money in account 1 to cover your investment needs (plus a little extra if you wish). You'll learn more about this process in Steps 6 and 7.

6. You will find the bank statements from account 1 easy to reconcile each month and account 2 will be no different from your present personal checking account.

WHAT'S NEXT?

Remember, although account 1 is reserved for investment use only, you still have check writing privileges so that money remains readily accessible in the event of an emergency. Speaking of emergencies, that's the subject of our next discussion. Turn to **Step 4: Create an Emergency Fund**.

S T E P **4**

CREATE AN EMERGENCY FUND

One of the most counterproductive situations to impact any investment strategy is an unexpected need for a large sum of money. It wasn't foreseen, but suddenly you find that the only resources you have to remedy your financial predicament are the investments you just started. This type of situation is simply the result of poor planning. Unless you have the good fortune to sell those holdings for a profit, you risk losing all or part of the principal you invested originally. In other words, you could lose money on the deal.

So how does an individual investor avoid the repercussions of sudden, unexpected drains on financial resources? One sure way to have a hedge against the unexpected is to create what is called an *emergency fund*. This is nothing more than an account where you stockpile cash and keep it at the ready for, you guessed it, *emergencies*.

WHERE'S THE BEST PLACE TO MAINTAIN THE EMERGENCY FUND?

For starters, you just opened two bank accounts, right? One account was for your investments and the other one was for your personal expenses.

Each account may require a minimum balance to avoid possible service charges or in order to accrue interest. But those same accounts certainly don't have a *maximum* balance. So your first option could be simply to keep pouring money into these two accounts until you reach the level of cash you want to keep on hand at all times. If you are more adventuresome, and don't feel you'd be overwhelmed by the added paperwork and bookkeeping, you could establish what is called a *money market account*. A bank money market account should not be confused with a *money market mutual fund*. There is a difference. Money market mutual funds will be discussed in more detail in Step 7, in case you're not already familiar with them. But suffice it to say that a money market *account* offered by a bank, credit union or savings and loan invests your cash in anything it wants to, but all the earnings are not passed on to account holders. Whereas a money market *fund* is a mutual fund that invests in actual money market instruments like short-term certificates of deposit, U.S. Treasury bills, commercial paper and so on. The money market fund actually owns these investments and passes on to you all of its earnings after deducting a management fee. The bank money market account may be insured while the money market fund may not be. But the short maturity of a money market fund's investments make it very liquid and probably as safe as most insured bank money market accounts.

If your cash needs are small, then your two checking accounts may be all you really require. What they lack in terms of a competitive interest rate, they may make up in sheer convenience and accessibility. If you feel compelled to keep a large sum of cash at the ready, you might want to seriously consider either a money market account or a money market fund. Either one will probably have a more competitive interest rate than a regular checking account. One word of warning, money market accounts and funds have restrictions that some people find too limiting, their *minimum* check size is often $250–$500. This means you may have to write any check for at least $500 even though you might only need $200. Such a restriction can actually be a good feature if you might be easily tempted to spend your emergency fund resources were they to remain in your two checking accounts. You also may want to separate your emergency fund from the other accounts just so you can get to this money readily. Do whatever you think will work best for you—after all, it's your money.

How Much Should You Keep in the Emergency Fund?

There are no hard and fast rules, just general guidelines to this question. Again this decision is largely up to you and based on your personal situation. According to some experts, you should maintain a minimum of two months of living expenses on hand at all times for the unexpected. Others suggest you have an emergency fund balance equal to at least six months of expenses readily accessible before you tie up your money in long-term investments. Readily accessible doesn't mean stuffing dollar bills in a mattress. No, we're talking about keeping this money in federally-insured checking accounts, higher yielding savings or money market accounts. All three accounts should yield slightly more than your mattress and be a bit safer as well.

Use the information collected from your budget data (Step 2) to arrive at the monthly expense figure to calculate the amount of your emergency fund. In determining whether to use two months, six months or a level in between the two, base your decision on some common sense factors. If you were recently hired by a company in an industry where firms come and go in the night, then you might want to use the six-months standard. The same would hold true if you manage your own business and although the future looks bright, you realize it holds uncertainty as well. In that case, go for the higher end of the scale (four to six months worth of savings) for your emergency fund. Also, it's best to hold back more cash when your family includes children or you have extended family members residing in your home (parents, grandparents, brothers, sisters, etc.). With these added family responsibilities, the likelihood is greater that financial emergencies will arise and you'll want to handle them without touching your investments.

You could be one of the fortunate ones to have an income that exceeds your monthly financial needs and job security is not an issue in your career field. In that case, just two months of expense money might be adequate for your emergency fund. This latter category is where you frequently find single workers or couples with dual incomes, no children and little debt. But remember, you can't use formulas or apply general rules and adequately cover everyone's needs. After all, people have different perceptions of their job security and just how much cash on hand is enough. Use common sense and make a decision you can sleep with. It is also important that you not go to bed worrying if you've put too much money in investments and not enough in your emergency fund.

Make Your Emergency Fund Your First Investment

If you decided that six months of expenses were what you needed to have on hand at all times, then your first investment will be establishing this emergency fund. That will probably be a considerable sum which might take you some time to amass. Don't worry about how long it takes to bring the emergency fund to your desired level. Consider it your *first* investment and you'll rest better knowing the money is there to help carry you through a crisis, if one arises.

Use an Automatic Transfer to Create Your Emergency Fund

Should you choose to hold back six months of expenses, you may decide to open a money market account (or money market fund). In that case, after the mandatory initial contribution to open the account (often $1,000 or more), you can have your monthly disposable income moved to the emergency fund each pay period ($200 per month using our previous example).

You can request automatic transfers at the time you complete the application for the money market account and attach a voided check from account 1. The automatic transfers should begin on the first pay period following receipt and processing of your application, with $100 sent to your money market account from checking account 1. The same transaction will take place two weeks later at your next pay period (or other day you have specified), and so on. Or you could simplify matters and have the entire $200 transferred at the end of the month.

If the amount of money you are having sent to your money market account is substantial, then using two automatic transfers makes more sense. You would want more of your savings to be in the higher yielding money market account than in your checking account. Once the transfers go into effect, the money moves between accounts automatically. You do not have to do anything but balance your statements each month, verifying that your pay went into account 1 and then was diverted to account 2 and your money market account (if you have one). This arrangement will remain in effect until you request a change.

When you near your goal for the emergency fund you can give your bank written instructions to terminate the automatic transfers to the money market account. Then allow the monthly disposable income to accumulate in account 1. If your next move is to open mutual fund

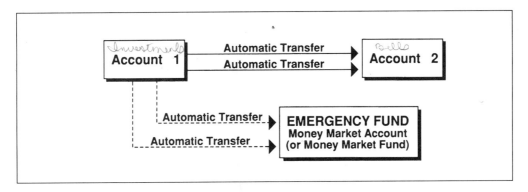

Automatic transfers can be used to build a bank money market account or mutual fund money market fund as your emergency fund.

accounts (as discussed in Steps 6 and 7), you'll use automatic transfers again. By the way, when you are transacting business it is best to give your instructions in writing. In the event a mistake occurs, you have written documentation as to what you requested, and it will make it easier to remedy any confusion.

If you do nothing more with the investment strategy outlined in this book than establish an emergency fund, you have accomplished something very important. You've created a financial safety net for yourself and your family, and that alone is a significant achievement.

In Review

1. Establish an emergency fund representing two to six months of expenses.

2. For convenience and ease of access, consider using the minimum balances in checking accounts 1 and 2 for small emergency funds (two months of expenses). For larger sums of money (six months of expenses), you may wish to open a money market account or money market fund.

3. If you do decide to establish a money market account (or money market fund) for your emergency fund, it would be in addition to checking accounts 1 and 2. Use automatic transfers from account 1 to move money to build this emergency fund.

4. Make the emergency fund your *first* investment.

What's Next?

You've got your banking organized and automated, you've established an emergency fund, so now it is time to start thinking about investing. But first, you should set some financial goals based on your monthly disposable income. Turn to **Step 5: Set Financial Goals**.

SET FINANCIAL GOALS

If you intended to visit Walt Disney World as part of your summer vacation, chances are you wouldn't undertake such an adventure without some advance planning. You would at least look ahead to the dates *you* wanted to visit and then arrange travel and hotel accommodations to suit *your* schedule. To make the journey by car, you would probably pull out your atlas and road maps, so you would wind up in Orlando, Florida, rather than Dallas, Texas. Then you would diligently lay out the route and begin the adventure armed with a destination (Walt Disney World), a set of instructions to get you there (your road maps) and perhaps a charted course (your daily driving goals). If the journey were too long and planning trips just wasn't your thing, you could always turn to professionals at the American Automobile Association (AAA) who do this kind of thing every day. In fact, the American Automobile Association is so up on what's going on, they'd even tell you where to stay if you needed to stop overnight en route and what areas to avoid because of road construction. In other words, the folks at AAA are trip-planning professionals who make their living providing this type of service.

When you move from the subject of a trip to Walt Disney World to a much longer journey, down the road to retirement, planning is equally as important, if not more so. You can make the arrangements yourself or call upon investment professionals for financial advice. Again, the choice is yours. Regardless of how you approach the tasks at hand, you have to decide where you're going and how you're going to get there. It's your vacation and your retirement, so the professional planners want to meet both your needs and expectations.

WHAT TO DO FIRST?

Financial planning should be looked upon as a road map or plan. To make certain the goals you have proposed are obtainable, you must have realistic expectations. You wouldn't leave California by car on Day 1 of your venture and expect to arrive in sunny Florida the next morning. That is neither safe nor realistic.

And the same logic should be applied when setting financial goals. In the previous budget example, the disposable income was estimated to be $200 per month or $2,400 a year after meeting all fixed and variable expenses (rent/mortgage, utilities, food, insurance payments, entertainment, miscellaneous expenditures, etc.). Obviously, when doing financial planning, don't expect to make $10,000 per year when investing $200 each month. It probably can be done, but such an outcome (making $10,000 a year by investing $2,400) is not realistic without an extremely high degree of speculation, risk and a great deal of sophistication. The deals where that outcome is possible are not intended for the average investor, so there is no sense in setting a goal like $10,000, because it is unrealistic and you are certain to be disappointed.

If our "average investor" sets aside $200 in January and each and every month thereafter, we can safely *predict* that by year's end the principal will be $2,400 ($200 × 12 months) not including any interest. The amount of money in excess of the principal invested ($2,400) will depend on the type of investment selected (bank savings account, money market account, U.S. saving bond, etc.). By sitting down and calculating how much you can save each month and establishing an objective for the amount of money to be accrued by the end of the year, you have actually set a financial *goal*.

REDEFINING SHORT-, INTERMEDIATE- AND LONG-TERM GOALS

When talking about an individual's financial planning, defining short term, intermediate term and long term may sound easy, but it is not. For example, a 25-year-old college student about to start her first job may think in terms of an income-producing career spanning 40 years with retirement at age 65. A 50-year-old auto worker could be eyeing his early retirement at age 55. While a 70-year-old retired schoolteacher living on a fixed income spends most of her time simply trying to maintain her present standard of living. To these three investors, short, intermediate and long term are relative, so each investor must set such goals in the perspective of his or her own personal situation. With this understanding, let's take a closer look at the various types of goals.

SHORT-TERM GOALS

There are no hard and fast rules that delineate the three levels of goals from one another. In fact, because financial needs, income levels and the number of years to save vary so widely with people of different ages, it is difficult to even define these levels of goals and have them apply to people of all ages and financial needs.

For the 25-year-old college graduate about to begin that first job, a five-year projection may be considered short-term given the potential to work for 40 or 50 years. Five years may represent the first major promotion opportunity within the company. To the 50-year-old auto worker, a

short-term goal might span two to three years for that next pay incre-
ment. While to the 70-year-old retired schoolteacher, investing over the
short term is defined by a period of six months to one year.

Consequently, think of short-term goals as being dynamic. If you
switch jobs, get a promotion or increase in pay you should reassess your
goals. Given your new station in life, you need to determine if you can
save more or less money each month. Either way, the change in your
monthly disposable income will affect your ability to reach those short-
term goals.

INTERMEDIATE-TERM GOALS

Beyond the estimated length for your short-term goals, you enter a period that takes you to your long-term projections. If short-term goals can
range up to 5 years, as with our college student, and retirement at age 65
is long term, then intermediate-term goals would fall in between these
two time frames.

LONG-TERM GOALS

Let's assume our college student has now entered the work force. If she
were to ask other new employees she met at work what their long-term
financial goals were (assuming they had some to start with), many of
them might equate *retirement* with long-term planning. Others might say
getting married or starting a family. After all, you save money not only to
buy goods and services that are essential to your lifestyle (e.g., a car, a
home, a summer or winter vacation) but to create a nest egg for those
years when you no longer work. As your income goes up and your assets
grow, you can also increase your long-term goals to include such items as
a second home, more frequent vacations or greater financial security in
retirement. But your basic long-term aim is to accumulate enough money
to provide you and your family with a retirement income to supplement
your monthly social security and your employer's retirement income

(if there is one). In retirement, you'd like to have an income sufficient to maintain a lifestyle close to what you enjoyed during your working years, if not better. One way to approach goal setting for each of these three time horizons is to follow four basic principles:

1. Set financial goals that are realistic (in other words, obtainable),
2. Be far-reaching in your expectations (set short-term, intermediate-term and long-term goals),
3. Regularly monitor your progress toward these goals and
4. Be prepared to adjust your goals (especially when you put money in investments where your principal is subject to price fluctuations).

SET REALISTIC FINANCIAL GOALS

Anyone can pull a number out of the air and say, "I want to have $10,000 in my accounts by the end of December." But we've already made the point that unless you have carefully reviewed and adjusted your budget, you won't reach such a goal. Merely wishing it won't make it happen. A realistic financial goal, therefore, is one that is arrived at by carefully establishing the amount of money coming in each month (income), subtracting your expenses (liabilities) and multiplying the difference by the length of time of your goal (short-term, intermediate-term or long-term). As your income increases, and hopefully it will, you can then take the higher income level into consideration and modify (increase) your short-term goals if your expenses do not go up as much or as fast as your income.

BE FAR-REACHING IN YOUR EXPECTATIONS

The point has been made that one of the best ways to be far-reaching in your expectations is to set short-term, intermediate-term and long-term goals. As you recall, goal setting is relative to one's age and the length of time over which those goals are sought. Nonetheless, let's explore this subject a bit further.

You could look up the meanings of short term, intermediate term and long term in a respected publication such as *Barron's Financial and Investment Handbook* written by John Downes and Jordan Elliot Goodman.[1] What you'd find is that all three terms are defined according to whether they are used in one of three applications: accounting, investment or taxes.

REGULARLY MONITOR YOUR PROGRESS TOWARD ALL GOALS

If you were to compare the results of two groups of investors, those who set goals and those who did not, in all probability the "goal setters" would come out ahead. But among the goal setters, those who regularly monitored their progress toward those goals would outdo those who did not. Setting goals, and realistic ones at that, is not enough. You must make it a point to at least do an annual review of your assets and liabilities, and determine how you are progressing toward your short-term, intermediate-term and long-term goals.

Definitions of short-term, intermediate-term and long-term.			
Time Frame	Accounting	Investment	Taxes
Short-term	1 year or less	1 year or less	6 months or less
Intermediate-term		Length of time depends on contexts (6 months to 1 year for a stock analyst and 3 to 10 years for a bond analyst)	
Long-term	Not applicable (but probably one year or more)	1 year or more and 10 years or longer for bonds	6 months or longer

Meeting, or exceeding, your goals is an incentive to carry on with an investment strategy. If you fall short of those expectations, then review and adjust your budget or revise your projections if they are not truly realistic. Regardless of the type of investment goal you are attempting to calculate, always write your estimates down on a piece of paper and keep them with your other financial records. You will want to refer to them periodically, and a written record is a lasting one.

BE PREPARED TO ADJUST YOUR GOALS

As you undoubtedly realize, not all investments automatically increase in value (appreciate) over time. Quite the contrary, certain types of investments can actually decrease in value (depreciate) and offer little or no return (interest or dividend). Others may not only increase in value, but do so while providing a return in the form of dividends and/or capital gains. These facets of investing will be discussed in more detail in subsequent steps. Nonetheless, it is important for you to realize that the fluctuations in the value of your assets should be taken into consideration when assessing your progress toward established goals.

If the value of your holdings are below projections due to unfavorable market changes, you do not necessarily have to recalculate your long-term goals, just adjust your short-term expectations. Hopefully, the unfavorable economic conditions will improve with time and enable you to get back on course. On the other hand, when your assets appreciate at a rate greater than you anticipated, be prepared to increase your short-term and intermediate-term goals. Set them higher and enjoy the growth in your assets. If the changes to your intermediate goals are significant, consider modifying your long-term goals to reflect those adjustments. Keep your original long-term estimates for later comparisons as well as their historical value. In other words, you can get a better perspective on where you are going when you can see where you've been.

Whatever you choose to do to modify your goals is uniquely personal.

Just make certain the changes reflect realistic performance expectations, because there is no sense setting unobtainable goals.

CALCULATING THOSE GOALS

Before you can begin setting any kinds of goals you must first determine the amount of monthly disposable income you have to work with. If you have not gone through the process described in Step 2, then do that soon. In the meantime, let's continue to use this example with an estimated $200 per month ($2,400 annually) to illustrate the process of setting some realistic goals.

FOR SHORT-TERM GOALS

For the sake of our example, we can define short term as two years. We'll assume you're new to investing but you envision having several decades over which to invest. In estimating the amount of money you'll have at the end of two years, start by projecting where you'll be by the end of the first year because that can be fairly simple. Multiply twelve (12) times $200 (our monthly disposable income), and you wind up with $2,400 plus interest. The amount of money above (or below) $2,400 will depend on the particular type of investment you've selected.

After you have read all 10 steps in this investment strategy and determined how to invest your money, you can make more realistic calculations. But because we haven't discussed mutual funds and individual stocks, let's assume you decided to invest very conservatively for the first two years and put your money in a money market account to establish your emergency fund. You can call your bank and ask them what your account balance would be if you continued to put in $200 per month for 12 months based on prevailing interest rates. Remember that interest rates will fluctuate, but you only want an estimate of your account balance after 12 months. You don't need to know an exact figure.

Rather than calling the bank every time you wanted an *estimate* of your return, do some simple arithmetic. If the interest rate on your account averaged 5% for the year, you could multiply 5% times your principal $2,400 and get $120. But not all the $2,400 will be in the account for the entire 12 months. In fact, only the first $200 would have been in that long, assuming it was deposited on January 1st. And the $200 deposited in December would not have been in the account for the entire 30 days. So you know that $120 would be too high an estimate for interest earned during the first year. For the sake of simplicity, let's say you actually earned $65. Now you will begin the second year with $2,465 and add another $2,400 over the next 12 months. Therefore, by the end of the two-year point you will have $2,465 from the first year and $2,400 of deposits from the second year. That will add up to a total of $4,845 plus the interest in the second year. If interest rates remained at 5%, you could calculate 5% times the $2,465 at the end of the first year which equals $123 of interest. Because you are again putting the same amount of money in the account per month ($200) at the same interest rate (5%) you could estimate another $65 of interest income for your second year contributions. That produces an estimated return of $253 ($65 + $123 + $65) over two years before taxes. Add that to the principal you put into the account (12 times $200, or $4,800) and your estimate for the account balance after two years would be $5,053 ($4,800 of principal plus $253 of interest income). By the way, an inexpensive business calculator can do these calculations for you quite easily.

FOR INTERMEDIATE-TERM GOALS

After estimating short-term goals, consider making projections of your assets over a longer period of time. Pick a time interval between what you consider short term and long term. Remember, these time references are all relative to one's age and personal situation. It is understood that looking into the future is not always easy and is generally considered nothing more than guesswork on your part. But you can make an *educated* guess of where you will be based on your monthly contributions and the previous returns on the investments once you've monitored your performance in reaching short-term goals.

Simply follow the same method you used to calculate those short-term goals: calculate the amount of principal you invest each year and multiply that amount by the number of years over which you are projecting. Be sure to make adjustments for pay increases and bonuses along with anticipated major expenses (car purchase, vacations, college tuition for your children, etc.) if you did not already include such estimates in your budget. Again, add an estimated return on your money each year. You will learn more about how to do that after you have selected a method of savings or investing (Steps 6 through 9).

FOR LONG-TERM GOALS

These are the most difficult projections to set realistically, especially for young investors in their 20s looking forward to the start of income-producing full-time employment or even for individuals in their 30s or 40s already established in their careers. Setting realistic financial goals over a period of 30 to 45 years is speculation, pure and simple, but good, productive speculation. Realism is added to those far-reaching estimates by monitoring your progress regularly and revising your earlier estimates as you obtain more accurate information over the years.

If you are single, 30 years old, make $60,000 per year, save diligently each and every month, then it might not be unrealistic for you to have a long-term goal of amassing one million dollars and retiring at age 62. After all, you have 32 years to reach that million-dollar projection and a good long-term savings and investing strategy will reward you with income over more than three decades. You do not actually have to *save* a million dollars, you merely have to provide enough of a principal to grow to that amount by the time you reach age 62. There is a big difference between putting a million dollars in an account and having investments earn that same amount of money over 32 years.

On the other hand, if you are 30 years old, married, making $25,000 a year and find yourself strapped with a large amount of debt (car and school loans), your financial situation and priorities are different from your single counterpart. Your interests may center more on buying a home and starting a family, so you have to spend more of your current income to cover your intermediate needs (family expenses, monthly loan payments, etc.). If you cannot save $200 per month at the moment, but find $75 a month a more reasonable estimate, then a long-term goal for your situation may be having a nest egg of $250,000 or more when you choose to retire at age 65.

Should you wonder why you even need to be thinking about long-term goals and projections of your assets at age 65, simply go back to Step 1 and review the discussion of the Princeton study. The point was made that Americans are poor savers and simply don't put aside enough money to support their retirement years. Perhaps this is related to the fact that most people do not actually sit down and set realistic long-term goals. Furthermore, they have no true idea of how much money they will need in savings and investment accounts to maintain their present standard of living in retirement.

A REALISTIC GOAL IS A FINANCIAL FORECAST

Obviously, setting goals is very individualistic and highly variable. Don't forget that the criteria for defining short-term, intermediate-term and long-term goals vary among different investors based on their perspective as well as the period of time over which they are working and saving. More importantly, what distinguishes a *realistic* financial goal from a more general aspiration or hope is the fact that you calculated your financial goal based on an *estimate* of your monthly and then yearly disposable income. So your projection into the future is not a wish or a dream but a financial *forecast* founded on your determination to put away a predetermined amount of money each and every month for a prescribed number of years. That total you arrive at is attainable, you simply don't know what your monthly and annual returns on that investment will be until you select the investment vehicles that suit your level of risk and complexity.

THE MECHANICS OF SETTING GOALS

Don't get hung up on numbers or definitions, at this point, but do sit down and put your thoughts on paper. Here's an easy way to get started:

1. Take a piece of blank, ruled paper and label it for the current calendar year.
2. Create 12 columns, label one for each of the twelve months of the year.
3. Make two rows, one for your *actual* savings and another for your *projected* savings. (This will allow you to determine how well you are adhering to your budget and monthly savings program. In other words, are you putting away $200 each month as you estimated you could?)
4. If you already have other financial holdings (certificates of deposit, money market accounts, U.S. savings bonds, mutual funds, individual stocks, etc.), you can make a row for each of these items separate from your actual income savings.
5. Have a third or final row entitled "Total" so you can sum the *actual* monthly savings from all your holdings and compare these figures to your *projected* savings.

Also make estimates of how much you will save each month, each year for the next five years, ten years, or as many years into the future as you want to project. Once you have set these financial objectives (goals) for yourself, monitor your progress in reaching these targets and do it regularly. Be prepared to revise these estimates as your financial circumstances change (promotion/layoff, pay raise/pay cut, buy a home, get married, have a child, etc.) and watch your assets grow.

After putting those goals (short-term, intermediate-term and long-term) on paper, store these documents in a folder that is readily accessible. Then monitor your progress toward reaching these goals by setting aside time to record your monthly and annual financial status on paper. For example, you can sit down on the first of each month, calculate your savings for the previous month and record that information. Also, set aside a time at least once a year to calculate your total assets and annual return on your investments. You can be conventional and do it in January for the previous year or select a special month in your life (your birth month, anniversary month, yearly bonus month, etc.) and make this annual estimate of your assets year-in and year-out. As your financial investments grow, the annual estimate becomes more involved and is transformed into a calculation of your **net asset value** (NAV) which is the difference between your assets (what you own) and your liabilities (what you owe). It has also been described as one's *net worth*. I prefer not to use the designation *net worth* because it is a calculation of *all* your assets including furniture, cars, clothing, jewelry and other personal property. Next time you read one of those articles in a financial magazine where they profile an individual's or a family's personal finances, take a closer look at how they determine assets and liabilities. Adding these tangible possessions tends to inflate the overall value (worth) of the positive side of the balance sheet (assets) and paint a rosier financial picture. Besides, how quickly do you think you could sell your car or clothing if you needed cash beyond your emergency fund on short notice? I prefer to measure only investments that are liquid, in other words, those you could withdraw from an account or sell tomorrow if you wished. These include such items as holdings in bank savings and checking accounts, money market accounts and money market funds, individual retirement accounts and 401(k) plans, stocks, bonds, mutual funds, certificates of deposit, U.S. saving bonds and treasury bills, bonds and notes. The assets that you can turn into cash in short order if you suddenly had to meet a liability (debt) are the ones I'd recommend you use to calculate your **net asset value**.

Monitoring increases in monthly savings gives a perspective on growth and reaching short-term goals. The annual reviews of net asset value provide a glimpse of your progress toward your intermediate- and long-term financial projections and goals. Never erase or throw away any of your long-term estimates. It is fun and sometimes amusing to compare the estimates of your total assets (including how much you actually contributed) and the performance of those investments (the actual returns) to your *estimated* contributions and returns.

Initially you may underestimate the performance of your investments; perhaps that is an unconscious attempt to ensure success. Whether the underestimation is psychological or due to poor math is irrelevant. What is important is that you meet and hopefully exceed your goals.

IN REVIEW

1. Determine your monthly and yearly disposable income.
2. Make short-term, intermediate-term and long-term goals based on your disposable income.
3. Make only *realistic* goals.
4. A realistic goal is a financial forecast!
5. Monitor your progress toward your goals (include at least an annual review).
6. Be prepared to adjust your goals periodically as the value of your assets changes (increases/decreases).
7. Save all your projections and compare them to the actual performance of your investments.

What's Next?

You know how much money you have to invest (disposable income) and you have set goals for yourself. Now turn to **Step 6: Develop a 3-Tiered Investment Strategy** to learn more about reaching those goals.

Notes

1. Downes, John, and Jordan Elliot Goodman. *Barron's Financial and Investment Handbook.* 2nd edition. New York: Barron's Educational Series, 1987.

DEVELOP A 3-TIERED INVESTMENT STRATEGY

In the preceding five steps the emphasis was on getting organized. You learned the value of establishing a budget and giving direction to money management by automating your banking and creating an emergency fund. Those steps were focused principally on laying the groundwork to a solid *savings* program. With that organization in place, you were then introduced to the need for goal setting.

While a savings program may be safe and secure, the yields on checking and savings accounts and even bank money market accounts provide little opportunity for true, long-term growth. Consequently, the next five steps focus on the *investment* side of your saving and investing program. Let's assume you automated your banking and your emergency fund is at a level where you can now invest that monthly disposable income. Like the approach to saving, you will first have to get organized and then formulate short-term, intermediate-term, as well as long-term financial goals for your assets at different points in time. To make these projections you need to establish a plan based on the types of investments you can afford at the level of risk you are willing to assume. The plan developed specifically to meet these goals might more accurately be called your *investment strategy*. When you arranged your banking, you chose the financial institution (bank, savings and loan, credit union, etc.), selected the type of accounts you needed (checking versus savings) and linked those accounts (through automatic transfers). Your first "investment" was the emergency fund and *you* decided how much money should go into that account based on a variety of factors (job security, family, etc.). In making these choices, in effect, you went through a series of decision-making steps along a course (strategy) to achieve an outcome (goal).

You will need to use that same energy to develop an investment strategy to have any hopes of achieving your long-term goals. The strategy need not be complicated but it should head you down a specific course toward those objectives. After all, you now have a disposable monthly income and a set of investment goals. The question then becomes one of how do you put that income to work to provide the maximum opportunity for growth without the fear of losing your money in the process? That's the challenge faced by you and every other investor.

One thing to keep in mind is that even the best financial plan is virtually worthless if it is never undertaken and given the opportunity to work. Beginning investors are often afraid to start investing, particularly if the economy appears weak and markets are volatile. They do not always understand how financial markets work or appreciate the natural tendency for prices of certain investments to fluctuate dramatically. Prudent market watchers, on the other hand, are accustomed to changing economic conditions and have ways to profit in both good times and bad.

Human nature being what it is, we relish the excitement of rising (bull) markets with inflated stock and mutual fund prices. As the momentum builds, so does our desire to participate in these "up" markets. But we all know the old saying, "What goes up must come down." So it is in the financial world that market "highs" are eventually followed by cyclical downturns to periodic "lows" where paper fortunes can be lost virtually overnight. And the moment those markets weaken and profit-taking begins, public confidence wanes along with the enthusiasm to continue "putting good money after bad." So in normal market "corrections" or major declines, it is not uncommon for new investors to question their approach to investing and money management. Business columnists in the newspaper or the financial "experts" on television like to make predictions about the economy or when financial markets "are ripe for a correction." In other words, they are offering general advice for conservative investors to sell their stocks and mutual funds, prior to some anticipated decline to preserve their principal. Investors may even be advised to put all their money in more secure, government-backed securities (U.S. Treasury bills, savings bonds, tax-free or municipal bonds, money market funds, etc.), where cash is safer. A mistaken belief exists that investments should be sold and profits taken so investors' assets are preserved at all costs. Readers of these articles and viewers of these programs may not realize that every time they sell (liquidate) an investment in a personal account, they must account to the government for any profit or loss at tax time. But there is no reportable gain or loss realized unless a holding is actually sold.

Unfortunately this simplistic view of dealing with rising and declining markets is shortsighted, at least in terms of the long-term investor.

SAVING VERSUS INVESTING?

Remember, the practice of putting money away with the intent of preserving those assets, or not risking the capital, is probably best described as **saving**. But when you want assets to grow and increase in value, you talk in terms of **investing** those dollars for a future reward.

In Step 4 you learned how to create an emergency fund to cover your living expenses for a period up to six months. Think of the money in checking accounts 1 and 2 as your savings. As mentioned earlier, the emergency fund represents your **savings** and it should be your *first* investment. These savings represent an investment intended to protect you and your family in the event of unexpected financial demands.

The money you accumulated in excess of your immediate expenses and beyond what you need to maintain in your emergency fund can be put aside, **invested**, for the future. So look upon *saving* as protecting your present and immediate future needs and *investing* as providing added security for you and your family over the long-term.

"INVESTORS VERSUS TRADERS"

It's not uncommon for long-term investors to have outlooks on the economy and events in the financial markets that differ markedly from the so-called "experts." Why is it that in uncertain times many financial gurus feel so compelled to sell a stock after a poor quarterly report or indications of an unprecedented weak performance by a company? Why do the experts want to get out of the stock market entirely when the nations economic reports look troubling? Why do they advise parking your cash in an interest-bearing account that's probably yielding 4% or less at the first sign of change? Why is it that they react so swiftly to events rather than waiting to see what the real impact might be? And why do they urge everyone to join the mass exodus? They won't be the ones struggling at tax time to figure out what was bought when and for how much to calculate a capital gain or loss. It will be you and your accountant or you and your calculator. And what happens if they were wrong and their predictions do not come to pass? Those who sold their holdings are left with cash in hand. Eventually they'll have to resume their search for other suitable investments or accept the low-yields of those fixed interest accounts. Otherwise, they have to wait patiently for those same experts to tell them when it is safe to buy other investments.

After giving this much thought, I eventually concluded that what distinguishes the so-called "experts" from everyone else in terms of their perspective on the financial markets, the economy and investing, in general, is based on one crucial element. Time! To understand this concept you have to appreciate the difference between "investors" and "traders."

For beginners, it is more important to put money into investments that provide a greater reward the longer they are held. In other words, hold the philosophy of a long-term "investor." You want to establish a business association with the mutual funds and stocks you own that will hopefully last for years. Obviously, some years will be better than others. With a perspective that is not oriented toward the short-term, falling share prices (of stocks and mutual funds) do not necessarily signal it's time to sell. Quite the contrary, the cyclic downturns can be viewed as opportunities to buy more shares at a lower price (strengthen your positions).

Not to take anything away from the "financial experts;" they may very well be making accurate economic assessments. It's just that they often have a much shorter outlook on financial matters. As a group, it is their job to look for the ideal time to "sell" assets and advise clients what and when to purchase other investments. They actively move in and out of markets, liquidating certain holdings and purchasing others for their clients in response to the changing market conditions. In effect, they are "traders" who follow the markets closely and make it their business to find opportunities to make money buying different investments on weakness and selling others on strength. For that strategy to be profitable, the investments must be followed very closely because timing can be everything.

If you are concerned about these normal daily, weekly and annual fluctuations, you can find ways to insulate your investments from such changes, if that were important to you. There are professional money managers who make their living "trading" for individual clients as well as mutual funds. Furthermore, the longer the period over which you invest, the less concerned you need be with day-to-day changes in interest rates, in the economy and on Wall Street.

WHAT DO YOU HAVE TO KNOW ABOUT INVESTING?

Undoubtedly you've heard the old saying that the three key features for success in selling real estate are "location, location, location." You could probably follow that same lead and say the three most important aspects of investing are "diversification, diversification, diversification."

WHAT DO YOU MEAN BY DIVERSIFICATION?

Turning to Barron's *Finance and Investment Handbook* once again, diversification is defined as "spreading of risk by putting assets in several categories of investments—stocks, bonds, money market instruments, and precious metals, for instance, or several industries, or a mutual fund, with its broad range of stocks in one portfolio."[1]

Let's use a practical example to illustrate how diversification is important to an investor. Say you've worked for the ABC Brick Company for 10 years and accumulated $20,000 in the company's retirement plan. One of the options available to you when you began your retirement program was to buy stock in the company through payroll deduction. It sounded great at the time because employees could buy the shares at a 10% discount, so naturally you signed up immediately. Here it is 10 years later and the entire $20,000 is invested in the ABC Brick Company. Business has been good over the years, but now layoffs and personnel downsizing are rumored because of increased foreign competition. You haven't paid much attention to that retirement account because, after all, you planned to continue working. Besides, retirement is another 20 or so years down the road. But with the recent rumors, talk in the plant cafeteria has turned to the economy, pending "pink slips" for some new hires and the sudden decline in the value of the company's stock. After checking the business section of the newspaper, you see that over the last year shares of ABC Brick Company actually have decreased in value by more than 25%. When assessing the performance of your retirement account you come to the alarming conclusion that buying shares of the ABC Brick Company was not as good an investment for you over the last 10 years as you had once thought.

Don't panic; the ABC Brick Company may still be a good *long-term* investment because of its strong management and the recent upgrading of several large pieces of machinery. Yes, there will probably be layoffs and more downsizing, but the company has introduced robotics and made a concerted effort to modernize the physical plant. So selling your shares in the company may not be the answer, at least right now.

Unfortunately, you've put all your retirement eggs in one basket. The entire $20,000 is invested in one company, and that may be a good show of loyalty, but it does not make sound business sense. What this retirement plan lacks is *diversification*. For as the ABC Brick Company goes, so goes that retirement account of yours.

You needn't turn very far for a real life example of this scenario. Simply look at what happened to the value of International Business Machines (IBM) stock in 1992. It started the year at $89.00 per share, hit a high of $100.38, but ended the year at $50.38 a share. The stock price fell $38.62 by year's end with each share of IBM losing 43.4% of its value during those 12 months. Imagine if you retired from the company in 1992 what the impact these events would have been on your retirement had you been fully invested in IBM stock? You were relying on the $4.84 per share dividend for income and price appreciation of the shares for growth. Now the strategy that brought you to this point must be reconsidered. You could continue to hold on to the stock and hope it rebounds. But unfortunately, a reduction in the share price of IBM was not the only disaster to befall stockholders of this company. On January 26, 1993, IBM announced a 55% reduction in the annual dividend from $4.84 to $2.16 per share. When 1993 ended, IBM closed at $56.50 and its annual dividend had been reduced to $1.00 a share. There went the income portion of that investment for retirees counting on their IBM holdings to supplement their company retirement and Social Security benefits.

It may be a bit late to do much for the IBM employees who just retired with most of their retirement account in the company's stock. But with 20+ years ahead before retirement, you can certainly do something substantial to change your ABC Brick Company retirement plan. You could reduce the amount of stock you purchase to, say, 20% of your annual retirement assets and spread the balance of your money among other types of investments offered by the company's retirement plan (growth stock mutual funds, income mutual funds, balanced mutual funds or perhaps a small portion in fixed income investments). You can also start paying more attention to your retirement account and be prepared to move money among the various accounts to maintain your diversification.

WHAT'S YOUR TOLERANCE FOR RISK?

It is easy to tell someone to transform their assets into a more diversified group of investments, but what are the alternatives? Why can't you just keep all your money in a safe money market account?

Whether you're speaking about a personal account (taxable) or a retirement account (not taxable until money is withdrawn in retirement), there is no way you can obtain growth from either a money market or savings account. By growth I mean having your assets increase in value (appreciate) at a rate greater than inflation and your tax liability. Without growth, inflation is certain to erode the true value of what you own. Say you put $10,000 in a money market account and left it in there for 10 years including all the income it produced. You will most definitely wind up with more money that you began with (from the interest accrued), but your principal would not have grown. Ten years from now, do you think $10,000 will have the same buying power it has today? It certainly will not; you can count on that. In a bank saving account or money market account, those dollars are barely keeping up with inflation and taxes. Remember the performance comparison between fixed income investments and growth stocks from Peter Lynch mentioned in Step 1?[2]

You should not keep all your assets in fixed income investments if you have a long period over which to invest those dollars. To provide an element of growth to an investment, you'll have to assume some level of risk.

WHAT IS RISK?

Risk can be defined as a "measurable possibility of losing or not gaining value" and at least 10 types of risk have been identified.[1] One closely related to this discussion is *risk of principal* defined as the "chance that invested capital will drop in value."[1] Note that both these definitions have a negative connotation. They emphasize the possibility that the value of your investment will decrease or simply remain the same over time rather than appreciate.

But risk has a partner, reward, and as the old saying goes, "nothing ventured, nothing gained." As far as investments are concerned, risk and growth are intimately related. If you seek maximum growth, you generally have to assume a certain level of risk. If you choose to avoid risk all together to preserve your money (capital), then inflation and taxes are certain to erode the value of those investments over time.

ARE THERE LEVELS OF RISK?

Yes, there are. You might hear people refer to an investment as high risk, moderate risk or low risk. These are broad categories but they are intended to describe and compare different types of investments. To a New York City school teacher, investing $5,000 in oil exploration in Oklahoma might be considered high risk. Despite the outstanding management and modernization, purchasing more ABC Brick Company stock still holds a moderate degree of risk to your principal over the short term. In contrast, putting that same $5,000 into an account at Suburban Federal Savings Bank insured by the FDIC (Federal Deposit Insurance Corporation) has very little risk.

HOW MUCH RISK IS TOO MUCH?

This is a difficult question to answer and one that is best left to each prospective investor. Obviously if you are a healthy 25-year-old worker looking ahead to a career spanning 40 or more years, you should consider investments that assume more than average risk. At the other end of the spectrum, if you are retired or looking retirement in the face, your emphasis should be on producing income, preserving your principal yet assuming sufficient risk to provide growth to your assets. Without the potential for appreciation, inflation will eat away at the buying power of your retirement dollars and lessen your standard of living. The bottom line is that to get growth in a portfolio, you have to take some degree of risk. Just bear in mind that if you play it too conservatively today, you'll wind up paying for it tomorrow.

DETERMINE YOUR COMFORT LEVEL

No one can tell you how much risk to assume in an investment strategy. That is really an individual decision. Finding that right balance between risk and safety is something you have to decide for yourself. You, and only you, should establish the level of risk you feel you can accept. I refer to this as your comfort level. Be honest when determining your tolerance for risk. Could you sleep at night if you learned the stock market went down 50, 100 or 250 points in one day? Would you worry yourself sick about the daily fluctuations of stocks and mutual funds and have to check the paper each morning to see how much money you *lost*? Or could you accept these fluctuations as the normal, cyclic changes of dynamic markets and ride through any rough periods knowing such events are to be expected? People are so different in their attitude and behavior that no one investment is suitable for everyone. It is best to match individuals with investments that suit their nature yet still provide an opportunity to meet their needs and goals. It's like the question, "Is the bottle of wine half empty or half full?" As you learn more about investing, you will develop a better sense of your comfort level, or what is appropriate for you in terms of risk, length of the commitment and the potential returns.

DEVELOP A 3-TIERED INVESTMENT STRATEGY

The philosophy of a 3-tiered investment strategy is a simple one that I devised for myself and continue to use successfully. The strategy emphasizes diversification and is flexible enough to accommodate your individual level of tolerance for risk (your comfort level). Furthermore, if you wish, you can develop and maintain your investment portfolio entirely on your own (be self-directed), use a financial consultant (stockbroker, certified financial planner, etc.) or any combination of the two (seek professional advice on an "as needed" basis only). The advantages are that you create the strategy (as will be described) and do as much as you want or seek as much help as you need to put that plan to work for you. Just remember, the less decision making others do, the more of your money goes to work for you.

If you find you enjoy the time spent researching and monitoring your investments, as I do, then the more capable you will become in making investment decisions by yourself. In Steps 7, 8 and 9 each of the three tiers will be described in detail, but here's a glimpse into the 3-tiered strategy and how to get started.

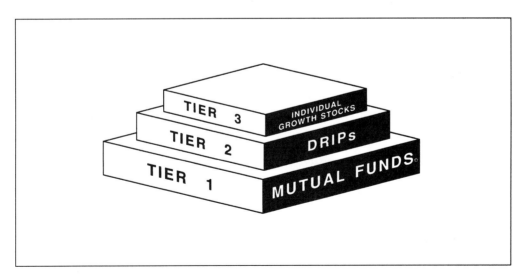

The 3-tiered investment strategy.

TIER 1 (MUTUAL FUNDS)

Regardless of what type of investment strategy you create, you'll want to make certain it rests on sound footing. One of the best foundations for any individual investor is in mutual funds. After establishing an emergency fund, your next investment will be to create a diversified portfolio of professionally managed mutual funds. As explained in Step 7, there are hundreds of different mutual funds spread across a number of groups or families. In fact, you can probably find a fund with just about any type of objective and risk level you want. Also, you don't need a lot of money to open a mutual fund account. In some cases, all that is needed is a commitment of $25 per month and no initial investment is required. In return, you get professional management, so the day-to-day decision making is left to the hands of seasoned money managers.

Furthermore, mutual funds not only offer convenience and professional management but generally these are investments you can hold onto for a number of years and not worry too much about. Of course there are exceptions, but by and large, it is the soundness of mutual funds that gives your financial strategy its stability.

TIER 2 (DRIPs)

While mutual funds provide a starting point for a portfolio, they should not be looked upon as your sole method of investment. Remember the importance of diversification? Once you feel more confident in your financial decision making, you should consider purchasing stocks that pay dividends and offer dividend reinvestment programs (referred to as DRIPs or DRPs). With a DRIP account, you arrange to have the quarterly dividends used to purchase full and fractional shares of stock rather than receive the cash. You can also make *periodic* optional cash purchases (OCPs) to buy additional shares for your account, often with as little as $10 a month. The structure of these plans varies from company to company. Many times the fees and expenses incurred in buying these stocks are actually paid by the respective company for shareholders with DRIP accounts.

The value of a DRIP is that over the years the price of a stock should increase along with the amount of the dividend. Through dividend reinvestment and optional cash purchases, you add more shares to your account on a regular basis. The few shares you purchased initially will multiply manyfold over the years you participate in the dividend reinvestment program. You buy those shares regularly at the various "highs" and "lows." Once in retirement, you can stop making optional cash payments. You either allow your dividends to be reinvested (if you *don't* need the cash) or ask for your dividends to be paid to you quarterly (if you *do* need the cash). When structuring your DRIP portfolio, you can even pick companies with staggered dividend payment dates to receive a check each and every month throughout the year to supplement your other income.

TIER 3 (INDIVIDUAL GROWTH STOCKS)

The third tier in this 3-tiered investment strategy requires more knowledge of the financial markets as well as a greater familiarity with the process of buying individual stocks. The objective here is to put that knowledge and newfound experience to work. Using either a discount or a full-service broker, you research and seek out information on stable "Blue Chip" companies, new or emerging companies, existing companies that are presently undervalued or out of favor, cyclical firms or companies about to make a turn around, etc. You do not necessarily buy these investments for any current income (dividends). On the contrary, you time your purchases because the stocks are priced attractively and you hope their value (stock price) will increase dramatically over time. This activity sounds risky, and it is to some degree, but the level of risk is only what you determine it to be based on the type of stocks you select. If you read about an interesting company but think the risk is greater than you want to assume, simply don't buy the stock. Wait for another opportunity. The stocks in this tier should not be "fly-by-night" companies. In fact, you want to purchase shares only in companies you would like to maintain in your portfolio for a number of years, unless you intend to increase the level of risk.

This is the tier of the 3-tiered strategy in which you would include companies like **Wal-Mart**, **Microsoft**, Apple Computer, etc. when they first went public and offered their shares to the general public. If you were not there at the beginning, you at least know to be looking for similar opportunities today. Then again, do you think Wal-Mart has peaked? Simply visit a Wal-Mart Store or a Sam's Discount and decide for yourself. If you foresee continued growth for this or any other company, track the stock, get a feel for an attractive price and then buy the stock when it reaches a level you can accept.

With the 3-tiered investment strategy, you begin by creating a diversified foundation in mutual funds (Tier 1). Once that foundation is sound, you then add quality growth stocks offering DRIPs, dividend reinvestment programs (Tier 2), to further diversify your portfolio. Selecting individual growth stocks (Tier 3) requires more of a commitment of time and effort, but it also offers tremendous opportunities for growth.

After you've come to know how the 3-tiered investment strategy works, use the information to suit your individual needs. If you do not want to move on to Tier 3 because you find it intimidating or too time consuming, that is perfectly okay. Expand your knowledge of mutual funds, refine your skills at selecting stocks with good DRIPs and limit your portfolio to Tier 1 and Tier 2 type of investments. Or stay with mutual funds for awhile if you want to leave the decision making to professional money managers entirely. But bear in mind that should you choose to invest *exclusively* in mutual funds, that can limit the diversification of your portfolio. Nonetheless, make your investment strategy work within your comfort level. If you ever reach the point where you are overwhelmed by the responsibility and decision making, you can turn to professional financial advisors for guidance. But armed with your increased knowledge of investing and financial markets, you will be in a position to better understand the recommendations of the financial professionals who assist you.

A NOTE TO FOREIGN INVESTORS

As you will learn from the discussions in Steps 7, 8 and 9, there are a wide range of investment opportunities in each of these three tiers. However, foreign investors should be aware that they are actually making two investments when they purchase a U.S. mutual fund (Tier 1), stock for a DRIP account (Tier 2) or an individual growth stock (Tier 3). For example, Canadian investors wishing to purchase a mutual fund directly from an American firm must do so in U.S. dollars. In effect, their first transaction is to sell Canadian dollars and buy U.S. dollars. Their second transaction is to use those U.S. dollars to purchase shares in the mutual fund they selected. This same process would be repeated for the buying of either Tier 2 or Tier 3 stocks.

When it comes time to liquidate those assets, the shares would be sold in U.S. dollars and must then be converted to Canadian dollars. This analogy is the same for transactions in Mexican pesos, the British pound, the Japanese yen, etc. As you can see, foreign investors must consider the effects of both currency exchange rates as well as the value of the particular investment they wish to purchase. Fortunately, long-term investors have the added advantage of making periodic purchases and timing sales to take into consideration the effects of exchange rate volatility and share price fluctuations.

IN REVIEW

1. You are to become an investor, not a trader.
2. Diversification is important in your investment strategy.
3. Understand the different levels of risk (low, medium, high or a combination of the three).
4. Establish your comfort level for risk.
5. A 3-tiered investment strategy includes: mutual funds (Tier 1), DRIPs (Tier 2) and individual growth stocks (Tier 3).

WHAT'S NEXT?

You now know what the 3-tiered investment strategy is. The next step is to explain more about each of the three individual tiers and how they can work for you. Turn to **Step 7: Invest in Mutual Funds (Tier 1)** to learn more about mutual funds.

NOTES

1. Downes, John, and Jordan Elliot Goodman. *Barron's Financial and Investment Handbook.* 2nd edition. New York: Barron's Educational Series, 1987.
2. Lynch, Peter with John Rothchild. *One Up on Wall Street.* New York: Simon and Schuster, 1989.

INVEST IN MUTUAL FUNDS (TIER 1)

The subjects presented in Steps 7, 8 and 9 are more complex than any discussed in the previous six steps. Therefore, it's important that you read the following material carefully, refer to the glossary when necessary and don't hesitate to reread sections you don't fully understand at first. But be sure to read the entire book to familiarize yourself with the concepts behind each step. Take your time and read at your own pace. Take notes and write your thoughts and questions down as they come to you and are still fresh in your mind. In this way, you won't forget a key point or question you want to pursue later.

The description of the 3-tiered investment strategy presented in Step 6 was intended to provide you with a brief overview of the different components and how they relate to one another. You should not only possess an *understanding* but a working *knowledge* of each of the three tiers. Don't be overwhelmed by the amount of detail presented. Steps 7 through 9 have to be comprehensive to be of any real value to investors with diverse goals. If you're not interested in certain types of investments, read over those sections quickly and focus on what you think will be most helpful to you in creating your *personal* financial strategy now. Then review these sections later when you have an even better understanding of investing. Use the resources in the Appendixes to open up new avenues of information gathering and knowledge. Take your time, read and work at your own pace. You'll probably find that you can reread many of the steps six months or a year from now and gain further insight into the subjects discussed. Because this book focuses on developing an investment strategy, the information is less likely to appear "dated" than other publications. Let's start off with a discussion of mutual funds, which will serve as the foundation of your investment strategy.

A mutual fund can be defined as a "fund operated by an investment company that raises money from shareholders and invests in stocks, bond, options, commodities or money market securities."[1] Such investments provide individual investors with both diversification and professional money management for a stated management fee. Furthermore, mutual funds may invest your money in a variety of different objectives and with varying levels of risk. Investors should assess their tolerance for risk before selecting specific mutual funds for their investment portfolio.

As you can see from this description, mutual funds are not at all like the savings accounts offered by your local bank. Quite the contrary, they

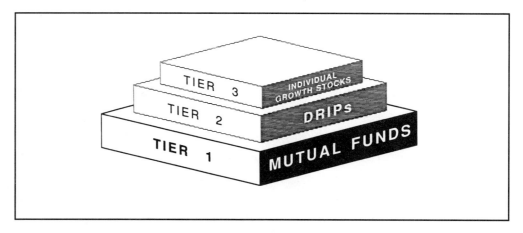

Mutual funds serve as the foundation (tier 1) of your personal investment strategy.

are rather diverse investment vehicles covering a spectrum of investment opportunities from conservative to aggressive and from low risk to high risk. But it is this diversity that attracts so many investors and has lured their dollars away from low-yielding fixed investments in banks to the attractive returns of mutual funds. In fact, the transition has been so great that according to a 1993 cover story in *Business Week*, investors were pouring more than $1 billion per day into mutual funds.[2] Citing data for the period from 1975 to 1992, the article reported that in 1975 mutual funds attracted only 2% of investors' assets compared to 37.4% held by commercial banks and 18.8% in thrifts (savings and loans and credit unions). By 1992 those figures were dramatically different. Mutual funds had literally exploded in popularity to the point where they accounted for 11.4% of assets in contrast to 26.8% for banks and 10.5% for thrifts. Not only was the percentage of assets far greater in 1992 than in 1975, but the shear value of this increase was almost beyond belief. The combined worth of mutual fund assets was estimated to be $1.7 *trillion*—that's $1,700,000,000,000,000,000. This value was spread across an array of more than 3,700 mutual funds in 1992 (3,737 to be exact according to *Smart Money)* in over 30 categories.[2,3] In 1993 the number of stock and bond mutual funds had blossomed beyond 4,200,[4] and indications are this upward trend will continue.

THE VARIOUS KINDS OF MUTUAL FUNDS

Granted, mutual funds are indeed rather diverse investment instruments. The question then becomes how do beginning investors make sense of such a complex subject and select funds that are appropriate for them? Two key features that help differentiate mutual funds are 1) whether they are open or closed-ended and 2) if they are load or no-load funds.

OPEN-END VS CLOSED-END MUTUAL FUNDS

Most of the funds you will see advertised on television and read about in magazines or newspapers are *open-end* mutual funds. The designation *open end* simply means that shares of the funds can be bought and sold at their net asset value (NAV). The investment company managing the funds is able to issue new shares for investors who want to buy more shares. In other words, as interest in a particular fund increases, more shares are created and sold to meet investors' demands. But the flow of money works both ways, and the firm will also sell (redeem) any shares at the NAV at the close of the business day in which a sell order is received. Some, but not all, funds charge a fee for redemptions.

Conversely, *closed-end* mutual funds offer a *limited* number of shares for sale, and those shares are sold on a stock exchange rather than by an investment company. As with any sale on a stock exchange, there must be a person willing to buy those shares in order for them to be sold. Transaction fees are also incurred with the sale or purchase of closed-end mutual funds and paid to the brokerage firm for executing these transactions much like what is done with stocks. Because beginning investors may find *closed-end* mutual funds somewhat complex, this book deals only with the more easily understood and commonly purchased *open-end* mutual funds.

LOAD VERSUS NO-LOAD MUTUAL FUNDS

A mutual fund may be listed as a "load fund" or a "no-load fund." The word *load* refers to a sales charge paid by investors to purchase shares. The rate (amount) of the sales charge (load) is clearly stated in the mutual fund's prospectus as a percentage of the dollar amount invested and can range up to 8.5%. If you look at the listing of mutual funds in the business section of your local paper or a financial publication like *The Wall Street Journal*, you'll see three key columns: NAV, Offer Price and NAV Change. The "NAV" is the net asset value of one share of the mutual fund and the "Offer Price" is the price you must pay to buy that share. The "NAV Change" is the amount the NAV increased (+) or decreased (−) in value of that one share from the previous day's close.

A *no-load* fund will have only the "NAV" price listed together with the "NAV Change" (if available that day). The "NAV Offer" will appear as NL for No Load. Obviously, if the NAV Offer listing is greater than the NAV listing, then that fund is a *load*-fund and the difference between the two prices is the amount of the *load* (sales charge) investors must pay to purchase one share.

For the examples in the figure below, we see that Fidelity Investments' Balanced Fund (listed as "Balanc") is a no-load (NL) mutual fund and on the previous day the NAV went down one cent ($ −.01). In that same listing, you'll also find **Fidelity's Growth and Income Fund** (listed as "GroInc"). This is a load-fund which you could have bought for $19.83 per share and would have sold for only $19.43 per share on that particular day. The $0.40 difference in value between the share prices represents a 2% sales charge (load) paid by investors to purchase *each* share. Also note the NAV for the Growth and Income Fund actually went up five cents ($ +.05) in value from the previous day. Obviously it is in your best interest to hold onto this *load* fund until the NAV reaches or exceeds $19.83 in order for the value of each share to meet or exceed the original purchase price, should you wish to sell your shares.

One drawback to selling mutual funds is that you do not know exactly how much they sold for until the trading day is over and the NAV has been published. The final NAV price is based on the closing price of all

	NAV	Offer Price	NAV Chg.
Fidelity Invest:			
Balanc	12.44	NL	−.01
GroInc	19.43	19.83	+.05

Representative listings of a no-load and a load mutual fund as they would actually appear in the newspaper using Fidelity Investment's Balanced Fund and Growth and Income Fund as examples.

the stocks and other securities owned by the fund at the close of that business day. In comparison, when stocks are sold, you can set a price (limit) in advance of the sale so you know how much you will receive per share if the transaction (sale) is executed at the price you specified. This is an important difference with open-end mutual funds.

CLASSIFICATION OF MUTUAL FUNDS BY NAME

When describing mutual funds, at least five general types have been identified: common stock funds, income funds, balanced funds, bond funds and money market funds.[3] But this classification is limited in its usefulness because these designations are broad and actually include more than one kind of fund. For example, under the heading common stock, you will find funds with differing objectives: growth, aggressive growth, growth and income in addition to index funds.

But at least these names enable you to appreciate the concept and picture a mutual fund not as a single entity but as a multitude of investment possibilities. Next time someone mentions they just bought a mutual fund, you can feel more comfortable asking the question: "What kind of mutual fund did you buy?"

CLASSIFICATION OF MUTUAL FUNDS BY OBJECTIVE

If the response to the previous question was not one of the five names of funds just described, it is probably because that person was identifying the fund they just bought in terms of its financial objective. For that matter, there are many different categories of mutual fund investment strategies (objectives). One major feature that differentiates the various strategies is their approach to obtaining growth and income. Some funds seek returns through capital gains (profits from the sale of investments) and/or income (money received from investments). Those that do generate income will distribute that revenue to you, and you are going to have to pay taxes on the proceeds received in any personal accounts. That income could be from dividends or dividends and capital gains distributed during the current year. Other mutual funds don't focus on income or capital gains but, instead, provide growth for investors simply by having the price of the fund's shares increase (appreciate) with time. Because you don't receive any current income, you don't pay any taxes until you actually sell those shares. Here are brief descriptions of those various categories:

Aggressive Growth Funds. These funds are designed to obtain maximum capital gains rather than current income. They are considered aggressive because of their high level of risk, so share prices can fluctuate dramatically over a short period of time. Investors turn to aggressive growth mutual funds when they want capital appreciation (increased share price) with little or no income distributions. People wishing to avoid a tax liability also find aggressive growth mutual funds attractive. Because there is little or no income (capital gains or dividends) distributed, there is no taxable income, just the potential for an increase in share price (appreciation) over time. It is only when shares are actually sold that a capital gain or loss is reported to the Internal Revenue Service (IRS).

Growth Funds. The growth mutual funds invest primarily in common stock with the intent to achieve capital gains rather than income. There are a number of different growth funds with varying levels of risk. Conservative growth funds invest in the more established companies with a proven track record of performance. As a group, growth funds are less risky than the aggressive growth mutual funds.

Growth and Income Funds. The growth and income funds invest in common stocks that offer growth (through price appreciation) and income (from dividends). Generally, they purchase shares in companies with a history of increased earnings (growth) and dividends (income), and these funds tend to be more conservative than pure growth funds. The growth and income funds differ from the balanced funds because they obtain their income from stocks rather than bonds.

Income Funds. The income funds exist for investors intent on receiving current income without regard for growth (capital gains). The income is derived from bonds as well as stocks. Fluctuations in interest rates, therefore, do affect the share price of income funds. Like the various bond mutual funds, when interest rates decrease, the share price of the funds increases and vice versa. Nonetheless, income funds are geared toward more conservative investors wishing to avoid high risk.

Balanced Funds. As the name alone might imply, balanced funds try to strike a "balance" in providing both capital gains and income. They invest in stocks for the capital gains and bonds for income while attempting to preserve investors' principal. Consequently, balanced funds are less risky than pure growth-oriented mutual funds.

Asset Allocation Funds. This relatively new type of fund was created to provide investors with a blend of investments to include stocks, bonds, international investments, precious metals and cash. Such an asset mix reportedly offers instant diversification plus the ability to move money among the various investment categories in response to changing market conditions. This flexible strategy is designed to lessen volatility while still providing capital appreciation and current income.

Index Funds. The index funds are a type of common stock fund which purchase shares of stocks found in various market indexes. They are designed to mirror the changes in the particular index to which they are matched. Given the strict guidelines for the makeup of an index, a fund can be structured to match one and only one index (the Dow Jones Industrial Average, the Standard and Poor's 500 stocks, etc.). Index funds typically have large minimum investments, and many are geared toward institutional investors such as pension funds, college endowments and bank trust departments. A few funds are available for the individual investor. You'll learn more about stock indexes in Step 9.

International Funds. International funds purchase shares of non-U.S. companies as well as in bonds issued by foreign companies and non-U.S.

governments. Your investment dollars go outside the United States, in other words. Consequently, the return on your investment is affected mostly by foreign-currency exchange rates. These funds are more aggressive by design and not necessarily suitable for conservative investors.

Precious Metal Funds. The precious metal funds invest in foreign and domestic companies that mine gold and/or silver (two precious metals). Such funds naturally mirror the changes in the value of gold and silver, inflation and political factors to a lesser extent. Historically, precious metal funds have been considered a hedge against inflation and dramatic political changes around the world. Recently, they appear to be less affected by political factors and more influenced by the simple dictates of supply and demand.

Money Market Funds. The money market funds are very conservative and pose little risk to one's investment because they purchase high-quality, short-term securities in the money markets including certificates of deposit, treasury bills and commercial paper. Commercial paper refers to short-term obligations issued by banks, corporations and other borrowers with maturities ranging from 2 to 270 days. Money placed in money market funds is very liquid (accessible) via check writing privileges. However, the minimum check size can range from $250 to $500. Because of the low risk to principal, money market funds offer competitive interest rates, but no growth potential. They are useful to the individual investor primarily to "hold" cash in an income-producing account as part of an emergency fund or between transactions (sales or purchases) while awaiting future purchases.

Bond Funds. There are a number of mutual funds that invest in a wide array of bonds issued by U.S. and foreign corporations, federal and state governments, agencies of the U.S. government, as well as local municipalities. Depending on a fund's objective, some may generate taxable income while others yield non-taxable revenue. In addition, the risk level of a particular bond mutual fund is based, in part, on the type, quality and length of maturity of the bonds it holds. Typical categories that may appear under the heading of bond funds include the following:

Corporate Bond Funds invest in high-quality corporate bonds and provide investors with current income.

Corporate High-Yield Bond Funds opt for higher rates of return by investing in lower rated (BBB rating) "junk" bonds to generate current income.

U.S. Government Bond Funds generate current income by investing in a variety of securities offered by the federal government and/or its agencies.

U.S. Treasury Bond Funds offer shareholders the safety of holding only U.S. Treasury securities backed by the U.S. Government along with current income and protection of one's principal.

Short-Term and Long-Term Municipal Bond Funds buy bonds offered by municipalities and states and their agencies to generate current tax-free income. Short-term bonds generally are less risky compared to long-term bonds with maturities ranging up to 20 years.

Short-Term and Long-Term State Municipal Bond Funds purchase municipal bonds from a particular state to provide shareholders with current income that is free of both federal and state income tax.

Mortgage-Backed, GNMA or "Ginnie Mae" Funds offer both current income and stability by obtaining income from mortgage-backed securities issued by agencies of the U.S. Government such as the Government National Mortgage Association (GNMA).

International Bond Funds invest in debt securities from non-U.S. companies and corporations for their income.

Global Bond Funds invest in debt securities from both U.S. and non-U.S. companies and corporations for current income.

Specialized Funds. A number of mutual funds may actually fall into a subgroup of a previous, larger category or simply don't readily fit into an existing classification at all. Consequently, in some publications you may find them listed separately. Two examples include sector funds, which specialize in one particular area (biotechnology, energy, food, health care, leisure, utilities, etc.) and funds that actually invest in other funds (an index fund of mutual funds rather than stocks). It is also quite possible that you may find asset allocation funds categorized as a "specialized" type of mutual fund in other publications.

OTHER POPULAR DESIGNATIONS FOR MUTUAL FUND CLASSIFICATIONS

Not all publications or references adhere to the categories of mutual funds as described. The very popular financial publication, *Money Magazine*, for example, uses many of the designations for the larger groups: balanced (Bal), equity income (EqI), growth (Gro), growth and income (G&I), but adds other more specific groupings expanding or modifying some of the five basic types: maximum capital gains mutual funds (Max), mortgage-backed securities (MBS), small-company growth (SCG), high-grade tax exempt (HGT), high-yield corporate (HYC), high-yield tax exempt (HYT), short/intermediate-term taxable (STT), international (Intl) and world income (WI).

The Wall Street Journal uses a classification system developed by Lipper Analytical Services, Inc. to group mutual funds into 27 categories under four headings (stock funds, taxable bond funds, municipal bond funds and stock and bond funds). Some of the categories include several different investment objectives (see table next page).

You may even see other descriptions of mutual funds in the course of your reading. As long as you understand what these basic categories represent, you'll be able to identify the objective of almost any fund you read about.

Mutual Fund Categories in *The Wall Street Journal.* *

Stock Funds

1. Capital appreciation (CAP)—capital appreciation

2. Growth and income (G&I)—growth and income

3. Growth (GRO)—growth

4. Equity income (EQI)—equity income

5. Small-company (SML)—small company growth

6. Sector funds (SEC)—health/biotechnology; natural resources; environmental; science and technology; specialty and miscellaneous; utility; financial services; real estate and gold oriented

7. Global (WOR)—global; small company global

8. International (non-US) (ITL)—international; European region; Pacific region; Japanese and Latin American; Canadian

Taxable Bond Funds

1. Short term (BT)—adjustable rate preferred; adjustable rate mortgages; short U.S. Treasury; short U.S. Government and short investment grade

2. Intermediate (BID)—intermediate U.S. Treasury; intermediate U.S. government investment grade corporate

3. General U.S. Taxable (BND)—general U.S Treasury; U.S. government; GNMA; U.S. mortgage; general bond; target maturity; flexible income; Corporate debt A-rated and corporate debt BBB-rated

4. High Yield Taxable (BHI)—high current yield

5. World (WBD)—short world multi-market; short world single-market and general world income

Municipal Bond Funds

1. Short term (STM)—short municipal debt; short term California

2. Intermediate (IDM)—intermediate municipal debt; intermediate California municipal debt; intermediate New York municipal debt

3. General (LLM)—general municipal debt

4. California (MCA)—California municipal debt

5. Florida (MFL)—Florida municipal debt

Table continued

---

6. Massachusetts (FDMA)—Massachusetts municipal debt

7. New Jersey (MNJ)—New Jersey municipal debt

8. New York (DNY)—New York municipal debt

9. Ohio (MOH)—Ohio municipal debt

10. Pennsylvania (MPA)—Pennsylvania municipal debt

11. Single-State Municipal (SSM)—all single-state municipal debt, except California, Florida, Massachusetts, New Jersey, New York, Ohio and Pennsylvania

12. High Yield Municipal (HYM)—high yield municipal debt

13. Insured, All Maturities, All Issuers (ISM)—insured municipal debt, California insured debt; New York insured debt

Stock & Bond Funds

1. Blended funds (S&B)— flexible portfolio, global flexible portfolio, balanced, balanced target maturity, convertible securities and income

---

MUTUAL FUND FAMILIES AND GROUPS

In response to investor demands, many, but not necessarily all, of the advisory companies that operate mutual funds offer a number of different kinds of funds (*load* and/or *no load*) with varying investment objectives. Consequently these investment companies have been referred to as "families" or "groups" of funds, meaning they offer a variety of ways to invest your dollars under one company's general management.

The 1993 *Business Week* article on mutual funds mentioned previously also identified the 25 largest fund managers, their total assets and their share of the mutual fund market (Appendix A).[2] To get a feel for the magnitude of investors' love for mutual funds, all you have to do is take a close look at the three leading fund managers in the United States. It was reported that the nation's single largest mutual fund management company was the Boston-based **Fidelity Investments** with a family of well over 100 *load* and *no-load* funds. The assets of **Fidelity Investments** amounted to approximately $164.3 billion or 10.2% of market share as of September, 1992. The list of Fidelity funds appears in the business section of the newspaper under four separate headings: Fidelity Advisor, Fidelity Investments, Fidelity Selects and Fidelity Spartan. Fidelity's next largest competitor and the second largest management company was Merrill Lynch with 81 mutual funds, $107.6 billion in assets and 6.7% of the mutual fund market. Both Fidelity Investments and Merrill Lynch offer brokerage services and the potential to purchase closed-end mutual funds, stocks, bonds and a variety of other types of investment. Third on this list was the Vanguard Group from Valley Forge, Pennsylvania which had 52 no-load mutual funds, $92.6 billion in assets and 5.8% of the mutual fund market as of September 1992.

Two other popular families are the **Twentieth Century Mutual Funds** and the **Janus Group**. The Twentieth Century Family of Funds is managed by Twentieth Century Investors, Inc. of Kansas City, Missouri. This particular family had only 12 *no-load* mutual funds to choose from, but has over $17.3 billion in assets or 1.1% of the mutual fund market. The equally popular Janus Group of Denver, Colorado, with a more modest holding of 10 *no-load* funds, had over $6 billion of assets. Even though the assets of the Janus Group amounted to more than $6 billion it did not make the list of the 25 largest funds. Remember, there are now over 4,200 stock and bond funds offered by a number of families from all the different categories.[4] A listing of many of the mutual fund "families" to be found in the business section of your newspaper is contained in Appendix A along with their respective telephone numbers.

Stock mutual funds have become so popular that in 1992 a record $9.9 billion flowed into these investment vehicles in the month of November alone.[5] Think of what that represents. In just 30 days, nearly $10,000,000,000 of new money went into the coffers of these mutual fund managers to invest in a variety of financial sectors. That's astonishing and further illustrates how important mutual funds have become to small investors as well as the financial markets themselves. That milestone lasted a mere two months before it was surpassed in January 1993, when contributions reached a whopping $10.2 billion level.[6] By October of 1993 stock mutual fund contributions reached a record $13.3 billion.[7] Also, when 1993 ended Fidelity Investments offered more than 150 mutual funds, Merrill Lynch's funds had grown from 81 to 94, Vanguard's had increased from 52 to 58, Twentieth Century offered 14 instead of 12 funds and Janus' list of mutual funds grew from 10 to 12.

How Do the Mutual Funds and Fund Families Work?

The various investment companies that oversee individual funds, families or groups of funds are in the business of pooling your dollars with those of other individuals following a particular investment strategy (objective). The funds' day-to-day operations are handled by one or more fund managers. These managers monitor the financial markets and direct the buying and selling of investment instruments that are in line with the funds' objectives.

Because of the fickle nature of the financial markets and differences in risk tolerance, a portion of a mutual fund's assets is maintained as cash to meet the demands of investors who wish to sell shares. In other words, the fund manager knows from experience that at any given time, a certain number of people may want to sell part or all of the shares in the fund to get their cash back. That's all part of the game, so to speak. So you need not worry if you have to redeem shares in an *open-end* mutual fund, all you have to do is get your sell order placed well before the close of business the day you decide to sell.

What Do Mutual Funds Do with Investors' Money?

Each potential investor receives a fund prospectus to read before investing in any mutual fund. That document outlines the investment objectives of the fund: growth, current income, both growth and current income, etc. The prospectus also tells how your dollars will be invested, what the fees are for the fund and indicates who the investment adviser is to the fund. In addition to this information, you should also find a statement of the performance of the fund over a stated period of time. The length of this historical information will vary because some funds have been around longer than others. You'll be able to find out how much of a dividend and/or capital gains were paid per share along with the opening and closing price of a share for the last few years. These historical data provide a clue to the *past* performance of the fund and the fund manager(s). If you want to compare the performance of several similar funds, you can use the data in the prospectuses, but make your comparison over the same investment periods (1 year, 3 years, 5 years, etc.). There is a movement to permit investors to expedite this process by direct purchasing without the required mailing of a prospectus.

But don't rush. It's better to take your time and become familiar with the funds you think you might like to purchase. Call or write for annual, semi-annual or quarterly reports if you are particularly interested in seeing a list of the assets (investments) presently in the fund's portfolio.

WHY ARE MUTUAL FUNDS SO POPULAR?

Institutional and average investors alike have moved much of their money from conservative holdings, such as CDs and money market accounts, and poured billions of dollars into mutual funds. There are any number of reasons why mutual funds have become so attractive to both institutional investors and the "average" investor:

THERE'S MORE MONEY TO INVEST

One of the leading reasons mutual funds have become so popular might be that more people have money to invest. In 1977 mutual fund assets amounted to $50 billion. By 1992 that figure had leaped to an amazing $1.7 trillion with the last $600 billion invested just since 1990.[2] And 1991 saw a record $38.3 billion infusion into mutual funds. But that record paled in comparison to the $77.8 billion investors poured into mutual funds for the year 1992.[8]

And those record levels were achieved despite the fact that Americans are not considered good savers at all. As I mentioned previously, the United States reportedly has a savings rate of less than 5%, which is the lowest in the entire world.[9] Remember that Japan and Singapore have savings rates of 20% and 42% respectively. Imagine saving 42% of your income! On average, Americans may not save as much money per capita as people from other nations, but that doesn't mean they aren't interested in putting what they do have away for a rainy day. They've taken to mutual funds and in a big way.

PROFESSIONAL MANAGEMENT

With interest rates as low as they have been for the last several years, more and more people have turned to mutual funds to obtain professional management of their money and higher rates of return. Buying a mutual fund may be one of the least expensive ways for small investors to start a sound investment program. After all, you have someone making the daily decisions on what to buy, when to buy, as well as when to sell. All you have to do is select the mutual fund that is right for you.

PERFORMANCE

Perhaps the single, most compelling reason mutual funds have become so popular, especially with small investors, is their performance. You need only look back to the stellar returns of 1991 to see why. The February 1992 issue of *Money Magazine* featured the top performing 1991 equity (stock) mutual funds as well as the taxable and tax-exempt bond funds.[10] The *Money Magazine* report was prepared by Lipper Analytical Services and included 1-year, 3-year and 5-year compounded annual returns to January 1, 1992. Just looking at the performance of the top 20 funds for the five categories of stock mutual funds, the percentage returns were extraordinary. For example, ranked by five-year performance as the number 1 growth mutual fund for 1991, **Twentieth Century Ultra Investors**, posted a 1-year return of 86.5%, an average annual return of 40.8% for 3 years and 27.6% per year for the last five years. The number 20 growth fund, had a 1-year return of 48.3% with 3-year and 5-year levels averaging 29.6% and 20.0%, respectively. By comparison, the averages for the entire category of growth mutual funds based on 1-year, 3-year and 5-year average annual gains were 41.9%, 18.8% and 14.5%, respectively.

As astonishing as an 86.5% one-year gain might seem, the Twentieth Century Ultra Investors Fund was not among the top five 1991 *stock* mutual funds. In reaching just the number 5 ranking, Financial Strategic-Health Sciences (a sector fund) had a 1-year gain of 91.8% and that was overshadowed by the number 1 stock fund, Oppenheimer Global Biotechnology with a 1-year total return of 121.4%. In 1991 the average *stock* fund had a 1-year return of 31.4%.[11] In contrast, 1992 did not see the spectacular gains so common in 1991. The average growth mutual fund had 1-year, 3-year and 5-year compound annual returns of 12.1%, 13.4% and 13.1% respectively.[12] The top ranked growth fund in 1992 (also based on five-year performance) was the Kaufmann Fund with gains of 14.5%, 22.9% and 33.2% during these same time periods. And the number 1 stock mutual fund for 1992 was Fidelity Select Savings & Loan, which posted a huge 53.8% 1-year return,[12] but stock funds in general averaged only 8.88% for the year.[13]

Obviously, the performance data for funds in 1992 do not compare to the levels of 1991. But the fact remains, the long-term gains (5- and 10-year returns) are at levels that outstrip fixed-income investment offered by banks or even the best money market fund. Over the long haul, mutual funds give the small investor the potential for growth without the responsibility of day-to-day management. Furthermore with "no minimum" enrollment programs, mutual funds are more affordable than ever before.

"NO MINIMUM" ENROLLMENT PROGRAMS

Were you aware that you could open a mutual fund account for as little as $25 per month with no initial investment required? And did you know you'd be buying some of the best names in the mutual fund business? If you didn't realize such programs exist, don't feel bad, because you're not alone. Until a few years ago, most funds required a minimum initial investment to open any account. In other words, you could not think about submitting an application to open an account without being prepared to write a check for a substantial sum: $1,000, $2,500 or even $3,000. So you would have to accumulate that much cash before you could even get started. Not only that, but you'd have to put all your investment "eggs" in one basket, that one mutual fund. Fortunately for the small investor, that has changed to a large extent. Although there are families of funds that continue to maintain these high initial investment requirements, the more progressive management companies have introduced "no minimum" enrollment programs. And these programs are offered by some of the better known families of funds, not the poor performers. Now more people with modest incomes can become mutual fund "investors" in addition to bank "savers."

There are no fees or expenses associated with the "no minimum" enrollment options, but there are some rules. You must agree to make a minimum monthly automatic transfer until your account balance reaches the fund's normal initial investment level which could be $1,000, $2,500, etc. Read the fund's prospectus and look for the section that discusses making automatic monthly investments. The fund family will probably have what is commonly called an "Automatic Monthly Investment Program," "Automatic Investment Plan" or some similar name. Such plans are nothing more than a way to arrange monthly automatic transfers of money from your bank to your mutual fund account. If you select a family of funds that offers this service, specific details can be found in a fund's prospectus or you may call the fund advisor for more information. What you'll need to know is the minimum amount of money you can transfer and if there are set dates each month for automatic transfers. Different groups of mutual funds have their own sets of rules for these programs, so transfer dates and amount may vary widely.

The benefit to beginning investors is that *you* determine both the amount of the transfer as well as its timing. Some mutual fund families allow you to make automatic transfers as low as $25 per month *with no money down* (examples include Oppenheimer, Putnam and Value Line). With funds from Alliance Capital, Sierra Trust, Templeton, and United, the low $25 automatic transfer option is available but you have to make an initial investment ranging from $25 (Templeton) to $500 (United). The Janus Group and Twentieth Century Investors, for example, do not require an initial investment, merely a minimum automatic transfer of only $50. But with the "no-minimum" enrollment programs, you must continue your contributions until you reach the standard initial investment for that particular family, which might be $1,000, $2,500 or even more. With Fidelity Investments investors can add to their account with $100 per month minimum automatic transfers after an initial investment of $2,500 (for non-IRA accounts). The customary minimum contribution for Fidelity mutual funds is $250 outside the automatic transfer option.

Once your account balance reaches the level of the standard initial investment, you may discontinue the automatic transfers, if you wish. But it is prudent to continue making these monthly purchases since the practice is a good way to build assets.

Signing up for a "no-minimum" enrollment program is actually very easy. You call the mutual fund family offering the plan and request a prospectus and application. When you complete the application form for the mutual fund or funds you've chosen, you'll see that you can check the "no-minimum" enrollment option. All you do is indicate how much money you want transferred each month from one of your bank accounts. You select the date you want the transfer made, indicate when you want the transfers to begin and mail in your application with a cancelled check. Often you do not even have to enclose any money with your application unless you want to. Your agreement to permit the automatic transfers is your entry into the "no minimum" enrollment program. From that point on, the transfer will be made automatically until you decide to make a change. It is that easy. You do not even have to make any additional arrangements with your bank; that will all be taken care of for you by the mutual fund.

DIVERSIFICATION WITHIN A MUTUAL FUND

Another attractive feature of a stock mutual fund is that a $25 investment may buy you part ownership into not one mutual fund, but the stock of dozens of individual companies. That's an awful lot of diversification for such a small amount of money. Few alternative financial opportunities offer that much diversity at such a low cost of participation. With the vast array of mutual funds, you can diversify within a particular industry (sector), across a variety of sectors or by following a particular market index.

DIVERSIFICATION BETWEEN MUTUAL FUNDS

Investors seeking added safety will find that many mutual fund families or groups offer an array of investment choices. As mentioned previously, Fidelity Investments, for example, has more than 100 mutual funds to choose from, some of which are no-load. Other families might not have as many choices, but they still offer funds with different investment objectives to enable the average investor to diversify between mutual funds within the same family. Furthermore, you can get that diversification with as little as $25, $50 or $100 a month. Remember, you can divide your dollars between two or more mutual funds ($50 will get you two $25 per month automatic transfers with one investment company or $100 will get you two $50 per month transfers with another).

DIVERSIFICATION AMONG MUTUAL FUND FAMILIES

Mutual fund families offer so many choices of funds because they would like to attract *all* your investment dollars. Once you join "the family" through your ownership of one of its funds, you'll also probably receive literature related to the family's remaining funds. But you may find other funds, from entirely different groups with different management philosophies more to your liking. Does it make good sense to invest entirely in one family? There is no simple answer to that question. If you want to take diversification to its fullest, you will not let any one family have all your money. Investment strategies differ markedly among fund advisors and managers, but by mixing families as well as funds, you diversify your portfolio even further.

LIQUIDITY

Generally your money is only a telephone call away. Should you have to sell part or all of your fund shares, you can make one telephone call and place a sell order. You'll be offered the option to make what are called "telephone redemptions" when you fill out your account application. Otherwise, you may want to consider adding this service at a later date, if you think you might need to alter your investment strategy. If you don't select the telephone redemption option, you must send a letter of instruction to sell your shares. That order will be executed on the first business day it is received, and a check will be mailed to you shortly thereafter. This takes more time and also requires signatures from all individuals listed on the account. The check will be made payable to the registered owners of the account. So for a joint account, both individuals must make the sale requests.

CONVENIENCE

The low minimum initial investment, automatic transfers, professional management, diversification and liquidity all provide a high level of convenience to small investors. Day after day, month after month, your dollars are being pooled with those of millions of other Americans in an effort to make the highest possible return on your investment. With automatic transfers and automated banking, you have the convenience of going about your business every day. Money is transferred to your mutual fund accounts by wire on the days you specified and in the amounts you selected. You don't have to worry about writing checks or forgetting to mail a contribution because your mutual fund investing is automated. If you need to make changes, simply pick up the phone and speak to someone in shareholder services at the mutual fund. Now that's convenience.

SELECTING MUTUAL FUNDS TO MEET YOUR GOALS

By now you are at least familiar with all the various types of mutual funds and how they differ in terms of their objectives. The question becomes one of how do *you* select funds that will help you reach your financial goals. Perhaps you know what features to look for, and you at least have a sense of what type of funds might suit your objectives. Then again, you might be overwhelmed by all the choices and need some direction of how to begin the selection process. Try these helpful hints to get started:

DETERMINE YOUR RISK TOLERANCE (COMFORT LEVEL)

This is an extremely important decision making point, so you need to be honest with yourself. How comfortable are you when it comes to taking risks with your money? Just what level of risk are you really willing to assume? In other words, what's your "comfort level" for risk or risk tolerance? Are you a long-term investor with a desire to be at the high end of the risk spectrum? Or are you conservative by nature and more interested in lower-risk investments? Maybe you want to compromise by choosing two funds, one with only moderate risk associated with it and the other more toward the high end of the risk spectrum? Once you determine your "comfort level" for risk, you can direct your search to the types of funds that meet your risk tolerance.

FIND A FAMILY/GROUP OF FUNDS WITH CHOICES

With thousands of registered mutual funds to choose from and dozens of "families" competing for your investment dollars, you have many choices. Initially you might be better served to deal with the larger mutual fund families that offer you diversity and high quality customer service, so you can get your questions answered easily, day or night, weekday or weekend.

OMIT FUNDS YOU DON'T WANT

If you selected a mutual fund family with 20 different funds, the number of choices can be overwhelming initially. So make the selection process easier by deciding what you *don't* want to do with your money. If you're looking for growth at moderate risk and you want to avoid current income (to keep your taxes low), then don't even consider the low-risk bond funds and the high-risk aggressive growth funds. The fact that for tax reasons you'd prefer not to have income producing mutual funds means you may not want a growth and income fund, simply a growth fund. Don't forget, there are different types of growth funds, so you may prefer one with a moderate risk level. If you want capital appreciation as well as current income, focus on the growth and income funds. If you mainly want income with some growth, look into an income fund.

COMPARE SEVERAL MUTUAL FUNDS WITH THE SAME INVESTMENT OBJECTIVE

By eliminating the types of funds in a family that you don't want, you are then able to see if that family offers mutual funds that are in line with your financial objectives. Once you've narrowed the field and found funds with the investment objectives that you believe you will feel most comfortable with, you will want to look for similar funds in other families. It is extremely helpful to compare three or four funds with similar financial objectives in different families before making your final selection.

LOOK FOR NO-LOAD MUTUAL FUNDS

Given the choice, as a small investor you are probably better off choosing a *no-load* mutual fund over a *load* mutual fund. If you are trying to build your account by $25, $50 or $100 a month, you want all your money to go to work for you immediately. Besides, there is no assurance that the *load* mutual fund will outperform a *no-load* fund with similar objectives, so why pay the sales charge if you can't be guaranteed a better return?

John Kimelman, a staff writer for the biweekly magazine, *Financial World*, wrote an interesting piece on this subject in 1992 entitled *Unloading the Loads*.[14] In his article, Mr. Kimelman matched up 10 *load* mutual funds with 10 *no-load* funds with similar financial characteristics and compared their 3- and 5-year performances. He was able to show that 10 popular *load* funds have *no-load* counterparts with comparable results. There were other important points worth mentioning. First, many of the *no-load* funds actually outperformed the *load* fund they were compared to. And second, the percentage returns reported for the *load* funds for the three- and five-year periods were *before* the sales charge (load) had been deducted. In one example the 5-year average annual performance of a fund was reported as 7.74%. Factor in the effect of the 5.75% *load* and that average dropped to 6.47%. In contrast, the *no-load* fund used in the comparison had a 5-year average annual return of 7.9%.

For *load* mutual funds, part of the sales charge is paid as a commission to the broker or agent who sold the fund to you. Not all funds have an initial sales charge (*front-end load*) to purchase shares, some load funds choose to make you pay a fee at the time you sell your shares (*back-end load*). If you do decide to buy one of the outstanding *load* mutual funds, the impact of the sales charge may be less significant if the fund outperformed its peers and you keep the fund for a number of years. Just remember that *no-load* mutual funds don't pay a commission to sales people but market directly to the public, so there is no financial incentive for a broker to recommend a no-load fund. What's also important to recognize is that with a little effort on your part, you can often find a *no-load* mutual fund with similar objectives and overall performance to a loaded fund. When you do, all your money is invested and you are more apt to maximize the return on your investment.

COMPARE ANNUAL FUND OPERATING EXPENSES

For the sake of example, let's say you narrowed your selection to two mutual funds with the same investment objective and their performance data were similar for the last 5- and 10-year periods. They both offer a "no-minimum" enrollment program and a low automatic transfer is available. How do you separate the two and select the one that might be more appropriate for you? Compare their annual operating expenses, that's how! You'd be surprised at how vastly funds differ in what they charge shareholders. Annual expenses may range from as little as 0.25% to 2.50% or more. By the way, the Vanguard Group is known within the mutual fund industry for its low fees (some as little as 0.25%).

You'll find a listing of a mutual fund's expenses and fees in the prospectus under two separate headings: Shareholder Transactions Expenses and Annual Fund Operating Expenses. With a *load* fund, you will see the percentage of the sales charge under the first heading, Shareholder Transaction Expenses, along with other charges listed as: sales load imposed on reinvested dividends, deferred sales load, redemption fees and exchange fees. These are fees you would have to pay for the respective services. Under the heading Annual Fund Operating Expenses are the fees taken directly from the fund's profits. They may include the following: management expenses, investment advisory fees, 12b-1 fees and other expenses (distribution costs, shareholder accounting costs and miscellaneous expenses).

A word about the 12b-1 fees. These charges have been added to the list of expenses by some mutual funds as part of an effort to recoup the routine costs associated with distribution, marketing and advertising the fund. According to Monica Roman (*Smart Money*, 1993) only 36% of the 1,500 mutual funds in 1985 assessed 12b-1 fees compared to more than 50% of the 3,737 funds in existence in 1992.[3] And in 1991 the expense ratio for 993 equity funds averaged 1.55%.

Be sure to look for this information on expenses in a fund's prospectus. What is important to remember is that the fund operating expenses are expressed as a percentage and charged against the assets of the fund. So these fees are coming out of your potential profit. Obviously if annual returns for mutual funds are at the single digit level, you'll benefit more if your fund has a low total expense ratio. The difference between expense ratios of 1.0% and 2.5% is 1.5% more of assets to distribute to shareholders. In a comparison of two similar funds, if you determine all other things to be equal, consider the fund with the lower annual expense ratio.

HOW DO YOU FIND OUT ABOUT FUND FAMILIES AND INDIVIDUAL MUTUAL FUNDS?

Now that you have established your "comfort level" for risk, decided which types of mutual funds you don't want and which you do want, you are ready to begin the actual selection process. So how and where do you start?

The answer to this question is not as difficult as it may first appear. You're going to need advice and some good advice at that. If you don't know anything about the financial markets and investing, you can't very well pick one or two funds from a list of over 4,200 and have the assurance you made good decisions.

There are two types of advice you can get: that which you pay for and that which is free. You may call a stockbroker or financial planner to obtain a recommendation for a mutual fund or two. Invariably, it will turn out that the brokerage house you called will have what you want and you needn't look any further. The broker will be happy to establish an account for you, if you have enough money to open one. For that recommendation and service, you'll pay a service charge (load), but now you're on your way. Right? Not necessarily! You *don't* have to pay a load, but you *do* want the best mutual fund you can find that will waive the initial investment using a "no minimum" program and automatic transfers. Okay then, you should call a financial planner for a recommendation, right? Not necessarily! You want all your money to get into your account. If you hire a financial planner, you'll have to pay for that service.

So where do you go for that other type of advice, the *free* advice? The public library, that's where.

WHAT THE PUBLIC LIBRARY HAS FOR YOU

You'd be surprised at the wealth of information that is available to you free of charge at your local branch of the public library. You'll have to do a little homework because the information is found in at least five different sources (see Appendix B for a list of reference materials):

NEWSPAPERS

If the business section of your local newspaper leaves much to be desired, visit the library and go through *The Wall Street Journal*, the *Investor's Business Daily* or the money section of *USA Today*. These publications are a rich source of current news, information and frequently feature articles with specific investment recommendations. Don't forget that such recommendations are only as good as their source, and there are no guarantees simply because they appeared in well-respected publications. But be aware that you are often getting in-depth and insightful information that you will not ordinarily find in your local paper. These newspapers generally are published Monday through Friday with no Saturday or Sunday editions.

NEWSLETTERS

There are a number of financial newsletters that track mutual funds, individual stocks or the economy in general. These can be a great source of insight into what is "hot" and what is not. Ask your local librarian which ones they carry. Some examples include: *Mutual Fund Forecaster*,

United Mutual Fund Selector and *The Value Line Investment Survey* to mention only a few.

MAGAZINES

Many of the best and most reliable financial magazines are household names in America: *Barron's National Business & Financial Weekly* (referred to simply as *Barron's*), *Business Week, Financial World, Forbes, Fortune, Kiplinger's Personal Finance Magazine, Money Magazine, Smart Money* and *U.S. News and World Report* are a few worth reading.

Take the January 1993 issue of *Kiplinger's Personal Finance Magazine,* for instance. It included features on economic forecasts, retirement, investing and money management, among other things. The feature article of the February 1993 issue of *Smart Money* was "The Five Best Investments for 1993" and included some specific mutual fund recommendations. The lead story of the February 1993 issue of *Money Magazine* was entitled "The 12 Funds to Buy Now," and it also contained an extensive listing of 1,296 funds ranked by performance. That's an awful lot of information for the $2.50 to $2.95 cover price of these publications and well worth the cost, if you care to purchase any of them.

I've been a *Money Magazine* subscriber for years, and if I were asked to pick just *one* financial magazine for the beginning investor, it would be *Money Magazine* without a doubt. The articles and monthly features not only track mutual fund performance and make specific recommendations for investors with a wide range of investment objectives, but they present a host of saving and investing tips, strategies and recommendations in an easy-to-read style. One word of advice though, be patient. It may take you months until you reach a point where you understand everything you're reading if you do not have much of a financial background. Don't be at all embarrassed or become discouraged if you have to reread stories, or you don't fully understand the point of an article. Stay with it, and eventually things will all start to make more sense.

As you grow in your understanding of investing, you will want to expand your reading to other business and finance publications in addition to *Money Magazine*. When you visit the public library, browse through the magazine section for the other business periodicals. Another favorite of mine is *Smart Money* (*The Wall Street Journal Magazine of Personal Business*).

BOOKS

Financial books are a tremendous resource for beginning investors who have a lot of questions and want a lot of answers. If you have the time, you can use the vast arrays of books in the library to learn a lot about very specific aspects of investing or investment strategies. Be advised that books that make investment recommendations can be quickly outdated by changes in the dynamic financial markets. Rely more on the monthly magazines and daily newspapers for current investment guidance and insight. Read financial books more for their insight on investment strategies (like this one) or financial management and money saving tips, so you can adjust your budget to increase your disposable income.

REPORTS

A number of services publish reports on the performance of individual stocks and mutual funds. Three well-known services include the Standard & Poor's Reports and the Value Line Investment Survey on individual stocks and Morningstar Mutual Funds for mutual funds tracking. These reporting services are expensive, so not all libraries carry them.

Individual investors who find the information helpful can subscribe to such services to receive these regular reports with current news, ratings and recommendations. The subscription costs are more expensive than the other reference materials (magazines and newspapers). If you think you might be interested in this type of literature, you can arrange a trial subscription for an introductory price (three months of Value Line and Morningstar for $55). That's several hundred dollars when figured annually, but the information is well worth it if you have a lot of money to invest and want the convenience of home delivery.

Some report services are so highly specialized that they track only one family of funds. An example is Fidelity Insight which is an independent reporting service for tracking the funds run by Fidelity Investments.

COMPUTER SUBSCRIPTION SERVICES

For the sake of completeness it is probably at least worth mentioning that there are also a number of services you can subscribe to and link up with on your personal computer. However, this subject is a bit beyond the scope of a book for beginning investors.

If your money and your time are limited and you wanted to select just one source of information for your research, I'd suggest you start with the financial magazines. They are consumer oriented, the features are timely and you'll usually find specific investment recommendations. And after all, that's the sort of information you want.

CALL FOR A MUTUAL FUND PROSPECTUS

Let's assume you visited the library and while reading you selected four mutual funds you thought might be what you were looking for. What do you do next?

First, find the toll-free phone number for the mutual fund family or investment company that manages the funds (see Appendix A). Call and ask for a prospectus and an application for each fund. Do yourself and the customer service departments both a favor, don't call during prime business hours. Place your call early in the morning or late in the day, after the markets have closed. (By the way, the New York Stock Exchange hours are 9:30 AM to 4:00 PM Eastern Standard Time.) By calling in the off hours, you are more apt to get through to a representative and that will minimize your waiting time. The customer service representative also will have more time to spend with you. During the normal business day, these people are at their busiest assisting shareholders, and you'll either be placed on hold or you'll get a constant busy signal. So plan your call accordingly. Don't forget, individuals living outside the continental U.S. can also call or write directly to an American mutual fund or fund family for information.

Read the prospectus of all *four* mutual funds, and compare the funds in terms of performance, expense ratio, availability of "no-minimum" enrollment programs and service.

PERFORMANCE

The annual returns of the funds are best compared by looking at their relative growth (price appreciation) and income (dividends and capital gains), if any. This information will appear in each fund's prospectus and be highlighted in the literature you receive. Most of the top performing funds proudly display the percentage "cumulative total return" or "average annual rate of return" for their funds and compare this performance to some index or average. Look for the 1-, 3-, 5- and 10-year performance data, and write this information down for each mutual fund on a single piece of paper. Then simply see how each fund did over the last 10 -, 5-, 3- and 1-year periods.

Compare the change in the net asset value of a share price of every fund from 10 years ago until today. Look at the amount of capital gains and dividends distributed for an overall assessment of the fund's performance. You'll probably find that the flyer accompanying the prospectus contains the average annual returns for the fund over what they term the fund's life (the period from inception to the last period reported) with comparisons to the average for funds with a similar objective.

EXPENSE RATIO

As was pointed out earlier, you can find this information in the front of the prospectus. Obviously, the lower the annual expenses the better. If the performance of the four mutual funds is comparable for the last 3, 5 and 10 years and the objectives are the same, then give a close look to the fund with the lowest annual expenses.

"No-minimum" enrollment program

If you like the performance and find the annual expenses of several funds to be acceptable, then check to see if they all offer a "no-minimum" enrollment program. If you only have $100 per month to invest, consider the family/group of funds that will waive the initial investment and allow the lowest automatic transfer. That $100 potentially could be split up as $50 per month to two mutual funds or $25 a month to four funds with one family or limited to one $100 a month automatic transfer to another. Remember that if you select several funds, you'll want to be diversified and choose more than one *type* of investment objective.

Service

It may not seem important initially when you only have one or two mutual funds, but service quickly becomes a significant issue as your mutual fund portfolio grows. So you will find it beneficial if you can make your phone calls and transact business at home in the evening or on weekends. Unfortunately, not all mutual fund families offer service 24-hours a day, 7 days a week. Those that do make your life easier because a routine phone inquiry can be handled quickly and effortlessly from home at 9 o'clock at night or on Saturday. Getting calls through during normal business hours is not always easy, especially on days when the markets are particularly active. Besides, you might not have a job where you can get to a phone as frequently and as easily as you would like.

It goes without saying that you not only want prompt but courteous service. So before making your final fund selections, place several phone calls to the toll-free phone numbers at different times and see what happens. The service issue may impact your decision making, particularly if you find you constantly are greeted by a recording and placed on hold too long.

USE THE TELEPHONE TO GET YOUR QUESTIONS ANSWERED

If you are completely baffled by the prospectus and can't find the answers to your questions, then call the toll-free phone number and speak to someone at the investment company. Check to see what the hours of operation are for the customer service department before placing your call. Take your time and ask whatever is on your mind. Remember, no question is stupid if you don't know the answer. You will be surprised to learn how much the folks at the other end of the phone line are willing to assist you even with your rudimentary questions.

Do a little advanced planning before calling. You'll find it particularly helpful to first write your questions on a piece of paper. Then make your call and jot down the answers you receive. If you don't get the kind of response you wanted or you didn't like the individual you spoke with, then call back later. Chances are another representative will take your call, and you may find that person is better able to help you.

OPENING ACCOUNTS WITH NO MONEY DOWN

The fact that you do not have thousands of dollars to invest should in no way prevent you from establishing mutual fund accounts. Simply by selecting families of funds which offer the "no-minimum" enrollment, you don't need a lot of money to get started, just enough monthly disposable income to cover the amounts of your automatic transfers. So after you have your questions answered, start thinking about making a decision and choosing a mutual fund. If you researched four different funds, chances are you may have found at least one, or even two, to be more exciting than the others. Make your selection and complete the application form. If you agree to sign up for the "no-minimum" enrollment program, you may not have to put any money down.

On the other hand, if you have some cash you would like to invest immediately, you can write a check for any amount above the minimum because the required initial investment has been waived. Even if you do have the financial resources to make an investment of say $1,000, don't make that large an initial contribution if you don't have to. Use the automatic transfer option to add to your account on a regular basis.

INVEST BY "DOLLAR COST AVERAGING"

One of the best ways for beginning investors to build assets and to get the most for their money is to use a process known as "dollar cost averaging." This is nothing more than investing a fixed amount of money on a regular basis. You buy more shares when the market is low and fewer shares when prices are high. But the overall cost is likely to be lower than it would be if you invested a large sum all at once. When you participate in the "no-minimum" enrollment programs you are actually using a "dollar cost averaging" strategy.

HOW TO INVEST A LUMP SUM

Perhaps you are fortunate enough to have accumulated a large amount of money in a savings account which you now want to put into a mutual fund as a long-term investment. What's the best way to go about doing that?

First, you may want to avoid putting the entire sum into a new account at one time. If you invested everything at once, you might find you wound up buying the shares at an all-time high. Shortly after you get your statement, you see the market makes a "correction" and now your shares are valued at a price less than you paid for them. In other words, your timing was less than perfect. If you are a true, long-term investor, chances are this will mean very little in 10 years, but it is important to you today. So one sure way to maximize your buying power is to use a strategy based on "dollar cost averaging." Second, you might consider spreading that money across several mutual funds with differing objectives.

This is all part of a strategy I call "walking your money into your accounts." With this method you can open any number of mutual fund accounts you wish whenever you want. Because you are investing small amounts of cash over time, you don't have to worry about "timing" the markets since you are a long-term investor. You simply want to avoid paying the high initial investment that is required of most mutual funds. To do that you can use either of two methods to invest that lump sum:

SIGN UP FOR THE "NO-MINIMUM" ENROLLMENT PROGRAM

Sign up for this option at the time you complete your mutual fund application. Keep your cash in a bank account, and use automatic transfers to "walk" your money into your newly established mutual funds each month.

This allows you to use "dollar cost averaging" to get started and build those account balances. Once you've reached the required minimum investment, continuing the automatic transfers (even if it means you have to lower the amount you invest each month) will allow you to build a solid foundation in mutual funds.

USE A MONEY MARKET FUND ACCOUNT

If you already planned to use automatic transfers in the "no-minimum enrollment program," but have a large sum of money you wanted to move into the new mutual funds quickly, then consider opening a money market fund account also. Look at your application carefully, and you probably will see that the family has a money market mutual fund, so you can put as much of your cash in that account as you wish. For example, say you had $2,000 you were waiting to invest, you had $200 of monthly disposable income and there were two mutual funds in the family you thought would be ideal for you. The question before you is "what's the best method to get that money into your new accounts?" In your application you could arrange to invest your $200 monthly disposable income with one $100 per month automatic transfer at the beginning of the month (to the first mutual fund) and another $100 transfer two weeks later (to the second mutual fund). Also, at the time of application you could write a check for $2,000 and also put $200 in each of the two funds initially and deposit the balance ($1,600) into the money market mutual fund account. Then simply mail in your application.

Once your application is processed, you'll receive a confirmation of your purchases of $1,600 in the money market fund and $400 invested in whole and fractional shares of your two mutual funds. You also receive a confirmation of your authorization for the two $100 a month automatic transfers. The remaining $1,600 can be transferred into your accounts over the course of the next eight months. If the market makes a sudden correction (goes down), you can call and buy more shares of the two funds or simply leave your cash where it is in the event additional "corrections" occur over the short term. Simply by "walking" the money into your accounts over time "dollar cost averaging" is working for you. Even though it can take many months to transfer the entire $1,600 from the money market fund to the mutual funds, you're still getting a competitive return on that cash compared to a bank savings account.

Account Options

When filling out that application (called an account registration form), you will have several options other than the automatic transfers. Although the registration forms will vary, as will the options offered by the investment company or family of mutual funds, four of the more important features include the following:

Account registration

Your first decision is one of how to register these new account(s). If you are single, you will obviously list only your name. Married couples may wish to consult a tax specialist to determine if it is advantageous to open their account(s) in both names (joint accounts) or just one name (individual accounts). Joint accounts can be set up "as joint tenants with the right of survivorship," which means if one spouse dies, ownership passes to the surviving spouse.

DIVIDEND AND CAPITAL GAINS PAYMENT OPTIONS

If you selected a fund that generates capital gains and dividends, typically you will have three choices for handling that income produced by those accounts:

a. to reinvest both your dividends and capital gains (if any),
b. to receive dividends in cash and reinvest capital gains, or
c. to receive both the dividends and capital gains in cash.

Long-term investors can choose the first option, so any form of income (dividends or capital gains) is reinvested in the fund to purchase additional shares. Initially, the amount of income you receive invariably will be very small and perhaps not enough to buy one share. Nonetheless, the investment company will purchase a fractional share, add it to your current account balance and maintain those shares for you.

AUTOMATIC TRANSFERS

By this time you should appreciate the value of such an option and how it helps you bypass the high minimum initial investment. This feature is of tremendous value to all individual investors, not just beginners, and should be seriously considered whenever possible.

TELEPHONE OR MAIL REDEMPTION

This option establishes the method or methods by which you will later handle the sale of your shares. The telephone redemption option allows the investment company to take instructions to redeem (sell) shares from you over the telephone. The mail option indicates that the only way you will authorize the investment company to sell shares in your account is by a letter of instruction from you. Obviously, the telephone redemption option is not only convenient but it affords you the opportunity to sell your holdings quickly. In the event of a sudden financial demand that cannot be met entirely by your emergency fund, you can make a phone call and have shares sold without delay. Also, in the event the financial markets change rather dramatically and you want to bail out or take profits, you have the ability to act swiftly. However, the mail redemption option provides greater safety to your account, and diminishes the possibility of an unauthorized sale. But your letter will have to include the signatures of all owners exactly as they are registered. These signatures may have to be *guaranteed* by a bank official or registered stockbrokerage firm and getting all that accomplished takes time. Check with the investment company to be certain what their requirements are before you actually mail your application.

You may be offered two other redemption options that appear as "by wire" or "by mail." You are being asked to indicate whether you want the proceeds from any future sale mailed to you or wired to one of your bank accounts. For the "by wire" option, simply supply the name, address and account number where the funds should be sent. You will be charged a modest fee to have the funds electronically transferred, but it is well worth it if the amount of money involved is substantial. Besides, mail redemptions take more time to complete and letters can be misplaced, misdirected, lost, stolen, etc.

While on the subject of redemptions, you should also know there are programs that allow you to have money automatically *withdrawn* from your mutual fund account each month. This is simply a reversal of the automatic investment plans mentioned earlier. Instead of you sending money from your bank to your mutual fund account, the mutual fund makes the transfer of an amount of money you specify on a particular day of the month you determine. This may sound like an inappropriate subject for someone who is trying to *begin* an investment program, but it actually highlights how mutual funds can benefit you in retirement.

On the Vanguard Group's application under the heading Fund

Express Option you'll find information on setting up an "Automatic Withdrawal Plan." You fill in the amount of the transfer and the date you want the money wired to your bank account. Just keep this in mind for future reference.

Buying Mutual Funds Through a Brokerage Service

In the previous discussions one major assumption was made. That was that you were selecting *no-load* mutual funds you wanted to purchase, and you were opening those accounts directly with the mutual fund family or investment company that provides the day-to-day administration for shareholders. It was further assumed that you would not mind making the phone calls and doing all the bookkeeping that goes along with owning several different funds from more than one fund family.

Is there another alternative? Yes, indeed! You could establish a brokerage account and have the brokerage service handle all the administration for you. At the very mention of a "brokerage service," most individuals immediately associate that with an account designed principally to purchase stocks and bonds. But today's stockbrokers can provide a wide array of financial services with varying costs. The larger brokerage houses offer their own load mutual fund, yet they will also buy hundreds of mutual funds for your account, even *no-load* funds, if you want them to do so. For investors interested in keeping all their holdings in one account, this cuts down on their paperwork and bookkeeping. In other words, you supply the money and they handle the transactions for you. But there's a catch. Many brokerage companies are going to charge you a commission to buy or sell your fund shares, even the *no-load* mutual funds. To some extent, you are losing the benefit of purchasing a *no-load* mutual fund when you pay a fee to buy it.

This service took on a new twist when the discount brokerage service, Charles Schwab, established a program that enables its customers to buy and sell specified *no-load* funds and pay *no fees*. Offered under the name

Charles Schwab Mutual Fund OneSource,™ this service enables participants to purchase more than 200 mutual funds without paying a load,
transaction or bookkeeping fees. In other words, you buy and sell shares of
certain designated funds at their net asset value (NAV) the same way you
would if you dealt with the fund families directly. This program includes
many very well-known mutual fund companies: Barron Asset, Benham,
Berger, Capiello-Rushmore, Cohen & Steers, Dreyfus, Evergreen,
Federated, Founders, INVESCO, IAI, Janus, Kaufman, Lexington,
Montogomery, Neuberger & Berman, Oakmark, Rushmore, Schwab
Funds, Skyline, SteinRoe, Strong, Twentieth Century, United Services
and Yacktman to name a few. The expenses associated with the program
are borne by the mutual funds, and some restrictions apply, but call
Charles Schwab for details and a free prospectus (1-800-2NO-LOAD).

Sounds perfect, right? Well, not exactly. As you might imagine, there
are those restrictions. For starters, the minimum *initial* purchase requirements, established by the respective mutual funds, range from $250 to as
much as $25,000 through the Schwab program. The actual amount of
subsequent purchases varies among funds from $250 on up unless you
participate in Schwab's Automatic Investment Plan. Under this plan you
arrange automatic transfers to Schwab from one of your banks to a mutual
fund account on a date or dates you specify. Many of the funds permit
automatic investments of as a little as $50, and these transfers can be
made every two weeks, monthly or quarterly. However, you still have to
come up with the initial investment which is at least $250 worth of
shares. That may not be much money to some investors, but to folks just
starting out, it is a lot of cash. In fact, the buying power of $250 is greater
for investors when they manage their accounts themselves.

Not to be outdone, Fidelity Investments introduced a similar program
entitled Fidelity's FundsNetwork®, which allows investors to purchase
shares of mutual funds from companies such as Benham, Dreyfus,
Evergreen, Fidelity, Founders, Janus, Neuberger & Berman, SteinRoe
and Strong without incurring transaction fees. Berger Funds are also
available, but they include an asset-based sales charge (12b-1 fees). For

more information on Fidelity's FundsNetwork™ program and a complete listing of these participating mutual funds, call their toll-free number (800-544-9697). Other brokerage firms, such as Muriel Siebert & Company (800-872-0711) and Jack White & Company (800-233-3411) offer investors the opportunity to purchase certain *no-load* mutual funds with no transaction fees, so call these companies for details on their particulars program.

But remember, if you work directly with fund families that offer the "no-minimum" enrollment programs and automatic transfers, you can open several mutual fund accounts with no money down and as little as $25 per month with Twentieth Century Investors and $50 per month with the Janus Group. Several other fund families have minimum purchases of $100 per transaction. The trade off here is that you have to administer the accounts and keep track of the monthly statement. (The accounting aspect of investing will be discussed in more detail in Step 10.)

For the benefit of readers living north of the U.S. border, Fidelity Investments of Canada, Ltd., maintains an office in Toronto (see Appendix D). Call their toll-free phone number in Canada (800-263-4077) to learn more about the Fidelity's FundsNetwork.® That program is not only available to investors living in Canada, but individuals who reside in the United Kingdom, Saudi Arabia as well as Puerto Rico and the U.S. Virgin Islands. Charles Schwab does not maintain a Canadian office, so if you live outside the U.S., contact their nearest American office to obtain information on the Charles Schwab Mutual Fund OneSource™ program. Be advised that when establishing accounts in the United States and making transactions such business is conducted in U.S. dollars.

Don't Buy a Dividend!

By now you certainly realize that timing the purchase of mutual fund investments is not critical if you make regular, low, monthly automatic transfers. But if for any reason you decide to make a large, lump sum payment you should be aware of one potential mistake. That is the purchase of shares just before a dividend is distributed. What this means is that if you buy shares of a mutual fund, or a dividend paying stock, prior to the distribution of a dividend, part of the net asset value of that security includes the as yet unpaid dividend. So when you make your purchase, you wind up purchasing those shares at a price that includes the dividend, and that's how this became known as "buying a dividend."

Let's use an example to illustrate exactly how this might work. Suppose you have $500 and you wish to use it all to purchase shares of Mutual Fund X, because your research showed it was an outstanding fund and it fit your investment objectives. You just have to have it in your portfolio, and you want to start off by putting the entire $500 in as soon as you can. So you send in your application and open your account in Mutual Fund X, and your first purchase is at the price of $10.00 per share. The day after your confirmation statement arrives welcoming you to the fund and telling you how many shares you own, you read in the newspaper that Mutual Fund X has declared a dividend, a capital gains distribution or both, in the amount of $1.00. Great you say, right? Wrong! If you made a $500 investment you bought 50 shares. When the declared income is distributed to shareholders, you'll receive $50 ($1.00 for each 50 shares) or have that money reinvested in additional shares. But the share price of your fund will drop to $9.00 ($10.00 NAV minus the $1.00 distribution). For the sake of our example, let's say you opted for the $50 in cash. You have 50 shares but at a net asset value of $9.00 they are only worth $450 (50 X $9.00). With the $50 check you just received you still have your $500 initial investment, but you also now owe the IRS taxes on the $50 of *income* you just received. Gotcha! You just bought a dividend.

If you own shares in the fund as of a certain date, called the record date, you'll receive the dividend for each of your shares. It doesn't matter if you bought those shares one day before the record date or you have owned them for 10 months, as long as you were listed as what is called "a shareholder of record" by that specified date. In effect you purchased shares that included the cost of the dividend, so when that dividend was paid to you, that meant you incurred the tax liability for the income received, even if you had the dividend reinvested.

Mutual funds that pay dividends and capital gains typically announce the dates of these payments in advance. This information will appear in financial newspapers, such as *The Wall Street Journal*, but if you don't read these publications regularly you might not be aware of such announcements. In that case, call the mutual fund(s) you are considering purchasing. Ask if a dividend or capital gains distribution will be paid in the near future.

How can you avoid "buying a dividend"? Simply wait until after the dividend is declared (the "ex-dividend" date), when the price of the fund's shares have dropped to reflect the amount of money soon to be paid out. You'll see the symbol "x" after the fund name to indicate it is "ex-dividend." Now your $500 will enable you to purchase 55.56 shares of Mutual Fund X at $9.00 per share. You will then receive income at the fund's next declared payment date.

This strategy is most important when you intend to open an account and make a large initial contribution. If you go with the "no minimum" investment option, you may also want to check with the fund and start the transfers after any distribution that is about to be declared. Otherwise, send in your registration form and start the automatic transfer immediately. Don't attempt to start and stop your automatic transfers to avoid "buying a dividend;" it's probably more trouble than it's worth, particularly if your monthly contribution is small. Should you want to move $500 or $1,000 each month into one account, then it might be prudent to keep track of distribution dates, delay a transfer and have the transaction occur after the distribution. Judge for yourself whether you think the amount of money involved necessitates such special handling.

SET A TARGET FOR EACH MUTUAL FUND

Once you have your mutual fund accounts established with automatic transfers in place for account building, your work is not finished. You obviously aren't going to want your money to be automatically transferred to your mutual funds forever. Everything has its limits, including mutual funds. So set a financial goal for how much money you think is appropriate for you to invest in any one mutual fund. Base your decision on the amount of disposable income you have and how much other money you see coming in down the road. What is a reasonable expectation for you given your income and expenses, $3,000, $5,000 or maybe $10,000? Only you can determine what that level is, because you are the only one who knows what your earning capacity is and how much money you have to invest each month.

When you eventually meet your goal, what do you do then? The choices are many and are not limited to the following:

1. Add more funds with different financial objectives to your foundation in mutual funds.

2. Keep the number of mutual funds unchanged. Simply raise your goal for each fund (go from $3,000 to $5,000 or from $5,000 to $10,000, etc.). This will keep your life simple if your funds are doing well, otherwise be prepared for more record keeping associated with adding new funds.

3. Expand upon your financial foundation in mutual funds by adding Tier 2 investments (DRIPs—stocks with dividend reinvestment programs).

HOW MANY MUTUAL FUNDS SHOULD YOU OWN?

This is almost like asking someone how many pairs of shoes should they have. There is often no simple answer to this question. In fact, sometimes it is not necessarily how many do you want but how many can you afford? You start off with the basics, a pair of shoes for work and another pair for play. If you have the money, you can buy additional pairs of dress and casual shoes for both work and play. You can even find specialized athletic shoes for golf, running, aerobics, tennis, etc. The choices are many; the limiting factor is how much money you have to spend.

The same thing might be said of mutual funds. There are no standard answers to the question of how many mutual funds are enough. It is a very individualistic question and one that you are best able to respond to based on your personal finances, income potential and lifestyle. While one or two mutual funds may be appropriate for someone making $50 a month automatic transfers, six or eight diversified mutual funds might be what is needed for couples with a higher disposable monthly income of $1,000 or $2,000 per month. But try to diversify your investments over as varied a portfolio of mutual funds as you can, using the fewest number of funds possible. Some have suggested just one or two funds, when your assets amount to $5,000 or less.[15] When you have $100,000 or more to invest you can spread that wealth over nine to ten different types of funds. In all likelihood the ideal mix lies somewhere between three and ten mutual funds.

After becoming familiar with all 10 steps in this investment strategy, you will be better able to see where mutual funds fit into your financial plans. Perhaps you have little time or inclination to go much beyond mutual fund investing (Tier 1) at this point in your life. If so, you may be content to limit your investing to just two or three high quality mutual funds. On the other hand, you may be drawn to the challenges of choosing companies with dividend reinvestment programs (Tier 2) and selecting individual growth stocks (Tier 3). Perhaps your income potential is great, and you foresee regular increases in your disposable income, so you wish to explore as many options as possible.

IN REVIEW

1. Know the difference between *open-end* and *closed-end* mutual funds.

2. The price of a *load* mutual fund includes an up front sales charge (load) while a *no-load* fund does not.

3. There are at least five basic kinds of mutual funds: common stock, income, balanced, bond and money market.

4. Mutual funds classified by their investment objective fall into many different categories.

5. Other designations based on investment objectives also exist and are in use: maximum capital gains, small-company growth, world income, etc, but all fall into one of the previous groupings.

6. Know what a mutual fund "family" or "group" is and which families offer a "no minimum" enrollment option.

7. Recognize the importance of diversification *within* and *between* mutual funds.

8. Know how to select a mutual fund and how to use your public library.

9. Know what to look for in a prospectus and what options are best for you when completing an account registration form.

10. Feel free to use the telephone, call a mutual fund on a toll-free number and speak with a representative to get your questions answered.

11. Invest by "dollar cost averaging" to maximize your investment dollars.

12. If you have a lump sum to invest, "walk" the money into your accounts through regular transfers from a money market fund account and don't buy a dividend.

13. Set a financial target for each mutual fund account.

14. Open enough mutual funds as you can afford to get diversification.

15. Refer to Appendix A for a listing of major mutual fund families and groups.

WHAT'S NEXT?

With a financial foundation in mutual funds you not only have Tier 1 of your investment strategy established but you have a direction for that strategy. Due to the importance of diversification, you would be well advised not to stop here. To maximize the potential return of your disposable income, you can diversify further by participating in stock dividend reinvestment programs (DRIPs). Turn to **Step 8: Diversify Your Portfolio—With DRIPs (Tier 2)** to learn more about this exciting investment opportunity.

Notes

1. Downes, John and Jordan Elliot Goodman. *Barron's Finance and Investment Handbook*. 2nd edition. New York: Barron's Educational Series, 1987.

2. Laderman, Jeffrey M. and Geoffrey Smith. "The Power of Mutual Funds." *Business Week,* 18 January 1993: 62–68.

3. Roman, Monica. "Has Your Mutual Fund Become 'Fat and Bloated'?" *Smart Money,* February 1993: 35–36.

4. Conn, David. "Myriad rating systems confuse fund investors." *Dayton Daily News* (reprinted from *The Baltimore Sun*), 19 April 1993: 3.

5. Clements, Jonathan. "Mutual Funds: Stock Mutual Fund Sales Soared to $9.9 Billion Last Month, as Bullish Investors Shatter Record." *The Wall Street Journal,* 31 December 1992: C1.

6. Clements, Jonathan. Heard on the Street. "Mutual Fund Investors: A Major Force in Stock Market." *The Wall Street Journal,* 26 February 1993: C1.

7. McGough, Robert and Sara Calian. Mutual Funds, "Bond-Fund Buyers Ease Up in November." *The Wall Street Journal,* 30 November 1993: C1.

8. McGough, Robert. "Investors Ran to Stock Funds During January." *The Wall Street Journal,* 2 February 1993: C1.

9. Kadlec, Daniel. Street Talk. "Baby boomers are a bust on saving." *USA Today,* 28 January 1993: 3B.

10. Staff feature. "The Top-Performing Mutual Funds." *Money Magazine,* February 1992: 101–111.

11. Simon, Ruth. "The Best Funds To Buy Now." *Money Magazine,* February 1992: 90–99.

12. O'Connell, Vanessa. "The Top-Performing Mutual Funds." *Money Magazine,* February 1993: 87–97.

13. Watterson, Thomas. "Check Averages before tossing a fund." *Dayton Daily News*, Smart Money Investor Section, 18 January 1993: 4.

14. Kimelman, John. "Unloading the Loads." *Financial World,* 24 November 1992: 48–49.

15. O'Connell, Vanessa. "How Many Funds Should You Own?" *Money Magazine,* March 1993: 63.

S T E P

DIVERSIFY YOUR PORTFOLIO—WITH DRIPS

With the 3-tiered strategy, mutual funds form the financial foundation of your investment strategy (Tier 1). You carefully select funds that meet your comfort level for risk and have objectives in line with your approach to reaching financial goals. But it is important that you not allow mutual funds to remain your *only* option to avoid concentrating your assets in just one investment arena. To this foundation you may want to add a portfolio of diversified dividend-paying stocks that offer a dividend reinvestment program, often referred to as a DRIP or DRP. Surprisingly, few small investors are even aware of the existence of such plans despite the fact they are offered by many well-known companies.

JUST WHAT IS A DRIP?

A DRIP is simply a program that allows stockholders to use the dividends they receive to purchase more shares of a company's stock. Most plans also provide an option for participants to make additional cash purchases

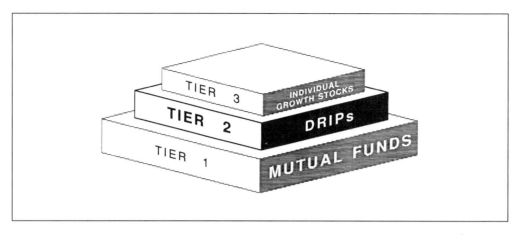

Dividend reinvestment programs (DRIPs) are added to your mutual fund foundation to complete the second tier in your 3-tiered investment strategy.

at times other than dividend payments, so DRIPs are best described as *automatic dividend reinvestment and common stock purchase plans.*

What this means for you as a shareholder enrolled in such a program is that each quarter, when dividends are distributed, the proceeds (dividends) are automatically applied to the purchase of additional shares (*reinvested*, in other words). With the option to send in money on a regular basis, you can buy even more shares through what are frequently called optional cash payments (OCPs). Some plans may refer to them as optional investments, cash purchases or something to this effect. Regardless of what they are called, it is important to know that many companies accept OCPs of as little as $10 per month. A $10 investment is an unheard of minimum even compared to mutual funds with "no minimum" enrollment programs. The frequency of the investment for the OCPs varies with each program from weekly to once a quarter, but monthly purchases seem more common. The OCPs are entirely optional, so participants send in the extra cash only when they want to, provided those payments meet the minimum level specified by the company's plan.

How Many Companies Offer DRIPs?

There are literally hundreds of companies and closed-end mutual funds that have such plans (over 800 hundred are listed Appendix C). I will make an additional reference recommendation, and this one will save you a great deal of time. In 1992 Charles B. Carlson published a book devoted entirely to dividend reinvestment plans entitled *Buying Stocks Without a Broker*.[1] This is a superb publication and one that you are sure to find not only informative but easy to read. In fact, it might best be described as a single-source guide on the subject of dividend reinvestment programs. The $16.95 cost of the soft-bound version is well worth the price of admission to DRIPs. The book has seven chapters and six appendixes full of very useful information. It even contains specific stock recommendations for five different model portfolios for investors of all ages: from the "playschool portfolio" for that college education to what Mr. Carlson describes as the "golden years portfolio" for individuals near or at retirement. You'll find company names, addresses, phone numbers and descriptions of their dividend reinvestment programs and basic features. All this in plain English. If you don't wish to buy the book, at least borrow a copy from your local library and give it a good read (if you can ever get folks to return it).

It is not uncommon for companies to switch transfer agents or to make modifications to their dividend reinvestment plan from time to time. The information contained in Appendix C was updated at the time of publication to be as current as possible, given the potential for frequent changes. Nonetheless, you'll find the listing contains the company name, its stock symbol, the exchange where it is traded, the minimum amount of their optional cash payment (OCP), as well as the name and phone number of the transfer agent administering the plan.

With that introduction behind you, it is now time to discuss the value of dividend reinvestment programs in a bit more detail.

HOW DOES A DRIP WORK?

To become eligible to establish a DRIP, you generally must own at least one share of stock in a company that pays a dividend and offers a dividend reinvestment program. Check the listing in Appendix C if you are interested in a particular company. You can also find this information under the heading "Dividend Data" in the Standard & Poor's Reports contained in the public library reference section.

While the general rule is one share of stock is sufficient for participation in a plan, a few companies do require applicants to own more before being eligible to enroll (for example, **AT&T** requires 10 shares). That requirement will be plainly stated in the company's plan description. Some companies will even help you get started by buying that first share directly through them rather than a broker (Appendix C). Unfortunately, those companies are few and the vast majority do not offer this service, so be prepared to buy whatever number of shares you need either through a full-service stockbroker or discount brokerage service. A partial listing of brokerage firms is included in Appendix D if you don't already have a brokerage account.

New stockholders generally receive information about the company they've purchased to include quarterly or annual reports along with a prospectus and an application for the dividend reinvestment program. It is important that the share(s) you purchased be registered in your name. You cannot have the stock held in a brokerage account or what is called "street name." So at the time of purchase, state that you are buying the shares to initiate a DRIP and ask to be issued a stock certificate. Allow six weeks or more from the time of your purchase for the document to arrive. By the way, you'll receive a single stock certificate whether you purchase one, 10 or 100 shares.

Once you become a registered shareholder, with stock certificate in hand, you can mail in your application to the plan administrator along with an optional cash payment if you so choose. Be sure to list your name on the DRIP application exactly as it appears on the certificate. And remember, when you purchase that stock through a brokerage account, the certificate will be issued to the individuals listed as the registered owners of the account. In other words, if you have an individual brokerage account you can expect to receive a certificate in your name only. If you wish to open DRIP accounts with your spouse, it is much easier to purchase those initial shares through a *joint* brokerage account so all stock certificates are immediately registered in both names. Stock ownership can be transferred from individual to joint ownership *after* the sale and *before* a certificate is issued or even *after* the stock certificate has actually been issued in one person's name. However, such transfers merely add delays and another layer of paperwork for all concerned. So plan ahead.

Except for those few companies that will buy your initial shares for you, most DRIP programs are administered by a transfer agent which is usually a commercial bank. The transfer agent performs all the administration for the plan: maintaining records, issuing and cancelling stock certificates and handling general issues for stock owners. You can write for DRIP information to a company's department of shareholder services, but you'll send your application and any checks for OCPs to the plan administrator, if the two are not one and the same. When the bank receives your payment, they will send you an acknowledgment. Shortly after the actual purchase date, a second statement will be forwarded to you indicating the amount you invested less any service charge, the number of shares purchased and the total number of shares held by you (your stock certificate) and held by the plan administrator in your account.

REINVESTING DIVIDENDS

Once you've enrolled in the DRIP plan, and it comes time for the company to distribute (pay) a dividend, your proceeds will be used to buy both full and fractional shares of stock. The purchase is generally made at the prevailing price of the company's stock at the time of the distribution. If you only own one share and your dividend is very small, you might wind up with 1.0257 shares in your account after the first dividend distribution. By following the price of your DRIP stock in the newspaper or on television you'll see that the stock will go what is called "ex-dividend" and the letter "x" will appear after the listing in the newspaper. That is the period between the announcement of the dividend and the actual dividend payment date. Typically the stock's price moves up by the amount of the dividend as you approach the ex-dividend date only to fall by the amount of the dividend after the date of the distribution. The same pitfalls for "buying a dividend" in a mutual fund explained in Step 7, apply here in buying dividend-paying stocks.

A statement will be sent to you either quarterly or after each purchase if you make optional cash payments in non-dividend paying months. The account statements will itemize the transactions for your account up to that last purchase. DRIPs are also referred to as "automatic" dividend reinvestment accounts, because once you enroll, the reinvesting is done for you automatically.

OPTIONAL CASH PAYMENTS (OCPS)

If it isn't already clear, you don't have to wait until a dividend is paid to purchase additional shares for your account. By using optional cash payments you can invest regularly and with very little money in most cases. The beauty of the OCP option is that this feature is truly "optional." If you want to send in $10 one month and buy 0.20 shares of a $50 stock that's fine with the company. You can also choose to send $500 the next month and buy 10 shares; it's your decision. Or you may opt not to send in any money at all, and that's okay too.

But by making regular OCP payments of a fixed amount each month, you can take advantage of "dollar cost averaging" as was recommended for your mutual fund accounts. An even better way to use the optional payments is to establish a minimum amount to be paid every month, but add a little extra cash during months when the stock's price is down. Just be sure to stick with your minimum when the price rises. In this way, you not only dollar cost average but take advantage of buying opportunities (downturns in the markets).

Costs Associated with a DRIP

Anytime stocks are purchased there are going to be commissions and fees to be paid by someone. One of the nice features of DRIPs is that whether you reinvest all your dividends or supplement them with additional cash payments, many companies absorb some or all of the fees for plan participants. This is not necessarily true of every company, because some impose nominal service charges or reduced brokerage commissions for each transaction. The fact that your money is pooled with other shareholders dilutes your costs and those savings are passed on to you. Review each plan description so you know exactly what the associated fees are (if any), otherwise you might find your low optional cash payment may be consumed even by "modest" fees. For example, if you sent in a $25 check as an OCP, and it was subject to a $5.00 transaction fee, you'd be assuming a 20% expense ratio. You'd have to increase your OCP to $100 to knock that fee down to just the 5% level.

All in all, the expenses are far less than you would pay if you were to attempt to execute a similar transaction elsewhere. And besides, you won't find many stockbrokers interested in regularly executing an order for $10 or $25 worth of a stock, even if that bought you the equivalent of one share. This is an important service to have available, particularly if you want to make rather large OCP payments and purchase blocks of stock to add to your holdings over a relatively short period of time.

When you sell all or part of the shares in your DRIP account, you'll be assessed the customary brokerages fees and a small related service charge. Again, because those shares are pooled with those of other plan participants, the commissions you pay on a sale are also less than what you'd be assessed outside the DRIP. This is especially true if you sell a small number of shares or what is referred to as an "odd lot" (less than a block of 100 shares).

STOCK PURCHASE DATE

The date on which shares are purchased for plan participants varies among companies, so read the prospectus to determine the purchase date for the stocks you buy. It may be the 1st, the 5th, the 7th, the 15th or the last business day of the month. Be advised that OCPs do not earn interest while the money is held awaiting the stock purchase date, so time the mailing of those payments accordingly. You don't want that money out of your bank account any longer than necessary, because you'll lose interest on your payment. By the way, you can write these checks from either account 1 or account 2, whichever is easier for you to administer.

DO ALL COMPANIES PAYING DIVIDENDS OFFER DRIPS?

Unfortunately, the answer to this question is no. If every company that paid dividends offered DRIPs, then life would be a bit easier for the small investor. But such is not the case, and that's one reason why Tier 3 (Selecting Individual Growth Stocks) exists. For now, review the list of companies offering DRIPs that is contained in Appendix C to get an appreciation of how many well-known and high-quality companies allow you to buy stocks through these programs.

HOW DO YOU KNOW WHICH COMPANIES TO SELECT?

Seasoned investors typically follow a number of financial publications, do a great deal of reading and often know what sectors of business are "hot" and which are not. They also can differentiate a fad from a trend, or at least they think they can. They know how to pick a company that appears to have a bright future.

Beginning investors not only must learn where to find information but how to interpret it and what to do with it once they've got it. That's why *Money Magazine, Fortune, Forbes, Financial World, Business Week,*

Smart Money, The Wall Street Journal and the myriad of other financial publications are so useful. They include feature articles on companies and make recommendations about their future (see Appendix B).

One sure way to get started immediately is to use Mr. Carlson's book *Buying Stock Without a Broker*. Chapter 7 contains over 200 pages listing company after company, so all the hard work has been done for you. Browse through those pages and see which companies and business sectors appeal to you and where you'd like to put your money. Mr. Carlson has gone so far as to include his favorite DRIPs along with a number of other selections for people with different financial objectives. He has included a portfolio for folks with a long-term growth strategy, one for those interested in sticking with "Blue Chip" stocks and another suited to a steady income producing retirement strategy. You may have heard the term "blue chip," but don't exactly know what it means. It's used to describe common stocks of nationally recognized companies with a long track record of increasing profits and consistent dividend payments backed by quality management, service and products.

A word of caution: these companies and portfolios represent Mr. Carlson's preferences, so compare these selections to the recommendations of the other research sources you locate in the public library. When you find several investment advisors recommending the same company, at least you have safety in numbers. You can identify companies that are worth a serious second look and in-depth assessment from two principal sources before you decide if they are right for your Tier 2 portfolio:

TAKE RECOMMENDATIONS FROM FINANCIAL PUBLICATIONS

There is a wealth of information on the past performance of hundreds of companies in the many financial books, magazines, newsletters and reports that exist today (Appendix B). I've already mentioned how you can use the book *Buying Stocks Without a Broker* to your advantage. If you don't like those recommendations, read current and back issues of several financial magazines (*Business Week, Financial World, Forbes, Fortune,*

Money Magazine, for example) and then browse through a stack of *The Wall Street Journal* and *Barron's* until you find reports and recommendations on stocks that look promising from your perspective.

There are a number of different approaches to selecting stocks for you from these choices. Perhaps you'd like to start out with a couple of low-risk suggestions, then look for reports on "Blue Chip" stocks. Take the list of stocks, go over to the Standard & Poor's Reports and look up their past performance, determine if they offer a DRIP (look in the Dividend Data section) and study the rate of increase in the share price *and* the dividend. Collect reports for each company and take time to examine their content and compare performance levels.

USE YOUR OWN INSTINCTS AND COMMON SENSE

You can also use the common sense approach to identifying stocks that may be appropriate for your DRIP portfolio. Just look around and analyze what you see from your perspective in life. If you like to eat out a lot, who has the best food for the best price? Is it **McDonald's**, Wendy's or **KFC** for the best fast food according to your taste? What's your favorite soft drink or beer? Where do women get the best quality and price on clothing these days? And if you want to buy something at discount where do you go, Kmart, Sears, **Wal-Mart** or Woolworth? Check out what's new and hot in the supermarket. When you start getting answers, then find out who owns the product or service you feel is a leader in the field. Head back to the library and review the S&P Report for that company. Focus your search on companies that are well entrenched and avoid fads and trends unless you are prepared to assume their high levels of risk.

DON'T FORGET TO DIVERSIFY!

Remember our earlier discussion on the need for diversification. Make sure you don't unintentionally duplicate your mutual fund's portfolio with your DRIP selections. If you do, you're not getting the diversification you sought. Try to add companies from a variety of business sectors and avoid concentrating your holdings in just one area. If you think you might be leaning toward stocks that your mutual funds own, don't buy anything until you've checked it out. Obtain a quarterly, semi-annual or annual report from your funds. They will include a list of the companies they hold in their portfolio. Unless the stocks you select are particularly exciting, you will wind up owning more of the same. That is not always bad and may be something you cannot avoid if you lean toward conservative stocks and mutual funds. If you can diversify, do it.

WHERE ARE STOCKS BOUGHT AND SOLD?

The stock of companies you will purchase for DRIPs will be bought and sold (traded) in one of three major organized marketplaces: the New York Stock Exchange, the American Stock Exchange or the "over the counter market."[2]

THE NEW YORK STOCK EXCHANGE (NYSE)

This is recognized as the oldest and largest exchange in America with the well-known address of 11 Wall Street in New York City. Here bonds, common stocks, common stock equivalents (preferred stocks or bonds which can be converted to common stock) and a variety of other financial instruments (option, rights and warrants) of large companies are bought and sold by members of the exchange. Of all the exchanges, the NYSE has the strictest requirements for membership, yet it lists over 1,500 of some of the largest companies that trade publicly. In fact, the large size of many of the NYSE members led to its nickname, "The Big Board." Here you'll find the likes of **AT&T,** Blockbuster Entertainment, **Coca-Cola,** Walt Disney, **Eastman Kodak**, General Motors, Hewlett-Packard, IBM, Xerox, etc., just to name a few.

The American Stock Exchange (AMEX or ASE)

The AMEX is also located in New York City. It is on this exchange that the stocks and bonds of small- to medium-sized companies are bought and sold, unlike the NYSE where the shares of big firms are traded.

The Over the Counter Market (OTC or NASDAQ)

The OTC is not an organized exchange per se, like the NYSE or AMEX. Instead, securities are traded by a telephone and computer network (called the National Association of Securities Dealers Automated Quotations, NASDAQ for short). Operated by the National Associated of Securities Dealers (NASD), the over-the-counter market historically was home to mostly small companies that were unable to meet the requirements for listing on the NYSE or the AMEX. However, many companies that met the requirements for listing on the other exchanges have chosen to remain on the OTC market because of the opportunity for trading by numerous securities dealers. One company that has remained a stalwart on the NASDAQ is the computer software giant **Microsoft**.

Regional Stock Exchanges

A number of other exchanges are registered with the Securities and Exchange Commission and exist outside of New York. But the purchases you make to initiate dividend reinvestment programs will probably be for companies traded in one of the three major markets (NYSE, AMEX and OTC).

Stock Indexes and Averages

There are a number of different methods to measure changes in the value of certain groups of stocks or the stock market in general. Some of the more widely mentioned indexes are: The AMEX Major Market Index, the AMEX Market Value Index (AMVI), the Dow Jones Industrial Average (DJIA), the New York Stock Exchange Composite Index, the Standard & Poor's Composite Index of 500 Stocks, the NASDAQ-OTC Price Index, the Value Line Composite Index and the Wilshire 5000 Equity Index:

The AMEX Major Market Index consists of 20 "blue chip" industrial stocks and is intended to mirror the Dow Jones Industrial Average.

The AMEX Market Value Index (AMVI) contains more than 800 stocks from all the major industry groups bought and sold in the AMEX.

The Dow Jones Industrial Average (DJIA) is made up of 30 "blue chip" stocks from the NYSE making it one of the most quoted indexes in the financial community and includes: **AT&T**, Alcoa, Allied Signal, American Express, Bethlehem Steel, Boeing, Caterpillar, Chevron, **Coca-Cola**, Walt Disney, DuPont, **Eastman Kodak, Exxon,** General Electric, General Motors, Goodyear, IBM, International Paper, **Merck**, 3M, **McDonald's**, J.P. Morgan, **Philip Morris**, **Procter & Gamble**, Sears Roebuck, Texaco, **Union Carbide**, United Technologies, Westinghouse and Woolworth.

Standard & Poor's Composite Index of 500 Stocks is more commonly referred to simply as the "S&P 500." This index is composed largely of stocks drawn from the NYSE but it also includes some listings from the AMEX and the OTC market. It represents 80% of the market value drawing on 400 industrial stocks, 60 transportation issues and 40 financial companies.

NASDAQ-OTC Price Index is based on over 3,500 stocks and includes all companies quoted on the NASDAQ but not traded on any of the exchanges.

Value Line Composite Index is derived from 1,700 stocks from the NYSE, the AMEX and the OTC market that are tracked by the Value Line Investment Survey.

Wilshire 5000 Equity Index is the largest and most comprehensive measure of U.S. equities based on 5,000 stocks from the NYSE, the AMEX and the OTC market and produced by Wilshire Associates.

HOW DO YOU BUY THAT FIRST SHARE?

The decision of whom to call upon to execute the transaction (purchase the stock on an exchange) can depend on how your stock selections were made. If you did all the research and the decision was entirely yours, all you need is someone to execute the deal—buy the shares for you. In that case, you may simply want to get the job done for the cheapest price. Contact several discount brokerage companies as well as some full-service firms, and price shop. Be sure to ask what their minimum commission is, particularly if all you want to do is buy one share. A list of both full-service and discount brokerage companies is present at the end of this book in Appendix D.

On the other hand, if you've narrowed your list of potential DRIPs for your account from 828 to 10, you may want professional advice in distilling that list to one or two choices. In that case, decide if you would feel more comfortable getting help from a full-service broker who might be able to make specific recommendations on your list of 10 stocks. Then have the broker purchase the shares for you and pay the full brokerage commission. If you want advice, be prepared to pay for it. If you don't need advice, don't pay for what you don't want or need.

In my own limited survey, I've found that the full-service brokerage firm of **Dean Witter Reynolds** offers an excellent opportunity to purchase one share of stock. They charge 10% of the stock price plus a $2.35 service charge. If you wanted to purchase just one share of Coca Cola at

$43.00 per share, you'd pay a commission of $4.30 and a service charge of $2.35 for a grand total of $49.65. My discount broker would have charged me the price of one share, $43.00, plus a minimum commission of $38.00 or a total of $81.00 for the *same* transaction. The difference in cost between the two purchasing methods is $31.35.

If you intend to make a number of stock purchases, you may want to talk with a broker at Dean Witter, or some other full-service brokerage firm in your area and shop around for the services you want. If you merely need someone to buy single shares of the stock you've already selected, then consider finding a new "account executive" (stockbroker). This is a person who probably has the time and inclination to help you, knowing full well that you are self-directed (making your own investment decisions). You may not find a lot of folks willing to make those one share purchases, but they are out there. You can also visit a stock brokerage firm as a "walk in" (without an appointment), because there is sure to be someone available to help you, then see how things go. If you don't like what you hear or how you are being treated because you are not looking for financial advice, simply say "thank you" and leave. Look elsewhere or get on the phone and call other brokerage companies.

With a company such as Dean Witter you can open an account with relative ease, putting in a few hundred dollars in their money market fund. When you can make your selections, call your account executive and have the funds transferred from your money market fund to pay for the shares you buy. The Dean Witter broker I work with did everything he said he would do, and there was never a complaint when I placed my first small orders (3 shares of Home Depot and 6 shares of Rubbermaid). He only brought in $38.93 worth of commissions for the firm, but he made one customer happy: me. Even now when I call with a question, I get a prompt courteous response. Next time there's an order to be placed for a few shares for a Tier 2 investment (to start a DRIP) or a block of shares for a Tier 3 purchase, I'll see if the full-service brokerage company can equal or beat my discount broker.

A word of caution, though. Check with the brokerage company you select because what money you save on commissions, you may have to pay later as an annual account service charge. And ask if there are any fees associated with the account you establish, because a few brokerage firms now charge customers $50 to *close* an account. Some brokerage houses also require an account maintenance fee for accounts that are not active (don't place a sufficient number of buy or sell orders). In that case, the discount brokerage companies may be more economical in the long run, especially if you don't intend to purchase stocks on a regular basis. You'll see how a full-service brokerage account and knowing a stockbroker can be of help to you in Step 9.

Appendix D also contains a listing of the names, addresses and phone numbers of several brokerage houses (discount and full-service) with offices in Canada. They include the large discount broker, Fidelity Investments of Canada, Ltd., as well as established, full-service firms such as Edward D. Jones & Company, CS First Boston Corporation, Goldman Sachs Canada, Merrill Lynch Canada and Morgan Stanley Canada, Ltd. Look for an office near you and call for more information. Better yet, make arrangements to actually visit a branch office and speak with an account representative about opening a brokerage account. Don't hesitate to call one of the other listed U.S. firms if you want to comparison shop and don't mind conducting business over the phone and by mail.

How Many DRIPs Should You Own?

There is no magic number to answer this question. Mr. Carlson contends an investor can obtain sufficient diversification across many industries by creating a portfolio of 13 to 17 DRIPs,[1] but I've chosen to exceed that recommendation. If you find it easy to identify quality dividend-paying stocks with attractive dividend reinvestment programs, then use this recommendation as a yardstick. Otherwise, set your own sights and make up a Tier 2 portfolio for yourself. Start out modestly with one or two, and add to your holdings as your income increases. Remember, you can often open a DRIP immediately by buying one share directly through the company, thus avoiding the need for a brokerage service altogether (Appendix D). But make your DRIP selections based on the quality of the company as an investment and not because it is convenient to enroll.

HOW MUCH MONEY SHOULD YOU PUT IN EACH DRIP ACCOUNT?

One way to answer this question is to apply the same logic used to put limits on your mutual funds. Set a goal for each DRIP account as you would with any other investment. You can use any number of methods. Two particular approaches that might interest you are the following:

SET A MAXIMUM DOLLAR CONTRIBUTION

Base your goal on the amount of disposable income you have to invest each month as well as your overall income. Set a realistic goal to contribute $3,000, $5,000 or even $10,000 across as many DRIPs as you can afford to support. Once you reach an established goal, discontinue making optional cash payments and simply allow your dividends to be reinvested. In other words, you'll eventually let the account accrue more shares on its own by using only the dividends to buy more shares. You then buy another stock and open an additional DRIP account for a company in an area not represented in your DRIP portfolio to add diversification.

SET A GOAL FOR THE NUMBER OF SHARES YOU WANT TO OWN

Instead of looking at the DRIP account in terms of the amount of *money* you put into the account, you can view it in terms of the number of shares you'd like to own before discontinuing optional cash payments. The number of shares in turn will determine the amount of the total dividends you'll receive. If you purchase a stock that pays a small annual dividend, you might be inclined to contribute to that account until you own enough shares to have a significant annual dividend payment.

It doesn't make much difference how you go about establishing the goals for your DRIP accounts, as long as you set targets for them. Once you reach those targets, open another account and expand your Tier 2 assets.

WHY ARE DRIPS SO VALUABLE?

By this time you've familiarized yourself with mutual funds and now know more about how to inexpensively purchase stock in a company. The stocks you pick for your portfolio should offer both current income and growth not only through price appreciation but periodic increases in the annual dividend. It is possible that you will also pick companies which mutual funds identify as worthy of adding to their own portfolio. So you may have some duplication in your assets.

As the companies you own grow and interest in them increases, more investors will want to share in that ownership with you, either directly (through direct stock purchases) or indirectly (through a mutual fund). As you may recall, in 1992 investors pumped over $77.8 billion in stock mutual funds compared to $38.3 billion in 1991 and $13.3 billion in October 1993 alone.[3,4] What did those mutual fund managers do with all that money? They kept a portion in cash to meet the redemption (sell) orders of some shareholders, but for the most part they were out searching for quality stocks to purchase. That means it is quite possible some of those funds purchased shares in the companies you identified. Think about it. If a company's balance sheet reflects solid earnings and profit growth and regular dividend increases (more income for you), the price of their stock is bound to rise as more investors become aware of that performance. With the law of supply and demand and only so many shares available, the value of your DRIP account should also increase over time and provide you with an added growth component to your portfolio (capital appreciation). With a DRIP you can build your stake in these companies with just $10, $25 or $50 a month and create a meaningful investment in only a few years.

Successful companies often reward their shareholders by declaring "stock dividend" or "stock splits."

STOCK DIVIDENDS

A stock dividend is the payment of a corporation's dividend in the form of additional shares of stock rather than cash, but the actual value of the stock does not change. This sounds strange, but it benefits shareholders because their assets (number of shares) increase without a tax liability. As an example, if you owned 20 shares of ABC Brick Company and a 5% "stock dividend" was declared, you would then receive one additional share and increase your ownership to 21 shares. At the same time, the share price would be adjusted downward, so the value of 21 shares equaled that of your original 20 shares. With no increase in value you have no immediate capital gains. The distribution was declared because the earnings and performance of the business were good and the reduced price should attract more investors to purchase the stock. As the stock's popularity increases, hopefully so too will its share price. Then your 21 shares will be worth more, and you'll see the benefit in the stock dividend.

STOCK SPLITS

Like a stock dividend, a stock split is designed to reward stockholders by increasing the number of shares they own. However, when a stock split requires an increase in the number of *authorized shares* or a change in the *par value* of the stock, shareholders must actually vote to approve this action because it represents a change to the corporate charter. Nonetheless, this is a very popular way for a company to reward stockholders without actually paying out cash. Typically, the company's stock is divided ("split") in a ratio of 4 for 1, 3 for 1, 2 for 1, 3 for 2 etc., but again the total value of the shares does not change because the share price is adjusted (reduced) to match the "split." In a 2 for 1 stock split, an investor with 100 shares valued at $40 per share winds up with 200 shares at a price of $20 per share immediately after the split. Some believe that more investors might be attracted to a $20 per share stock than a stock trading at $40 per share, otherwise ignoring the balance sheet and true worth of the company. If all goes well the stock price gradually increases, and should it return to $40 a share, shareholders can look forward to doubling their investment.

A "stock split" is also regarded as a way a company can express confidence in the value of its stock and splits are frequently followed by dividend increases according to *USA Today* columnist Daniel Kadlec.[5] That same view is shared by *Chicago Tribune* financial writer Andrew Leckey.[6] The lower share price following a split is believed to draw more potential investors to a stock.[5] Mr. Leckey reported that many investors prefer to purchase stocks in the $30 to $50 range.[6]

The number of stock splits in the 1990s has increased from 73 in 1991 to 159 in 1992 with the record being 225 splits of no less than three shares for two in 1983.[5] It is not uncommon for a stock's price to increase after the announcement of a split, only to have the post-split price continue upward.[5]

Not all splits produce an increase in the number of shares for shareholders. On occasion, a company with a low-priced stock may reduce the number of outstanding shares using what is called a "reverse split." In this instance, shareholders wind up with *fewer* shares after the split without any change in market value. For example, let's say the ABC Brick Company has 5 million shares of stock outstanding with each share valued at $2. If it executes a 1 for 5 stock split, then there will be 1 million shares on the market, each selling for $10 per share. There is no actual increase or decrease in market value, but the company used the "reverse split" in an effort to make their shares more appealing to potential investors who might otherwise shy away from a $2 stock.

Both the "stock dividend" and "stock split" benefit participants in dividend reinvestment programs, because they ultimately increase the value of one's holdings. After all, the intent of a DRIP is to acquire additional shares over time with the expectation that eventually both the number of shares and the amount of the dividend will have increased substantially.

THAT DIVIDEND INCOME IS TAXABLE

The dividends generated from the shares in DRIP accounts are reportable as taxable income, even when you reinvest that money to purchase more shares of stock. But if your stock splits, you do not have to pay taxes on the additional shares you receive. The total *value* of your investment did not actually change at the time of the split. Should your shares later go up in value, you will have to report that increase as a capital gain only if you sell those shares. In January of each year the plan administrator will send you a form 1099-DIV listing the dividends, capital gains (if any), and other distributions you received. You will also have to report as income any fees paid by the company on your behalf. This would include brokerage commissions and related fees that were not charged when shares were purchased for you. A copy of the 1099-DIV form is sent to the Internal Revenue Service, so be prepared to claim what is reported as income for your account when you file your income taxes. Talk with your tax preparer if you have other questions related to income from your DRIP accounts.

THE NUMBER OF DRIPS MAY INCREASE

Evidently the growing appeal of dividend reinvestment programs to individual investors has not gone unnoticed. The number of companies offering DRIPS could increase along with the services they offer. For example, the **Exxon Corporation**, which already permits individuals to purchase stock directly through them, has expanded its services to allow shareholders to establish individual retirement accounts and even arrange automatic transfers to purchase shares.

While companies such as Exxon are eager to expand their shareholder services and DRIP program, other firms have found it necessary to curtail their plan due to skyrocketing administrative costs. But apparently stock transfer agents are eager to expand their services. They want to offer to buy and sell more stock in more companies directly to individual investors thereby by-passing brokers altogether. If this expansion of services by transfer agents were to come about, it would certainly transform the way business is presently conducted to open DRIP accounts.

My guess is that "traders" will continue to use conventional methods to purchase and sell their shares in individual stocks. Long-term "investors," on the other hand, will probably jump at the chance to buy shares directly through a company or its representative (a transfer agent) and use optional cash payments (OCPs) to dollar cost average. But picking the right company is the key to any investment strategy. One should view a DRIP like any other investment. There are good DRIP stocks and there are bad DRIP stocks. But it is simply nice for individual investors to have more options.

The Value of DRIPs in Retirement

If creating a large nest egg of investments for retirement is one of the driving forces behind your interest in developing and undertaking a savings and investing program, then the DRIP portion of your assets can have a measurable impact on that outcome.

For example, suppose you have just three DRIPs in all. You stopped making optional cash payments some years earlier, and now you're at the point where you want to actually start receiving the income from those investments. If you planned it right, you could have selected stocks with staggered dividend payment dates. In other words, one stock pays quarterly dividends in January, April, July and October. The second makes distributions in February, May, August and November. The third company distributes dividends in March, June, September and December. In effect, you have each month covered by a dividend payment from one of your three DRIP accounts, thereby assuring you of a monthly rather than a quarterly income from this portion of your portfolio.

THE POWER OF DRIPS

It was already mentioned that you can achieve long-term growth using your dividend reinvestment plan through three main avenues: *appreciation* (increase in the *price* of your shares), *stock splits* (increase in the *number* of your shares) and *rising dividends* (increase in the income from your shares). To illustrate the power of DRIPs and how they can impact your investment strategy, let's use some real-life numbers.

For the impact of *appreciation* you need only look around the corner at your neighborhood **McDonald's** for a shining example of a "Blue Chip" stock. Looking through the January 1993 issue of *Kiplinger's Personal Finance Magazine,* I came upon an article written by Dan Moreau entitled "McDonald's: 95 billion burgers served and a lot more to come."[7] The article briefly reviewed the rise of McDonald's from its humble beginnings and included some interesting information on its sales and profits since the company went public (was sold on an exchange) in 1965. Of particular note were the performance data for 1991, 1992 and the projections for 1993. Citing an analyst for Value Line Investment Survey, the article reported that 1992 earnings were expected to be 15% higher than 1991. The price of a share which was $30 in the middle of 1991, ended 1992 at $48.75, up 63% for that 18-month period. Mr. Moreau quoted another analyst who anticipated McDonald's stock would rise as high as $50 to $52 per share in 1993. An increase to the $52 level would represent a price appreciation of 73% from the $30 per share level. While the stock price takes off, the dividend remains at a meek $0.40 per share but the advantage here is that this increased appreciation has not created any taxable gain (unless the shares are sold). This is especially important to individuals interested in avoiding investments that add to their tax burden. How did McDonald's actually do in 1993? The stock closed at $57 on December 31, 1993 with its annual dividend set at $0.43 per share. At that price level, the stock appreciated 90% from its mid-1991 value of $30 per share. Now that's a nice McGain.

That information came from an article in a well-known magazine. You could turn to those Standard & Poor's or Value Line Reports I keep mentioning for the next example on stock splits and rising dividends. If you don't know what these references look like or where they are found, all you have to do is ask a librarian and in a matter of minutes you'll have a wealth of information at your finger tips. Check the date of the volume you pick up to make certain you're using the latest information.

In this next example we'll use data on the leading consumer product company, **Procter & Gamble** which is listed on the New York Stock Exchange (NYSE) under the symbol PG. For the period, 1986 to 1993, Procter & Gamble had a 2 for 1 split in 1989 and another in 1992.[8] To put the effect of stock splits into perspective, you need only examine and compare the price of the stock and the level of its dividend during this period.

By the way, if your local library doesn't carry the Standard & Poor's *Stock Market Encyclopedia*, perhaps the reference librarian can direct you to a similar publication for tracking individual stocks. The data are drawn from a company's annual report, so regardless of what reference you use you should find basically the same information. For example, Procter & Gamble actually traded in the $58.88 to $45.25 price range in 1993 before ending the year at $57 per share. But if you go to one of these reference sources to look up the price in 1986, it will appear to have sold at an *adjusted* high price of $20.63 and a low price $15.88 per share. When I say *adjusted price*, I mean that the reported data already have the effect of the 1992 and 1989 2 for 1 stock splits factored into them. In actuality, Procter & Gamble ended 1986 trading at over $76 per share. I must admit that when I first looked at these numbers I did not take that into consideration and, consequently, overestimated the increased value in the stocks I was following. It was not until I realized that with the stock splits factored in, all I needed to do was compare the increase in stock price over the time period being analyzed. In other words, it would be incorrect to think that 100 shares of Procter & Gamble increased to 200 in 1989 and then to 400 by 1992 from the stock splits and at the same time the price of each share went from say $20.63 in 1986 to $57 by the end of 1993. It is important to remember that when studying a research report presenting the data with an adjustment for the stock splits, comparisons should be made between the changes in share *price* and not the *number* of shares. So each of the 100 Procter & Gamble shares may have been valued at $57 at the end of trading on December 31, 1993, but they had a price of $20.63 per share at the 1986 adjusted "high." Your actual cost in 1986 would have been over $7,600 (100 × $76).

Because all this may be new to you and you are more likely to have the business section of the newspaper handy than you are an annual report or a research report on a given stock, the following examples will be presented with *actual price levels* for the years in question. In other words, when I state a price for a particular stock I am reporting the closing price as it appeared in the newspaper. Consequently, with any of *my* examples you can go directly to today's newspaper and recalculate the value of those stocks using current price information. Hopefully, you will find this method of illustration easier to understand and appreciate.

At the beginning of 1986 Procter & Gamble, then yielding $2.60 a share in dividends, was priced at around $69.75 a share. Let's say you purchased 25 shares at this price directly through the company for a total investment of $1,744 (25 × $69.75). Because you purchased these shares through their dividend reinvestment program, the brokerage commissions were small. For the sake of this example, we'll ignore the commission but assume the dividends you received were reinvested. The annual dividend increased slightly each year so that by 1989 it was $2.80 a share and the company also announced a 2 for 1 split. After the split, your stake in the company increased from 25 to 50 shares, but the price of the stock decreased by one half to adjust for the stock split. The dividend continued to increase again in 1990 and 1991, and in June of 1992 the company rewarded stockholders with a second 2 for 1 stock split, so the number of shares in your account increased to 100. Meanwhile, the annual dividend in 1992 reached a post-split level of $1.10 per share. However, Procter & Gamble stock ended 1993 at $57 paying an annual dividend of $1.24 a share. That means your $1,744 initial investment was worth $5,700 (100 shares × $57) at the close of 1993, just eight years later. During this time, you also earned *at least* another $784 in dividends. With that income reinvested in your DRIP account, your total holdings were probably valued at well over $6,484. Now that's quite a return on your $1,744 purchase.

You might think that this example is not too realistic because not everyone has $1,744 to invest, and besides, that amount of money was worth far more in 1986 than it is today. In some respects that is true, but with the option to make additional cash payments you could have invested $100 a month and put that much principal together in less than two years and easily by the end of 1987. Or at the rate of $50 a month, beginning in 1986, you would have contributed more than $1,800 by the end of 1988. The first stock split did not occur until 1989, so the dividend reinvestment program allowed you to open the account, build it steadily with low monthly payments and still get much of the same rewards as the individual who plopped down $1,744 cash in a lump sum. Besides, with regular monthly payments, you used "dollar cost averaging" and probably had far more than 50 shares at the time of the first stock split.

The Procter & Gamble example is an interesting one because until July 1993, investors could purchase stock directly through the company including the first share. They had an unbelievably low minimum optional cash payment, $2 per month. However, the costs associated with the administration of the dividend reinvestment program made it prohibitive to continue with both the direct and the optional cash purchases. Today all that remains of the Procter & Gamble DRIP is the dividend reinvestment portion. Shareholders can no longer make monthly purchases through the company, but quarterly dividends continue to be reinvested for program participants. Any shareholder interested in buying new shares must do so through a brokerage service, have the certificate issued to them and have those added shares registered in the DRIP. This revamping of the Procter & Gamble DRIP was an unfortunate turn of events for the small investors, because the former program made it easy to enroll (with direct stock purchase) and well within the financial reach of any investor ($2 minimum monthly OCP).

Let's look at another example. This time we'll examine the history of the well-known soft drink company **Coca-Cola** (traded on the NYSE under the symbol KO).[9] In January 1986 the stock was selling around $84.50 per share and paying an annual dividend of $2.96. Say you purchased 10 shares at $84.50 per share, or $845 plus commissions, and opened up a dividend reinvestment account. You wanted your annual dividends to be reinvested to purchase more stock but made no further contributions. In the middle of 1986 the company announced a 3 for 1 stock split, so the number of shares in your DRIP account jumped to 30. By the middle of 1990, and much to your delight, Coca-Cola declared a 2 for 1 stock split so your DRIP account held 60 shares. Meanwhile, the dividend rose to a post-split level of $1.36 per share in 1990. Your Coca-Cola stock continued to increase in value in 1991, and the annual dividend was raised again. The upward trend did not stop there and in 1992, Coca-Cola declared yet another 2 for 1 stock split, bringing your account balance to 120 shares. And when 1993 ended, each of your 120 shares was worth $44.63 and paying an adjusted annual dividend of $0.68. During this eight-year period your initial investment of $845 for 10 shares grew to more than 120 shares as a result of stock splits and appreciated in value to $5,356 (120 × $44.63) plus you received dividends of at least $350 for a total investment worth over $5,713. For that matter, if you purchased 100 shares in 1986 for $8,450, you would now own well over 1,200 shares valued at more than $53,556 plus dividends (using the 1993 year end price).

Even more fascinating to consider is the fact that had you reinvested all your dividends during this same 7-year period and made an optional cash payment or two (two advantages of a DRIP account) over the course of eight years ($10 a month minimum for Coca-Cola and $2 a month for

Procter & Gamble), your returns would have been even *greater*.

These are just two examples of the power of DRIPs and how they can bring another dimension to your investment strategy and diversify your portfolio building upon your mutual fund foundation. More importantly, the power of DRIP is well within your grasp.

IN REVIEW

1. A DRIP is a dividend reinvestment program open to registered shareholders.
2. Most companies require that you own at least one share of common stock to be eligible to enroll in a DRIP.
3. Over 828 companies offer these programs, but not necessarily all dividend-paying stocks.
4. Optional cash purchases (OCP) allow you to purchase more shares of a company on a regular basis with a low minimum payment ($10, $25, etc.).
5. You can find out if a company offers a dividend reinvestment program from any number of sources (Appendix C, Carlson's book *How to Buy Stocks Without a Broker*, Standard & Poor's Reports, etc.).
6. Use these same financial publications to seek out companies that are leaders in their field and offer long-term growth in terms of stock price appreciation, stock splits and regular dividend increases.
7. Only a handful of companies enable you to make your initial stock purchase directly through them. So plan on establishing a brokerage account with either a discount broker or a full-service brokerage company (particularly if you feel you'll need advice periodically).
8. Diversify your DRIP portfolio and purchase as many stocks as you can across a number of business sectors.
9. Set a goal for each DRIP account either in terms of a dollar amount or a target number of shares based on your income level and the amount of your disposable income.

10. Dividend income you receive is taxable in the year in which it is received.

11. Each DRIP account can be a source of steady income in retirement.

12. DRIPs are a powerful investment vehicle that can provide long-term growth through capital appreciation (increase in the *price* of your shares), stock splits (increase in the number of your shares) and rising dividends (increase in the *income* from your shares).

WHAT'S NEXT?

At this point, you've established a greater understanding of stocks as well as the value of reinvesting the dividends they produce. But you also learned that not all stocks pay dividends and not all dividend-paying stocks have dividend reinvestment plans (DRIPs). So other investment opportunities await you, but you can't acquire them as you would a DRIP, and you may not find them among the stocks in your mutual fund portfolio. Or if they are owned by your mutual funds, their benefit is diluted by hundreds of other stocks. Turn next to **Step 9: Select Individual Growth Stocks (Tier 3)** to learn more about the third tier in this investment strategy.

NOTES

1. Carlson, Charles B. *Buying Stocks Without A Broker.* New York: McGraw-Hill, 1992.

2. Downes, John and Jordan Elliot Goodman. *Barron's Finance and Investment Handbook.* 2nd ed. New York: Barron's Educational Series, 1987.

3. McGough, Robert. Mutual Funds, "Investors Ran To Stock Funds During January." *The Wall Street Journal,* 2 February 1993: C1.

4. McGough, Robert and Sara Calian. Mutual Funds, "Bond-Fund Buyers Ease Up in November." *The Wall Street Journal*, 30 November 1993: C1.

5. Kadlec, Daniel. Street Talk, "Capital gains break could boost stocks." *USA Today*, 19 February 1993: 3B.

6. Leckey, Andrew. "Stock splits emotionally uplifting for investors." *Chicago Tribune*, 14 March 1993, sec. 7:8.

7. Moreau, Dan. Blue Chips, "McDonald's: 95 billion burgers served and a lot more to come." *Kiplinger's Personal Finance Magazine*, January 1993: 32.

8. Standard & Poor's Corporation. *Stock Market Encyclopedia* Standard NYSE Stock Reports, vol. 60, no. 186, 27 September 1993: 1868.

9. Standard & Poor's Corporation. *Stock Market Encyclopedia* Standard NYSE Stock Reports, vol. 60, no. 183, 22 September 1993: 562.

SELECT INDIVIDUAL GROWTH STOCKS (TIER 3)

Selecting mutual funds (Tier 1) probably will prove easier to accomplish and require less of a personal commitment to manage than selecting and tracking your DRIPs (Tier 2). But in return for the increased effort in developing these two components of your portfolio lie many opportunities for long-term growth enhanced by the option to invest regularly and build your assets through "dollar cost averaging." As you move from Tier 1 to Tier 2, the level of risk associated with choosing appropriate DRIP stocks and timing OCPs is greater than the "no minimum" enrollment programs of mutual funds using automatic transfers. So it is that the final component in this 3-tiered investment strategy, selecting individual growth stocks (Tier 3) can involve even greater risk taking. But the strategy draws on the knowledge and experience you gained from identifying and purchasing mutual funds and dividend paying stocks. In other words, you can learn to make educated decisions that are still within your "comfort level" (risk tolerance) and are appropriate for you as a beginning investor.

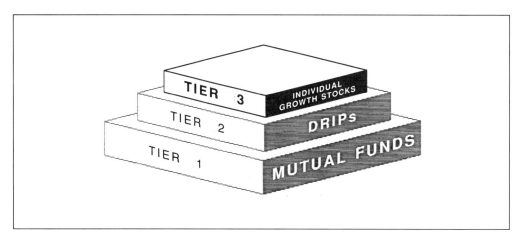

The selection of individual growth stocks is the third tier in the 3-tiered investment strategy.

The Advantages of Individual Growth Stocks

If you have an investment portfolio based on mutual funds and augmented by DRIPs, why would you need to add individual growth stocks? One answer is growth stocks are like automobiles in many ways. They come in a variety of shapes and sizes, but any one of them will get you where you want to go. In Tier 3, you want to reach your financial goals with the fastest and safest investment vehicles. To do that you have to keep your expenses and taxes low, so as many of your investment dollars go into these stocks as possible. One of the best ways to accomplish this is to minimize your current income and maximize appreciation. Okay, so how do you do that?

Look for growth stocks that do not pay a dividend or if they have a dividend it is not very significant. In fact, you want to avoid current income (a dividend) as much as possible and principally seek capital appreciation (share price increases or stock splits). If a company prospers, you want to be rewarded not with cash but with more stock. As examples,

Wal-Mart (dividend is $0.13) had 2 for 1 stock splits in 1987, 1990 and 1993; **Southwest Airlines** (dividend is $0.04) declared a 3 for 2 split in 1990, a 2 for 1 split in 1992 and a 3 for 2 stock split in 1993 (in addition to a 7.1% dividend increase); and Toys "R" Us (no dividend) split 3 for 2 in 1988, 1989 and 1990. Stockholders in these companies have seen both the number of their shares and the value of their investments increase significantly as a direct result of the stock splits. With low or no dividends, stockholders achieved an increase in the number of shares they owned without an increased tax liability. They may have seen the value of their stock double, triple or quadruple without realized capital gains to pay taxes on unless they decided to sell their shares.

Meanwhile, the income from interest and dividends and capital gains produced by mutual funds in Tier 1 or the DRIPs in Tier 2 are fully taxable if held in a personal rather than a tax sheltered account. Clearly, Tier 3 investments can not only offer real growth but growth without adding to your income taxes, and that is why individual growth stocks are important to your overall investment strategy.

WHAT MAKES TIER 3 INVESTING MORE RISKY?

Actually, two things. The first is the fact that unlike the small initial investment involved with mutual funds and DRIPs, you have to have more cash to invest when purchasing large blocks of stock in the Tier 3 strategy. By large I mean enough money to buy anywhere from 50 to 100 or more shares at one time. That, in turn, will require you to make a decision and back it up with a commitment of thousands of dollars for one purchase. Don't be intimidated, at least not yet. Wait until you've read about how this is done and what it can do for you before you pass judgment on the Tier 3 strategy.

Back to our discussion. The second factor that makes this component riskier than Tier 1 and Tier 2 is that the companies you buy are principally growth oriented, so they won't provide much, if anything, in the way of current income. Consequently, during the period in which you own them, your only reward will be the *expectation* that the price of stock will increase over time (capital appreciation). That approach in itself is riskier than buying a mutual fund or a DRIP, because those investments generally reward shareholders with dividends and/or capital gains semi-annually or annually in the case of mutual funds and quarterly with DRIPs. Not so with Tier 3 individual growth stocks. They are chosen not for their income but their growth potential. If there is no growth, there is no reward, pure and simple.

Obviously, for this strategy to work you'll have to do more research than you did when selecting mutual funds and stock for DRIPs. Fortunately, all the information you need is readily available, and it is as easy to find individual growth stocks as it is to find Tier 1 and Tier 2 investments. In fact, many of the financial publications recommended previously include feature articles highlighting individual stocks. A beginning investor who spends time at the public library reading *The Wall Street Journal* and browsing through an assortment of financial magazines is certain to find very specific stock recommendations by any number of financial "experts." The important thing is not to be overwhelmed by the process, because it is a lot easier to find this information than you might think. What helps the most is knowing what to look for, and that is what you will learn here in Step 9.

How Difficult Is It to Identify Individual Growth Stocks?

Not very difficult at all, in fact! There are literally thousands of companies listed on the various exchanges. You aren't expected to go through the particulars of each and every one to identify the best growth stocks for Tier 3. That is an unrealistic expectation.

Simply break the process down into two simple steps. First, and you've heard this one before, review the financial publications (newspapers, newsletters, magazines, etc.) in your local library just like you did when you were looking for stocks to add to your DRIP portfolio. The authors of the features in these financial publications have done much of the preliminary research for you already. Besides, their advice is *free*. So when you come upon an interesting article on a stock, write down the name of the company that's recommended and save the article. Second, go to the reference section of the library and examine the most current Standard & Poor's Reports on companies whose products or services you think make them leaders in their field or particular stocks you found were recommended in the articles you read.

USE FINANCIAL PUBLICATIONS

Appendix B contains a list of many of the better known financial publications. Take that listing to your library and see which ones are available to you there. If you still feel like a novice reading this type of information, then start your search with the more consumer-friendly publications such as *Money Magazine, Kiplinger's Personal Finance Magazine* and *Smart Money*. As you become more familiar with the terminology and the workings of the financial markets, you will then find it easier to read and enjoy *Business Week, Forbes, Financial World, Fortune Magazine,* etc. Don't wait to read *The Wall Street Journal;* it is an excellent newspaper full of valuable articles and reports, many of which contain specific stock recommendations and projections from the perspective of a variety of financial analysts. More importantly, *The Wall Street Journal* is a timely publication with current up-to-date reporting on political issues, the economy, the financial markets, business trends and the performance of individual stocks.

Another good way to illustrate how easy it can be to identify growth stocks is to provide a real-life example. It just so happens I use **Fidelity Brokerage Services** as my discount broker. Each month they provide me with a *free* copy of a newsletter prepared by the Standard & Poor's Corporation for **Fidelity Brokerage Services** entitled *Standard & Poor's*

Investor's Monthly. Along with my monthly brokerage statement, I receive their 8-page newsletter. The January 1993 issue contained a list of 40 stocks described under a heading as "Rapid Growth Stocks Currently Favored By Wall Street Analysts."[1] Granted, many of the names were unfamiliar to me, but there were also some companies everyone has heard of: **Gillette**, **Microsoft**, **Philip Morris**, Sara Lee, Tootsie Roll, Toys "R" Us, Tyson Foods and the ever popular **Wal-Mart**.

So an investor with a Fidelity Brokerage Account doesn't have to look very far for a place to start. That list contained information on per-share earnings, five-year growth rates up to 1991 and 1992, annual revenues, the stock's recent price and its 1992 price-earnings ratio. You could then take that list to the public library and review the individual Standard & Poor's Reports for each one of the companies. Compare the data you obtained and decide if any of these stocks might be of interest to you and then rank them on a piece of paper. Track the stocks over a period of time and look for an opportunity to make your purchase if and when you think the price is attractive and the time is right.

STANDARD & POOR'S REPORTS

You were introduced to the Standard & Poor's Reports in Step 8 when it was explained how you could look under the "Dividend Data" section to assess dividend increases and determine if a company offered a dividend reinvestment plan. Now you want to take those same reports, but look for information of another sort, appreciation (stock price increases) and stock splits.

On the first page right next to the "Current Outlook" section you'll see a chart of the stock price and trading volume for the past seven years. Remember, the **Procter & Gamble** and **Coca-Cola** examples? What you are looking for at this time is the number of stock splits and the change in stock price. Obviously, you'd like to see the stock price moving upward with frequent splits. Don't forget that the price of a stock may not move up rapidly if it splits frequently. That would be a wonderful outcome to have multiple stock splits and continuous price appreciation, but it is not realistic, because after a split, the stock's price is actually reduced. It takes time for the share price to rebound unless you are dealing with a very "hot" stock. Whether or not the company pays a dividend is inconsequential, because current income is not a goal of the Tier 3 strategy.

For another real-life example, let's look at a company named **Home Depot** which largely sells home improvement products through a chain of warehouse-type stores mainly in the Sunbelt and Northeastern states.[2] The stock is traded under the symbol HD on the New York Stock Exchange and paid an annual dividend of $0.12 per share in 1993. The chart in the Standard & Poor's report for Home Depot showed two rather dramatic things during the period 1986 to 1992. First, the stock price rose slowly between 1986 and 1990, then took off in 1991 and 1992. Second, since 1986 there have been *five* 3 for 2 stock splits, including one in 1987 which would help to explain why the stock price appeared to remain steady, and one 4 for 3 split in 1993.

Now let's put this stock split information together with some share price information to assess the stock's performance. As in those previous examples, I am quoting *actual*, rather than adjusted, share prices. Suppose you bought 200 shares of Home Depot at the beginning of 1986 for $12.50 per share. Your cost would have been $2,500 (200 × $12.50) plus commissions. The stock split 3 for 2 in 1987, so your number of shares increased from 200 to 300. In 1987 there was no stock split but the company started paying a small dividend but we'll ignore the dividend at this point. As I indicated, the stock started doing something unusual, it split 3 for 2 every year from 1989 to 1992. So the number of shares you owned increased by 50% in *each* of those years. In other words, you went from owning 300 shares in 1987 to 450 in 1989, to 675 in 1990, to 1,013 in 1991 and finally in 1992 you had a total of 1,519 shares of Home Depot. What was the price of the stock doing during this period? It may have been at $12.50 when you bought it in 1986 but by the close of 1990 it traded at $38.63, then jumped up to $67.38 per share by early 1992, but ended that year at the unbelievable price of $67.50 per share.

When you combine the benefit of stock splits (200 shares growing to 1,519) and appreciation (stock price rising from $12.50 to $67.50) in seven years, the numbers are staggering. If you stuck by Home Depot for the entire period from 1986 to 1992, your initial investment of $2,500 would have skyrocketed to a value of $102,533 (1,519 × $67.50), not including dividends. And you thought Procter & Gamble and Coca-Cola were success stories. Although the 4 for 3 split in 1993 brought your total holdings to 2,025 shares, the price of the stock retreated significantly and ended the year at $39.50, bringing the total value of your holdings to a mere $79,988 (2,025 × $39.50).

Now let's suppose you weren't such a visionary in 1986, and there was no way you were going to risk $2,500 on a relatively new company. That sounded too risky to you. Or say you live in the Far West and didn't hear about Home Depot until late in 1989. When you reviewed the S&P Report for the company, you saw two 3 for 2 stock splits, one in 1987 and another in 1989, so you followed the stock for awhile before deciding it was time to jump in. What's ahead for this investment now?

If you purchased 200 shares in early 1990 (at the 1989 closing price of $36.63) after witnessing the 3 for 2 splits in 1987 and 1989, your initial investment would have been roughly $7,326 (200 × 36.63). That's a far cry from the $2,500 needed in 1986. But your 200 shares would have grown to 300 as a result of that 3 for 2 split in 1990, to 450 from the 1991 split and by mid-1992 that fifth 3 for 2 stock split would have increased your ownership to 675 shares. So with Home Depot ending 1992 at $67.50 per share your 675 shares would have been worth $45,563. Not a bad three year return on your $7,326 investment, even after playing it a bit safe. In spite of the 1993 price decline, you would have ended that year owning 900 shares, after the 4 for 3 stock split, with a total value of over $35,500 (900 × $39.50) from a four-year investment.

These examples demonstrate the impact of long-term investing for growth and how Tier 3 investments have the potential to reach unbelievable heights. Equally as important, they also illustrate how you can still enjoy some of the benefits if you can identify a stock on the way up, even as late as 1990 in the case of Home Depot. And unless those HD shares are sold, this increase in value (appreciation) is not taxable. At the same time, as a long-term investor you should be prepared for price fluctuations as seen in 1993. By the way, Home Depot subsequently established a dividend reinvestment program (DRIP) in 1990. It would have been considered a Tier 3 investment when purchased in 1986 but with the advent of its dividend reinvestment program, I would regard it a Tier 2 investment.

One final example of a Tier 3 stock is Blockbuster Entertainment (listed on the NYSE under symbol, BV). In early January 1987 you could have purchased 200 shares for roughly $2,350 with the stock trading around $11.75 a share. The company made two 2 for 1 stock splits in 1988, another in 1989 and a fourth in 1991. So over the years you would have seen the number of shares in your account go from 200 to 400 (1988), then 800 (1988), then 1,600 (1989) and finally 3,200 (1991). On December 31, 1993, Blockbuster Entertainment closed at $30.63 a share (down from its high for the year of $34.25). Do that math and you find that 3,200 shares multiplied by a per share price of $30.63 equals an astonishing $98,016. Although Blockbuster pays a small dividend ($0.10 per share), it did not offer a dividend reinvestment program as of 1993.

HOW MUCH RISK IS INVOLVED?

The risk level for the stocks that fall into the category of "individual growth stocks" will vary from industry to industry and company to company. If you invest in a new sneaker manufacturer that hopes to compete with the likes of Nike® and Reebok® in their athletic shoe line, the risk to your money may be substantial. Compare this company to a recently created computer software firm that has an advanced multimedia software system or a biotechnology company with a unique diagnostic test. These three enterprises have different markets and levels of competition. All things being equal, the company with the greatest market and lowest risk may have better potential as an investment you'd be interested in owning.

There's no guarantee of a sure thing, but if you look hard and long enough, you are bound to find a company that has a unique niche in some industry. As an investment, this stock does not necessarily have to be one that is undiscovered and waiting for an investor like you to add it to your portfolio. Far from it. After all, Apple Computer, Intel, **Microsoft, Southwest Airlines** and **Wal-Mart** were not household names at one point. In fact, they were fledgling companies struggling to find their way in each of their respective fields. But some investors had the insight to buy these stocks and, hopefully, hold on to them long enough to become very rich stockholders in the process. This is not to say that you have to find the next Apple Computer. On the contrary, these examples are presented simply to illustrate that there are opportunities out there today as there were when these now well-known companies first emerged. The challenge to the individual investors is to separate the Wal-Marts from the local five and dimes.

Remember too that just because you were not there in the beginning does not mean you cannot benefit by buying a company that is still growing. The Home Depot example showed that an investment of about $7,400 as late as 1990 still would have grown to $35,500 in just four years. But you have to devote time to read and research these companies.

SOME POST-NAFTA EXAMPLES FOR U.S. AND FOREIGN INVESTORS

It wasn't long after the signing of the North American Free Trade Agreement that it became apparent how some U.S. businesses viewed the opportunities to venture north into Canada and south into the Mexican market. What's more, you don't have to look very far to uncover this information, it can be found in newspapers and financial magazines. I ran across the following examples simply by reading *The Wall Street Journal* and *Forbes* to follow some of my personal investments. Let's not only take a closer look at a few of these reported news events, but put this information into perspective with respect to our 3-tiered investment strategy.

THE CANADIAN MARKET

On January 17, 1994, *The Wall Street Journal* reported that Wal-Mart Stores Inc. had agreed to buy the Woolco Stores in Canada from Woolworth Corporation's Canadian subsidiary.[3] This agreement meant Wal-Mart would acquire approximately 120 Woolco stores and more than 14 million square feet of retail space in Canada. But the announcement momentarily hurt Canada's largest retailer, Zellers, whose share price dropped 12% on the Toronto Stock Exchange, and the stock of several other Canadian retailers also fell on fears of increased competition.

Meanwhile, there were some interesting events rising from the Canadian flour market. According to a report in the January 31, 1994, issue of *Forbes*, International Multifoods Corporation (traded on the NYSE under symbol IMC) has been the leader in the Canadian flour sales for some time and either first or second to Grand Metropolitan's Pillsbury division in the North America bakery mixes market.[4] But Multifood's dominance in Canada apparently now faces stiff challenges from **ConAgra, Inc.** (NYSE, symbol CAG) and Archer Daniels Midland Co. (NYSE, symbol ADM). A quick check of Appendix C reveals that Grand Metropolitan, International Multifoods Corporation and ConAgra, Inc. not only pay a dividend but all offer a dividend reinvestment program making them *potential* Tier 2 investment. Should your research find Archer Daniels Midland Co. or Wal-Mart Stores, Inc., to your liking, consider them *potential* Tier 3-type investments.

In February 1994 it was announced that Home Depot was venturing further into the Canadian home improvement market by agreeing to buy 75% of the Molson's Aikenhead's Home Improvement Warehouse chain. This union was to result in the formation of Home Depot Canada and lead to the immediate acquisition of five stores in Canada, with expectation of opening up to 14 by the end of 1994 and perhaps as many as 50 Canadian stores over the next five years.

THE MEXICAN MARKET

Wal-mart's venture into Canada was not its first foray across U.S. borders. In fact, according to another *Forbes* article it actually followed the company's joint venture with Mexico's largest retailer, **Cifra**.[5] Evidently, Wal-Mart and Cifra had been teamed up since 1991 but what changed recently was the relationship between the two companies. A clause allowing either partner to exit from their joint venture was dropped. The net result was that the two companies became more united and would "effectively operate as one in Mexico."[5]

Shares of Cifra are traded in the U.S. in the over-the-counter market as American Depository Receipts (ADRs) of the Mexican bolsa B shares. To obtain a quote of the share price you can either call a stockbroker or look it up in a business newspaper such as *The Wall Street Journal*. If you choose to look it up in the *Journal* you have to do a little maneuvering initially to get the information you need. First, go to the regular feature entitled "Foreign Markets" in the paper's Money & Investing section. Second, look under the heading Mexico, and you'll see the stock listed as Cifra B. The listing is in Mexican pesos, so you'll want to convert that price to your currency be it U.S. or Canadian dollars. Third, locate the feature entitled "Currency Trading" (also in the Money & Investing Section) and see what the current exchange rate is for the Mexican peso. Lastly, divide that exchange rate (in U.S. dollars) into the quote for Cifra B (in pesos) and you'll have the previous day's closing price for Cifra B ADRs in U.S. currency. In other words, if Cifra B appeared in the paper as 10.50 and the peso exchange rate per U.S. dollar was $3.113, then one share of Cifra B was last priced at $3.37 in U.S. dollars (10.50 ÷ $3.113 = $3.37).

These examples illustrate how investors living in Canada and Mexico can identify and perhaps purchase stock in U.S. companies to take advantage of expansion into their own market places and throughout North America.

TRACK THE COMPANIES YOU SELECTED

Unless you have money you want to invest immediately, take time to track the stocks you selected by recording their closing price periodically for several months or until such time as you have money to invest. Use whatever time interval suits your level of interest, once a week, once a month, once a quarter, etc. I've tracked stocks literally for years and still do. The value of this kind of information gathering is that you create a handy and inexpensive reference of the price fluctuations for each of the stocks you monitor. In addition to the 52-week high and low prices quoted daily in the newspaper, you have a more detailed record of the trading range for these shares. Consequently, you can develop an appreciation of when a stock is overpriced (don't buy it then) and when it is attractively priced (consider buying it if the fundamentals haven't changed).

HOW MUCH STOCK SHOULD YOU BUY?

This is not an easy question to answer. The obvious response might be "as much as you can afford," but that is not necessarily a correct one. If you wanted a general rule, try to at least buy in what are called "round lots." A round lot is a unit of trading composed of 100 shares as opposed to an "odd lot" which is any quantity less than 100. If you are thinking of trading in units other than 100, say 25 or 50 shares, you may pay more than the normal commission to buy or sell your "odd lot" of shares.

Buying Those Individual Growth Stocks

After you've tracked the stocks on your list for some time, you may eventually see an opportunity to make that first purchase.

Discount- or Full-Service Broker?

If the stock selection is yours, then consider using a discount broker to execute the transaction and minimize the commission expenses. On the other hand, if you have the money to invest in growth stocks, but lack the inclination to do the research and tracking, contact a full-service broker and ask for some recommendations. Perhaps you opened a Dean Witter account and had an account executive (stockbroker) buy single shares to begin your Tier 2 DRIP accounts. Call and ask what the firm is presently recommending in the way of growth stocks, if you want advice. Just be sure to clearly state how much or how little risk you are willing to assume (your risk tolerance). At this point you can ask the broker to send you additional information on any stocks recommended by the brokerage house. Just be sure to check out these suggestions before agreeing to buy them. If you establish an account with a full-service brokerage company, chances are that your broker will telephone you periodically with recommendations for ways you can invest your money. The calls may be welcomed at first as you learn how to make investment decisions on your own, but be prepared to politely decline offers for investment "opportunities" that you don't know anything about or don't quite suit your "comfort zone" for risk. Remember to stay with the investment strategy you created for yourself and avoid temptations that might take you off course.

If you have a list of stocks *you've* prepared, you now know how to do the research. Go to the public library and look up the most current Standard & Poor's report for each company. Review the sections in the report entitled: Current Outlook, Common Share Earnings, Important Developments, Per Share Data, Dividend Data, etc. Study the chart to see the trend in share price and look how often the stock has split, if at all. Review the current issues of the financial publications in the library (newspapers and magazines) for additional information on your selections.

PLACING YOUR ORDER

When you make the decision that it is time to buy a particular stock and you have enough money to purchase 50 or 100 shares, you'll find that a discount broker can probably complete the transaction less expensively than a full-service broker. To place your order simply call the discount brokerage service toll-free phone number and state that you wish to place a "trade." The person answering the phone will ask for your account number, so have it handy, and once they've confirmed that you are the owner of the account you'll be switched to a stockbroker. You may be advised by a taped message that you are on a *recorded* line. In other words, your conversation is being recorded in case there's a dispute after the transaction. You should ask for the current price of the stock (what is called a "quote"), so be prepared to provide the person assisting you with the stock symbol, BV for Blockbuster Entertainment, for instance. After you hear what the actual trading price is, place your order by stating exactly how many shares you wish to purchase at that price. You can also place your order for a different, lower price if you want to wait and see if the stock price drops. In fact, you can let your order at the lower price remain in effect for that day ("good for the day only") or let the order stand until it is filled or cancelled ("until cancelled"). It is probably more common to place an order for the prevailing price or what is called a "market order" or "at the market" trade if you want to be assured of completing the transaction that day at your quoted price.

If this all sounds confusing, it can be, at least until you've done it a few times. But don't be afraid to try it. When placing your first few trades, come right out and tell the person handling your order that this is all relatively new to you and you'd like their help in getting the order placed correctly. These are busy people, but you'd be surprised how helpful they can be. They'll explain what you need to do, what your options are in terms of placing the order and in many cases actually confirm your purchase while you are on the line. The process can be intimidating and scary at first, but you gradually learn how the system works, and you'll be surprised how quickly you can literally become an owner of Blockbuster Entertainment stock.

If your order was filled the day you placed it, the brokerage service will mail you a statement confirming your trade (the number of shares, the price per share and the brokerage commission) and indicating how much you owe them for the purchase. You'll be expected to pay that amount in full by the "settlement date," which is five business days from the date the stock was purchased. The settlement date will appear on the statement, so you know exactly when the money is due.

If you decided to open an account with a full-service brokerage company, you'll find the experience of buying your first shares of stock even easier. After all, you opened your brokerage account with a stockbroker, or account representative. All you have to do is call that individual, and he or she will gladly handle your purchase order and explain the procedures to you. You call this same broker for each and every transaction you want to execute where you want personalized service and advice. At the discount brokerage house, the representative you reached will give you his or her name and place your order with comparable efficiency. However, the discount broker is there simply to execute *your* orders. Remember, if you want to talk and get advice, you'll want to speak with a stockbroker from a full-service brokerage company.

Also, there are other ways to purchase stock besides paying cash for them in full. One is buying on credit using other assets in your account as collateral, and this is referred to as "buying on margin." You can discuss those alternative methods of purchasing stock with your brokerage service. You'd be advised to start out by buying only what you can actually afford to pay for in full in what is called a "cash account." By the way, you'd follow this same process to purchase one share of a stock to start a DRIP. The main difference is that you would ask to purchase one share and probably place a "market order" and have the transaction over within minutes. As you become more astute in stock picking, you may want to look into reducing your brokerage commissions even further by using what are called "deep discount" brokerage companies. Several such firms are included in Appendix D under the heading of discount brokerage firms.

FOLLOW YOUR INVESTMENTS

You can go to bed each night with little regard for your mutual funds, because you know the fund manager is responsible for the day-to-day investment decisions. But you'll have to follow your Tier 3 individual growth stocks much like you do your Tier 2 DRIPs accounts. If you are a long-term investor with money in a conservative, quality growth stock you probably don't have to worry too much about day-to-day price fluctuations.

Investors who select higher risk stocks with a full-service broker should anticipate an occasional short notice call from their account executive recommending the sale of their holdings in dramatic markets rises (take profits) or falls (cut losses). Personally, I find it more tolerable to select long-term growth stocks that suit more of a "buy and hold" strategy. Until you become more seasoned in the world of investing, you may be better off keeping your risks on the low side. As you gain experience and knowledge of the workings of the financial markets, you can try your hand at riskier types of investments, if that suits your fancy.

WHEN TO SELL?

No question is tougher to answer than one of when to sell an investment. *Buying* a stock is somewhat easier, because you can judge a price based on historical information. But knowing when to *sell* is much more challenging. In the case of growth stocks it is a matter of timing. If you sell too early, you are apt to miss the peak price level and wind up with only a portion of the profits you would have had if you only had held on longer.

Look at the Home Depot example. Shareholders who bought in 1986 and held on through 1992 made huge profits. The folks who were impatient and sold in late 1986 because the stock went nowhere for a year can only look back and weep. They selected the right stock but chose the wrong time to sell. On the other hand, if you sell too late you'll find yourself on the downside trying to unload a stock other investors don't want to buy. As a beginning investor, your strategy should be directed toward *buying* growth stocks rather than *selling* them. Nonetheless, you should not think that you can hold on to this or any type of investment forever.

One way to avoid some of the traps of missing a selling opportunity is to focus on long-term growth stocks. Remember you are investing for the future, you have many years to reach your financial goals and these growth stocks are going to help you get there. You need to avoid the temptation to be lured into speculative, high-risk ventures on the recommendation of some distant relative or a "tip" from some financial expert you bumped into at a party.

Just recall the trials and tribulations of International Business Machine Co. (IBM) in 1992. The stock lost 43.4% of its value over twelve months. Then in 1993 the annual dividend went from $4.84 to $2.16, a whopping 55% reduction. What happened to the price of IBM stock and its dividend serve as graphic reminders of the potential hazards that lie out there even to "Blue Chip" companies in the Dow Jones Industrial Average. The greatest safeguard against this potential pitfall is diversification to lessen the impact such a turn of events might have on one's investment portfolio. If IBM represented only a small portion of an investor's portfolio (directly and indirectly), the effects of these price and dividend reductions are not as great. It also points out that as investors near retirement, they must monitor their assets more diligently to look for indications of a decline in a company's growth.

Investors who might already own IBM stock must consider whether to retain the stock, ride through the lean years ahead and look to management to turn things around, or sell even if it means a loss. Fortunately, that is probably not a decision you have to make at this point. It is more important that you, as a long-term investor, should not become complacent and assume the growth stocks you picked today will remain growth stocks forever.

KEEP A WATCHFUL EYE ON YOUR GROWTH STOCKS

If there is something to be learned from the troubles that befell IBM and IBM stockholders, it is that investors can no longer maintain a "buy and hold" attitude indefinitely when investing. In a February 1993 article appearing in *Forbes*, David Dreman, Chairman of Dreman Value Management, LP and author of *The New Contrarian Investment Strategy*, wrote that long-term investors need to take a modified "buy-and-hold" stance."[6]

Instead of blindly thinking they can own a stock indefinitely, Mr. Dreman suggested a new approach, the "buy-and-watch" strategy. You buy "good quality stocks when the price is right and hold them as long as their fundamentals don't deteriorate."[6] You have to be on the alert for potential problems and be prepared to sell if the companies you own are weakening and losing the position they have long maintained while the competition roars ahead.

FOUR DANGER SIGNS TO WATCH FOR

I've summarized the four major "dangers signs" Mr. Dreman suggests investors in long-term stocks should watch for: the one-time restructuring charge, faltering performance, management glossing over problems and a deteriorating balance sheet.[6]

1. **The one-time restructuring charge.** A large write-off by the company is a clear sign of trouble, particularly if management gives a vague reason for that or for a reorganization. If there is a second major write-off, Mr. Dreman recommends you sell the stock.

2. **Faltering performance.** Watch the firm's revenue, profitability, return on capital and market share. Should they deteriorate while the company tries to move forward, consider this a warning sign.
3. **Management glosses over problems.** If the company's management fails to clearly address obvious problems, but instead tries to gloss over them, then consider this too as a sign of possible danger ahead.
4. **A deteriorating balance sheet.** If you see the company's traditionally strong balance sheet start to deteriorate with no apparent reason, consider that another strong warning.

DON'T VENTURE INTO GROWTH STOCKS TOO SOON

Take your time in reaching the Tier 3 level of your investment strategy. Don't be so eager to get there that you do not fully develop your mutual fund and DRIP portfolios. There will be plenty more opportunities for you in the years to come, so be patient and work your way up to this level.

I've known many an individual investor who had nothing more than a bank account or two and a full-service brokerage account. They had no mutual funds or DRIPs, and yet they were investing in highly speculative individual "growth" stocks. Before investing in any such ventures, ask about the nature of the investment, the company, what it did and anything related to earnings growth and a target price. The stocks may very well prove to be winners over the long-term, but undoubtedly they will be sold in the near term and the money reinvested into other "growth" stocks. I know. I've been there and played that game.

GOING IT ON YOUR OWN

Early on in my career as an investor I relied on the advice of stockbrokers for selecting individual growth stocks. What I did not know then was that I did not have to be so speculative (take high risks) in order to add "growth" to my portfolio. Taking the advice of "my" broker, I quickly learned that he was the decision maker, and I was merely the supplier of the capital to implement those decisions. When I invested thousands of dollars at a time, the transaction costs took a sizeable piece of the profits, even when the stock selections were winners. But when we lost, and I mean "we," because I agreed to risk the money, I had to absorb the transaction costs as well as the stock loss. As my interest in investing grew from these good and bad experiences, so did my understanding of financial markets, and I began to make more decisions on my own.

My first steps were tiny ones into well-researched mutual funds (Tier 1). I selected the funds and opened the accounts entirely on my own. Maybe that's not quite correct. I did get plenty of help from reading *Money Magazine*. To build those accounts I invested regularly, although this was before the days of the "automatic transfer." For diversification, I established a discount brokerage account and purchased dividend-paying stocks to open DRIP accounts that I managed (Tier 2). At the same time I relied on a discount broker to purchase individual growth stocks that I also selected. I expanded my reading to the resources of the library and *The Wall Street Journal* and began selecting individual growth stocks for my brokerage account (Tier 3). When I eventually compared the performance of my broker to what I had achieved for myself, I was astonished. I was actually making more money implementing my decisions for selecting mutual funds, DRIPs and individual growth stocks.

Finally, after a series of particularly bad losses, I closed my full-service brokerage account and redirected my money into the investments I selected for Tier 1, 2 and 3. So many years ago, everything changed for me when I became totally *self-directed*. In other words, I took complete control of all my assets and put *my* money where *I* wanted it to go. I have been making all my own investment decisions, both good and bad, ever since. This is not to say that you'd have the same experience with a full-service broker. Quite the contrary. There are many fine, honest stockbrokers in this world who make a sincere effort to help individual investors reach their financial goals using sound investment planning. It was my personal choice to take on this responsibility and decision making. That does not mean you should not include a stockbroker as a resource as you, too struggle to build your personal wealth and create a diversified investment portfolio. But my experience does show that going it on your own as you *begin* to invest is *not* impossible, however it does require a commitment of time on your part. The benefit is not only the increase in your net asset value but the satisfaction of identifying and using the many opportunities available to help you reach financial goals. Besides, the more you learn now about saving and investing, the better off you will be in the future as you approach retirement.

Remember too that you can also stop being "self-directed" and bring in a financial advisor (stockbroker, financial planner, etc.) at any time to help you select future investments. And even if you do choose to do that, at least you will be more knowledgeable about investment matters, so the decisions you make are more likely to be appropriate investment vehicles for you and your family.

IN REVIEW

1. It is not difficult to identify individual growth stocks (information is plentiful and often free).

2. Use the public library to research companies for which you find recommendations.

3. Make a list of potential stocks to purchase, and track them for several months.

4. Select only those individual growth stocks that fit your risk tolerance ("comfort level").

5. Buy stocks in "round lots" (blocks of 100 shares), not "odd lots" (less than 100), if you can.

6. Follow your investments (track them after your purchase).

7. Keep a watchful eye on your growth stocks, and look for warning signs to sell.

8. Don't jump to Tier 3 investing without first establishing a foundation in mutual funds (Tier 1) complemented by DRIPs (Tier 2).

9. Don't be reluctant to make your own stock selections and buy them through a discount broker.

10. Also, don't hesitate to ask a stockbroker for advice if you don't feel comfortable enough to go it on your own. Just stick to your strategy and tolerance for risk.

11. Don't be afraid to try going it on your own, being *self-directed*. You may be surprised at what you can do for yourself.

WHAT'S NEXT?

You've just gone through the entire explanation of the 3-tiered investment strategy. But before you go out and try to create and implement your own financial strategy, it is important that you have a plan to integrate all three tiers and monitor your progress toward your investment goals. Turn to **Step 10: Monitor Your Investments Regularly** to learn more about record keeping.

NOTES

1. Standard & Poor's Investor's Monthly. "Rapid Growth Stocks Currently Favored by Wall Street Analysts." January 1993: 6.
2. Standard & Poor's Corporation. *Stock Market Encyclopedia* Standard NYSE Stock Reports, vol. 59, no. 164, 24 August 1992: 1149.
3. Ortega, Bob, Patrick M. Reilly and Larry M. Greenberg. "Wal-Mart Agrees to Buy Woolco Stores in Canada from Woolworth Corp. Unit." *The Wall Street Journal,* 17 January 1994: A3.

Norman, James R. "Multidogs?" *Forbes*, 31 January 1994: 82.
5. Jaffe, Thomas. Streetwalker, "Buys on the bolsa," *Forbes*, 31 January 1994: 144.
6. Dreman, David. The Contrarian, Money & Investments Section: "A Buy-and-Watch Strategy," *Forbes*, 1 February 1993: 114.

STEP

Monitor Your Investments Regularly

Regardless of how far you go with this 3-tiered investment strategy (Tier 1, to Tier 2 or up to Tier 3) or any other investment approach, it is important to establish some method of organizing your financial records and monitoring your progress toward your stated goals. You should also identify which financial statements are important for tax purposes and retain copies of those records for future reference. Mutual fund dividends and capital gains, as well as DRIP dividends in personal accounts, will have to be reported as taxable income in the year in which they are received. You'd like to think the investments you selected are ones that will perform well for a number of years. Nonetheless, you must be prepared to sell a holding if it fails to meet expectation, particularly when you are dealing with individual stocks. Consequently, good record keeping is essential.

What Financial Records Should You Keep?

Once you actually begin investing, you'll develop a greater appreciation of what is important and which records must be maintained. Bear one thing in mind. When you sell a holding you must have documentation for both ends of the transaction (purchase and sale). Sales of taxable investments in a personal account must be reported to the Internal Revenue Service as either a capital gain (you made money) or a capital loss (you lost money). To do that you will use the statements furnished by your mutual fund (Tier 1), DRIP company or transfer agent (Tier 2) or your brokerage company (Tier 3). Also, keep copies of those records which document how much money you put into an investment (automatic transfers, OCPs and stock purchases).

TIER 1 INVESTMENTS

In the case of mutual funds, you will generally receive a confirmation for every purchase you make. So those *monthly* automatic transfers invariably generate *monthly* statements. If you stop the automatic transfers, then your statements probably will be limited to those months when a dividend and/or capital is distributed. The mechanics of administering mutual fund transactions are dynamic. To keep administrative costs down, one mutual fund I own discontinued the practice of sending me a written statement for my monthly automatic transfer. So every month, I now have to call a toll-free phone number to confirm the transaction and find out my new account balance. I'd prefer a written record, but that option no longer exists.

TIER 2 INVESTMENTS

With the Tier 2 DRIPs, the transfer agent or company will send you an *acknowledgment* upon receipt of your OCP (optional cash payment) and a complete statement after the next stock purchase to indicate how many shares were bought. Some stocks can be bought weekly, others monthly or quarterly. If a company you've selected buys stock once a quarter for DRIP participants, then you will receive an updated statement quarterly with acknowledgments for each check you sent in during those three months.

TIER 3 INVESTMENTS

The record keeping for individual growth stocks is often simpler and easier to follow, as well as to explain. After all, you are buying these investments principally for growth so you might not receive any current income (dividends). In that case, you'll need to document your cost (the total price you paid for the stock plus brokerage commissions) and the income from the sale (sale price less the sale commission). The difference between the two is your gain (if you made a profit) or your loss (if you didn't). The time span between your purchase and the sale may be years, nonetheless you must retain documentation for both ends of the transaction. In the event you received dividends, you will need to keep those records and include that income to calculate your gain or loss.

ORGANIZE THOSE FINANCIAL RECORDS

You may find it helpful to buy a document holder or even a small file cabinet to house your financial records. As your portfolio grows, so will your need for efficient record keeping. Make a folder for each mutual fund, DRIP, growth stock or brokerage account. Organize the folder or file cabinet in any way that makes sense to you. For instance, you may want to alphabetize the folders mixing mutual funds, DRIPs and stocks because it is simpler to find things arranged that way. But choose your own organizational method and set up the document folder or file cabinet accordingly.

When you receive a financial statement or an acknowledgment, file your copy in the appropriate folder. You might also find it helpful to create a visual record of your contributions and the amount of money you've invested in each holding by listing all payments on a piece of paper. Have a column for each month of the year at the top of the page and a row for each mutual fund at the left (Figure 1). List your automatic transfers and any other separate contributions. If you send an additional $50 to Mutual Fund 1 in February, record the date and check number in that block and so on. Below the mutual fund name, keep a running total of how much you've contributed to each fund to date. In that way it will be easier for you to see how far you are from your contribution goals. Set up a similar record for monitoring your DRIP accounts.

Computer whizzes will find any number of software programs that will perform these tasks with ease and speed. In fact, if you have a computer and the interest you can consider purchasing money management software. But that is not necessary at this point for the beginning investor. Everything that you need to do can be done without a computer initially. Once you've established a diversified portfolio, you can think about expanding your horizons and computerizing all your holdings. For now, keep it simple.

RETAIN PHONE NUMBERS AND ADDRESSES

You may find it necessary to communicate with your mutual fund, brokerage company or a transfer agent handling one of your accounts from time to time. To make that process easier, keep some of the literature you receive with statements that lists phone numbers and addresses. When you have questions about your DRIP account, you don't want to call or write the company's shareholder relations department. Instead, contact the transfer agent that actually administers the dividend reinvestment program.

Also, keep a prospectus and at least one recent quarterly or annual report on hand in the event you later have a question relating to investment strategy and policies, available services, fees, a company's product line or payment of dividends and capital gains. If you want to make an additional purchase in any one of your investments, it is prudent to check your records to ensure you don't "buy a dividend," but time your purchase to maximize its benefit.

Contributions to Mutual Funds for the Year 199__ *

	Jan	Feb	Mar	Apr	May	Jun	Jul	Aug	Sep	Oct	Nov	Dec	TOTAL (comments)
Mutual Fund 1 ($)**													
Mutual Fund 2 ($)**													
Mutual Fund 3 ($)**													
Mutual Fund 4 ($)**													

* For automatic transfers, record the date and the amount. For check deposits, record the check number, the date and the amount.

** Keep a running tally of how much money you have contributed to each of your accounts.

Set up a chart to record the contributions to your mutual funds.

Monitor Your Investments Regularly   179

Contributions to DRIP Accounts for the Year 199___ *

	Jan	Feb	Mar	Apr	May	Jun	Jul	Aug	Sep	Oct	Nov	Dec	TOTAL (comments)
DRIP Fund 1 ($)**													
DRIP Fund 2 ($)**													
DRIP Fund 3 ($)**													
DRIP Fund 4 ($)**													

* For automatic transfers, record the date and the amount. For check deposits, record the check number, the date and the amount.
** Keep a running tally of how much money you have contributed to each of your accounts.

Set up a chart to record the contributions to your DRIP accounts.

Learn the Tax Consequences of Your Investment Strategy

Aside from devoting time to identify and select good investment opportunities, you should know how your investment strategy affects your local, state and federal tax liability. In other words, you need to understand which purchases you make are going to generate taxable income and which are not *before* you actually make them. The following information is intended to acquaint you with this subject, but you are advised to call the IRS or consult a tax preparer, accountant or tax attorney for specific guidance on your tax responsibilities. At the very least you should know about:

The Form 1099-DIV

It was mentioned in Step 8 that you would be sent a Form 1099-DIV, or a substitute Form 1099, for each of your Tier 1 mutual funds and your Tier 2 DRIP holdings by the end of January. The form will list all the dividends and other distributions (capital gains, foreign taxes paid, non-taxable distributions, federal income tax withheld) and other information related to your investment. For those of you at the Tier 2 level, remember that for tax purposes any discounts, fees or commissions paid by the company for you are considered taxable income. These are the discounts that some companies included for the benefit of the shareholders. If you have Tier 3 growth stocks with small dividends, they too will generate a Form 1099. Be advised that these Form 1099s are also furnished to the Internal Revenue Service, so you want to make certain to report all this information on your tax return.

Remember that not all your investments will pay a dividend or capital gains. In fact, some mutual funds and stocks are valuable assets particularly because they do not distribute any revenue for investors. They are attractive for their price appreciation alone. When you eventually sell those shares, taxes will be due on any capital gains.

SWITCHING MUTUAL FUNDS

You read and hear a lot about telephone switching of mutual funds. This is a common practice of investors who try to time "highs" and "lows" in the market or sell mutual fund assets to take profits (in up markets) or prevent further losses (in down markets). When you move money from one mutual fund to another in a personal account (not a retirement account), be advised that each switch represents a sale (to get out of one fund) and a buy (to get into another). You'll also have to report those sales to the IRS on your income taxes. While fund "switching" is convenient and you read and hear financial advisors recommending "taking profits" or reducing "your position in stock," be aware that these moves do have tax consequences.

SELLING DRIPs AND INDIVIDUAL GROWTH STOCKS

When you sell all or part of your shares of stock in dividend reinvestment programs or growth stocks in your personal brokerage account, you also have to report the sale when you file your income taxes. The government wants you to indicate if you sold your holdings at a profit or loss, pay taxes on any gains and report losses to offset other gains within specified limits. Consult the IRS or your tax preparer for information pertaining to your individual holdings.

BE PREPARED TO PAY ESTIMATED TAXES

Once you reach the point where you have a significant amount of taxable income coming in from your investments each year (dividends and capital gains), you should estimate your taxes and file a 1040ES with the Internal Revenue Service. These are quarterly payments of the estimated tax on the income your investments generate. The IRS has a four-page set of instructions it will send you to determine if this income is at a level requiring the filing of a 1040-ES. If so, you can make quarterly payments by the middle of April, June, September and January each year.

Again, consult your tax preparer or call the IRS for more information, forms and guidance on when such filings are necessary.

"RIDE THROUGH AND BUY THROUGH" THE ROUGH SPOTS

You'll read countless articles and hear numerous financial experts make projections about the economy in the United States and abroad. You'll even hear some of these individuals make dire predictions and strong recommendations to sell your "equities" (stocks) and move your cash into safe, government-backed securities (U.S. Treasury bills, U.S. Savings Bonds, GNMAs, etc.). Before you pick up the phone or write that letter to your brokerage service or mutual fund transfer agent, stop and think about what you are being asked to do. If you are a short-term investor in need of protecting a part of your assets that is exposed to risky investments, then perhaps you should take such advice under serious consideration.

On the other hand, if you are a long-term investor, you should listen and learn, but not necessarily take any action. In fact, you may want to be prepared to buy more of your mutual funds, DRIPs or individual stocks. Don't lose sight of the fact that you are expecting the markets to have their ups and downs and your strategy is to *ride through and buy through the rough spots*. Remember, these "experts" are traders, trying to make money for themselves and their clients by buying low and selling high. So they look for opportunities that offer profit making and profit taking. They also prefer to sell promptly in down markets to avoid potentially big losses. As an investor, and not a trader, your view of the markets is not short-term. Recall the rewards of the **Home Depot** stockholders who held onto their shares from 1986 through 1992.

MONITOR YOUR HOLDINGS REGULARLY

It helps to listen to the nightly news and cable television financial programming to gain new insights into the financial markets and learn what's "hot" and what's not. This is time well spent if you listen and learn more about investing. Yet, it is no substitute and should not take time away from your efforts to chart each investment and monitor your progress toward those goals you set.

MUTUAL FUNDS (TIER 1)

You'd be advised to set aside a regular time not only to look up the net asset value (NAV) of your mutual fund(s) but actually to record that share price in a log. When just beginning your Tier 1 strategy you'll only have a few hundred dollars in a fund, so you needn't spend much time tracking this single investment. But you should be researching other mutual funds and other mutual fund families to identify additional investment opportunities you believe would be ideal for your portfolio. Chart those mutual funds to develop a share price history, so you know an attractive NAV when you see one. In other words, don't open one mutual fund account, set up an automatic transfer and consider your Tier 1 investment strategy complete.

Monitor the performance of your mutual funds as well as those which you would one day like to own. Eventually, you will get to a point where you can consider establishing a second, third, fourth fund, etc., and you'll have some of your own data to use for any assessment. Also look at market downturns as buying opportunities rather than occasions to sell. With mutual funds you can buy additional shares and open new accounts on any business day of the week, 52 weeks a year, and by monitoring your investments, you'll know when it might be wise to acquire more shares.

DRIPS (TIER 2)

Keep a regular eye on the price of the stocks in which you have DRIPs, because you may want to add more money to your "dollar cost averaging" program in those months when the markets are down. Chart the price of your stocks each week, once a month or quarterly, whatever you find works best for you. Be advised that the newspaper will only provide you with the high price, low price and last price for the past 52 weeks. You'll need to get price information outside these time frames yourself or from other sources (like the Standard & Poor's Reports and financial newsletters in the library). Timing is especially important because DRIPs vary widely in the frequency with which they buy shares, although many companies make purchases monthly.

If you see share prices heading down, consider adding a little extra to your account but maintain your minimum monthly investment even if the market is "up." After several years of regular monthly investing, hopefully you'll see that what you perceived as a "high" price yesterday is "low" in comparison to the prevailing price a year from now.

INDIVIDUAL GROWTH STOCKS (TIER 3)

If you're investing at the Tier 3 level you already know how important it is to follow your investments. In fact, you have to track your individual stocks closely to know when, or if, it is advisable to buy more shares. Here timing is everything, since you want to purchase shares of stock in round lots of 100 shares, if possible. By monitoring stock prices over a long period of time, you can become familiar with the trading (price) range of a given stock and add more shares to your account, if and when, you think the price is right.

KEEPING TRACK OF YOUR OVERALL PROGRESS

At the very least, you should determine your net asset value (NAV) on an annual basis and assess the year's progress toward your stated, written goals. Compare the value of all your investments to what you estimated them to be at different points in time (projections at six months, one year, five years, etc.). As your assets grow, you may find it helpful to do a weekly NAV check and retain a running record of the NAV level for each month during the year. So when you sit down to calculate your net asset value for July, you see the previous figures for June, May, April, March, February and January of that same year. You'll quickly see if the value of your portfolio is growing, remaining the same or shrinking.

As a beginning investor just starting out, your assets will be few and simple, so record keeping should be easy and take little time. As the number of your holdings increases and you move from a diversified mutual fund portfolio (Tier 1) to DRIPs (Tier 2) and then more selected stock picking (Tier 3), you can continue to do your record keeping manually or get help from a computer. The level of sophistication you employ will depend largely on the number and complexity of your investments as well as the amount of time you wish to devote to this activity. But with inexpensive computer software you can monitor and update your entire portfolio daily and recalculate your net asset value in a matter of a few minutes.

COMPARE YOUR PROJECTIONS TO "REAL WORLD" DATA

When you do your annual review and calculation of your net asset value, be sure to compare actual figures to your estimates. If you recall in Step 5 you were advised to put your projections on paper and keep them for comparison later on. This is really important, because it can be a form of positive reinforcement not only to attain a projected goal but to exceed it. That is success, and it is satisfying to learn that you can achieve what you set out to do.

If you overshoot your goals, then revise them and set your sights higher. In the meantime, work to refine your investment strategy and maximize the returns you are capable of receiving from your Tier 1, Tier 2 and Tier 3 holdings.

FINALLY, *STAY WITH YOUR INVESTMENT STRATEGY*

There are no short cuts to financial success, so stay with the strategy you create, and you'll realize the most from your efforts. Remember, this book was intended not to make specific investments, but to help you learn how to develop and implement a financial strategy to achieve *your* long-term goals. The time you spend in developing and implementing your own investment strategy will be well worth the monetary return and personal growth.

Once started you'll be surprised at how much you can do for yourself with only a little bit of effort. As you develop a more extensive strategy and your assets grow, so too will your understanding of wealth building. In the end, you will be much better able to manage your own investments and make financial decisions in retirement. Or, you can at least make participatory decisions with an investment advisor, should you wish to turn this responsibility over to a financial expert in your latter years.

IN REVIEW

1. Identify those financial records which must be kept.
2. Organize your financial records in a folder or file cabinet.
3. Save the phone numbers and addresses of your investments.
4. Know the tax consequences of your investment strategy.
5. The more you know about sound saving and investing strategies, the better you will be able to make financial decisions in retirement.
6. "Ride through and buy through the rough spots." Don't be afraid to buy in a "down" market.
7. Monitor the value/price of your holdings regularly and record that information for future use.
8. Keep track of your progress toward attaining your goals.
9. Compare your financial projections to the "real world" performance of your investments.
10. Stay with your investment strategy and strive to improve it.

WHAT'S NEXT?

Nothing and yet everything. That's the end of the discussion of the 3-tiered investment strategy. All that remains is for you to take what you have learned from Steps 1 through 10, formulate your own investment strategy, and then implement it using the techniques you've just learned. **Good luck!**

AFTERWORD

THERE ARE ANSWERS ALL AROUND YOU!

When I sat down to write this book, I had two main goals. First, I wanted to present the 3-tiered investment strategy I devised over the years. It has enabled me to give direction to managing my own money. Even to this day, it continues to work for me, so I wanted to share it with others. And second, I hoped to demonstrate to beginning investors that they are capable not only of developing an investment strategy but actually putting such a plan to work and becoming *self-directed*.

I believe those were realistic goals, and hopefully I've achieved them. If so, you should feel more knowledgeable and confident in making investment decisions for yourself. No longer is selecting a mutual fund, opening a DRIP account or buying individual growth stocks a mystery. Not only do you know the "hows" and "whys" of investing but you also know where to go for resource information. At the very least you should be far more aware of all the financial publications that are literally filled with *free* investment advice and recommendations.

Before you read this book, you may have asked yourself many questions: what should I do with my money? how should I invest my savings?

how do you find a good mutual fund or stock? how much money do you need to start a mutual fund? how much money do you need to buy stocks? what's the best way to start investing? and so on. If those were some of your questions, you now know you can find answers to them in newspapers, in financial magazines, in the reference section of the public library and on television.

In fact, the next time you read *Money Magazine* or *The Wall Street Journal* or watch the "Nightly Business Report" on your local public broadcasting stations, you'll see just how much more informed and knowledgeable you have become. You now know what to look for. Just remember that "there are answers all around you."

Mutual Fund Families

The following is a listing of many of the mutual fund families offering a variety of funds (both load and no-load). They are presented in the order in which they appear in the typical newspaper business section.

Name	Phone Number*	Name	Phone Number*
AAL Mutual	800-553-6319	American Capital	800-421-5666
AARP Investments	800-253-2277	American Funds	800-421-0180
ABT Funds	800-553-7838	American National	
AHA Funds	800-445-1341	Funds	800-231-4649
Aim Funds	800-347-1919	American Performance	800-762-7085
AMCORE Vintage		AmSouth Funds	800-451-8379
Funds	800-662-4203	Aquila Funds	800-437-1020
AMF Funds	800-527-3713	Arch Funds	800-452-2724
ARK Funds	N/A	Atlas Funds	800-933-2852
Advest Advant	800-243-8115	BB&T	800-228-1872
Aetna Funds	800-238-6263	Babson Group	800-422-2766
Alger Funds	800-992-3863	Bailard Biehl & Kaiser	800-882-8383
Alliance Capital	800-227-4618	Baird Funds	800-792-2473
Ambassador Funds	800-892-4366	Bartlett Funds	800-800-4612
American AAdvant	817-967-3509	BayFunds	800-229-3863

*N/A = phone number not available at the time of publication.

Name	Phone Number*	Name	Phone Number*
Benchmark Funds	800-637-1380	Evergreen Funds	800-235-0064
Benham Group	800-472-3389	FBL Series Funds	800-247-4170
Berger Group	800-333-1001	FFB Funds	800-437-8790
Bernstein Funds	212-756-4097	FFTW Funds	800-762-4848
Biltmore Funds	N/A	FMB Funds	800-453-4234
Blanchard Funds	800-922-7771	FPA Funds	800-982-4372
BNY Hamilton	800-426-9363	Federated Funds	800-245-2423
Boston Company Inst	800-221-7930	Fidelity Investments	800-544-8888
Boston Company Retail	800-225-5267	59 Wall Street	212-493-8100
Boulevard Funds	800-285-3263	First American Funds	800-637-2548
Bull & Bear Group	800-847-4200	First Investors	800-423-4026
CFB Market Watch		First Omaha	800-662-4203
Funds	800-232-9091	First Union	800-326-3241
CGM Funds	800-345-4048	Flag Investors	800-767-3524
Calvert Group	800-368-2748	Flagship Group	800-227-4648
Cambridge Funds	800-382-0016	Flex Funds	800-325-3539
Capstone Group	800-262-6631	Fortis Funds	800-800-2638
Cardinal Family	800-848-7734	Fortress Invest	800-245-5051
Colonial Funds	800-248-2828	Forum Funds	800-456-6710
Columbia Funds	800-547-1707	Founders Group	800-525-2440
Common Sense	800-544-5445	Fountain Sq Funds	800-654-5372
Compass Capital	800-451-8371	Franklin-Templeton	
Composite Group	800-543-8072	Group	800-342-5236
Conestoga Funds	800-344-2716	Franklin Mgd Trust	800-342-5236
Conn Mutual	800-322-2642	Fremont Funds	800-548-4539
Core Funds	800-323-3851	Fund Trust	800-344-9033
Crabbe Huson Funds	800-541-9732	Fundamental Funds	800-322-6864
Crest Funds Trust	800-782-7222	GAM Funds	212-888-4200
DG Investor	800-344-2488	GIT Invest	800-336-3063
Dean Witter	800-869-3863	GT Global	800-824-1580
Delaware Group	800-523-4640	Gabelli Funds	800-422-3554
Dimensional Funds	310-395-8005	Galaxy Funds	800-628-0414
Dodge & Cox	415-434-0311	Gateway Funds	800-354-6339
Dreyfus	800-373-9387	General Electric Invest	800-242-0134
EBI Funds	800-554-1156	Gintel Group	800-243-5808
Eaton Vance	800-225-6265	Goldman Sachs	800-762-5035
Emerald Funds	800-637-6336	Govett Funds	800-634-6838
Enterprise Group	800-432-4320	Gradison McDonald	800-869-5999

Name	Phone Number*	Name	Phone Number*
Guardian Funds	800-221-3253	Managers Funds	800-835-3879
Hanover Inv Funds	800-821-2371	Mariner Funds	800-634-2536
Harbor Funds	800-422-1050	Marshall Funds	800-934-3883
Heartland Funds	800-432-7856	Maxus Funds	800-446-2987
Heritage Funds	800-421-4184	Merrill Lynch	609-282-2800
High Mark Funds	800-433-6884	Merriman Funds	800-423-4893
Huntington Funds	800-354-4111	Metropolitan Life	
IAI Funds	800-945-3863	State St	800-882-3302
IBM Mutual Funds	800-426-9876	Midwest	800-543-8721
IDEX Group	800-624-4339	Monetta Trust	800-666-3882
IDS Group	800-328-8300	Monitor Funds	800-253-0412
INVESCO	800-525-8085	Morgan Stanley	800-548-7786
ISI Funds	800-645-3923	Mutual of Omaha	800-228-9596
Independence Cap	800-334-2292	Mutual Series	800-448-3863
Inst Fund Gp	800-821-7432	NCC Funds	800-622-3863
InvSer Optifd	800-245-4770	NYL Institute Funds	800-695-2126
Jackson National	800-888-3863	National Funds	800-243-4361
Janus Funds	800-525-8983	Nations Funds	800-321-7854
John Hancock	800-225-5291	Nationwide Funds	800-848-0920
Kemper Funds	800-621-1048	Neuberger & Berman	800-877-9700
Kent Funds	800-633-5368	Nicholas Applegate	800-551-8045
Keystone	800-343-2898	Nicholas Group	414-272-6133
Kidder Group	800-238-7753	North Amer Sec Trst	800-334-0575
Landmark Funds	800-846-1291	Norwest Funds	800-338-1348
Legg Mason	800-822-5544	Nuveen Funds	800-621-7227
Lexington Group	800-526-0056	One Group	800-338-4345
Liberty Family	800-245-4770	Oppenheimer Funds	800-525-7048
Liberty Financial	800-872-5426	Overland Express	800-552-9612
Lindner Funds	314-727-5305	PFAMCo Funds	800-800-7674
Loomis Sayles Funds	800-633-3330	PIMCO Funds	800-800-0952
Lord Abbett	800-874-3733	PNC Funds	800-422-6538
Lutheran Bro	800-328-4552	Pacific Horizon	800-332-3863
MAS PTF	800-354-8185	Pacifica Funds	800-662-8417
MFS	800-225-2606	Paine Webber	800-647-1568
MIM Funds	800-233-1240	Paragon Pt	800-525-7907
MIMLIC Funds	800-443-3677	Parkstone Funds	800-451-8377
Mackenzie Group	800-456-5111	Pasadena Group	800-648-8050
Mainstay Funds	800-695-2126	Penn-Royce Fund	800-221-4268

Name	Phone Number*	Name	Phone Number*
Performance Funds	800-524-2276	Sentinel Group	800-233-4332
Perm Port Funds	800-531-5142	Seven Seas Series	800-647-7327
Phoenix Series	800-243-4361	1784 Funds	N/A
Pierpont Funds	800-521-5412	Shawmut Funds	800-742-9688
Pilgrim Group	800-334-3444	Sierra Trust	800-222-5852
Pillar Funds	800-932-7782	Signet Select	800-444-7123
Pioneer Funds	800-225-6292	Sit New Begin	800-332-5580
Piper Jaffray	800-866-7778	Skyline Funds	800-458-5222
Portico Funds	800-982-8909	Smith Barney Shearson	800-544-7835
Preferred Group	800-662-4769	Society Funds	800-362-5365
T. Rowe Price Funds	800-638-5660	Stagecoach Funds	800-222-8222
Principal Presv	800-826-4600	Star Funds	800-667-3863
Princor Funds	800-247-4123	State Bond Group	800-437-6663
Provident Mutual	800-441-9490	State Farm Group	309-766-2029
Prudential Funds	800-225-1852	State Street Research	800-882-3302
Putnam Funds	800-225-1581	Steadman Funds	800-424-8570
Quantitative Group	800-331-1244	Stein Roe Funds	800-338-2250
Quest for Value	800-232-3863	Strong Funds	800-368-1030
RBB Fund	800-888-9723	Sun Eagle	800-752-1823
RSI Trust	800-772-3615	Sun America Funds	800-858-8850
Regis Fund	800-638-7983	TARGET	N/A
Rembrandt Funds	800-443-4725	TNE Funds	800-343-7104
Retire Invst Trust	800-231-5652	TRAK Funds	N/A
Rightime Group	800-242-1421	Templeton Funds	800-237-0738
Robertson Stephens	800-766-3863	Thomson Group	800-227-7337
Rochester Funds	716-383-1300	Thornburg Funds	800-847-0200
Rodney Square	800-336-9970	Tower Funds	800-999-0124
Rushmore Group	800-621-7874	Trademark	N/A
SEI Funds	800-342-5734	Transamerica	800-343-6840
STI Classic	800-428-6970	Trust for Credit Unions	800-526-7384
Safeco Funds	800-426-6730	20th Cent Mutual Funds	800-345-8765
Salomon Brothers	800-725-6666	USAA Group	800-531-8181
Schwab Funds	800-526-8600	UST Master	800-233-1136
Scudder Funds	800-225-2470	Union Inv	800-634-1100
Seafirst IRA	800-323-9919	United Funds	800-366-5465
Security Funds	800-888-2461	United Services	800-873-8637
Selected Funds	800-243-1575	Value Line Funds	800-223-0818
Seligman Group	800-221-784	Van Eck	800-221-2220

Name	Phone Number*	Name	Phone Number*
Van Kampen Merritt	800-225-2222	Wells Funds	800-776-0179
Vance Exchange	800-225-6265	Westcore	800-392-2673
Vanguard Group	800-662-7447	Westwood Funds	800-253-4510
Venture Advisers	800-279-0279	William Penn	800-523-8440
Victory Funds	800-782-7222	Wood Struthers	800-225-8011
Vista Funds	800-348-4782	Woodward Funds	800-688-3350
Voyageur Funds	800-553-2143	World Funds	800-527-9500
Waddell & Reed Funds	913-236-2000	Wright Funds	800-232-0013
Warburg Pincus	800-257-5614	Zweig Funds	800-272-2700
Weiss Peck Greer	800-223-3332		

A NOTE TO CANADIAN INVESTORS

ABOUT INVESTING IN U.S. MUTUAL FUNDS

Canadian investors interested in learning more about buying U.S. mutual funds should call or write the headquarters of a particular fund or fund family for account information, prospectuses and application forms.

You may actually be able to use the published toll-free numbers for some funds, while others will have you call a commercial international number. If you intend to invest directly in an American mutual fund, be sure to ask about transacting business in U.S. rather than Canadian dollars.

The 25 Largest U.S. Mutual Fund Managers*
(as of September 1992)

The Top Ten**

1. Fidelity Investment
2. Merrill Lynch
3. Vanguard Group
4. Dreyfus
5. Franklin Group
6. Capital Research
7. Dean Witter
8. Kemper Funds
9. Federated
10. Shearson Funds

The Rest

11. Putnam Fund
12. Prudential Funds
13. IDS Group
14. Scudder Funds
15. Nuveen Funds
16. T. Rowe Price Funds
17. Provident Institutional
18. MFS
19. Goldman, Sachs
20. Alliance Capital
21. Paine Webber
22. Oppenheimer Funds
23. AIM
24. 20th Century Funds
25. American Capital

* Laderman, Jeffrey M. and Geoffrey Smith. "The Power of Mutual Funds." *Business Week*, 18 January 1993: 62–67.

** Author's note: At press time, the 1993 rankings for the 25 largest mutual fund companies were not available. However, according to the following report, Fidelity Investments and the Vanguard Group were ranked 1 and 2 in size, respectively: Calian, Sara. Mutual Funds. "Stock Mutual Fund Sales End Year on a High Note." *The Wall Street Journal*, 31 December 1993: 15, 32.

REFERENCE MATERIALS

MAJOR NEWSPAPERS

Name	Publisher	Cost
The Wall Street Journal (published Mon–Fri)	Dow Jones & Company, Inc. World Financial Center 200 Liberty Street New York, NY 10281 (800) 628-9320	$149.00 (one year)
Investor's Business Daily (published Mon–Fri)	Investor's Daily, Inc. 1941 Armacost Avenue Los Angeles, CA 90025 (800) 443-3113	$139.00 (one year)
USA Today (published Mon–Fri)	Gannett Company, Inc. 1000 Wilson Blvd. Arlington, VA 22229 (800) USA-0001	$130.00 (one year)

MAJOR FINANCIAL/BUSINESS MAGAZINES

Name	Publisher	Cost
Barron's National Business & Financial Weekly (published weekly)	Dow Jones & Company, Inc. P.O. Box 7014 Chicopee, MA 01020 (800) 328-6800	$109.00 (one year)
Money Magazine (published monthly)	Time, Inc. Time & Life Building Rockefeller Center New York, NY 10020 (800) 633-9970	$35.95 (one year)
Business Week Magazine (published weekly)	McGraw-Hill, Inc. 1221 Avenue of the Americas New York, NY 10020 (212) 512-2511	$44.95 (one year)
Financial World (published biweekly)	Financial World Partners 1328 Broadway New York, NY 10001 (800) 666-6639	$37.50 (one year)
Forbes (published bimonthly)	Malcom G. Forbes, Jr. 60 5th Avenue New York, NY 10011 (800) 356-3704	$52.00 (one year)
Fortune (published bimonthly)	Time, Inc. Time & Life Building Rockefeller Center New York, NY 10020 (212) 522-1212	$52.95 (one year)
Smart Money (published monthly)	Hearst Company and Dow Jones & Company 1790 Broadway New York, NY 10019 (800) 444-4204	$24.00 (one year)

U.S. News and World Report (published weekly)	Mortimer B. Zuckerman, Inc. 2400 North Street, N.W. Washington, DC 20037 (800) 234-2450	$39.00 (one year)
Worth (10 issues per year)	Capital Publishing 82 Devonshire Street–R25A Boston, MA 02109 (800) 777-1851	$11.95 (one year) $18.97 (two years)

SAMPLING OF VARIOUS RATING SERVICES—MUTUAL FUNDS

Name	Publisher	Cost
CDA/Wiesenberger Mutual Fund Update (published monthly)	CDA Investment Technologies, Inc. 1355 Piccard Drive Rockville, MD 20850	$295.00 (one year)
Lipper Analytical Service Mutual Fund Profile (published quarterly)	Standard & Poor's 25 Broadway New York, NY 10004	$125.00 (one year)
Morningstar Mutual Fund Values (published biweekly)	Morningstar, Inc 53 West Jackson Boulevard Chicago, IL 60604	$395.00 (one year)
The Mutual Fund Forecaster (published monthly)	The Institute for Econometric Research 3471 North Federal Highway Ft. Lauderdale, FL 33306	$100.00 (one year)
The Value Line Mutual Fund Survey (published biweekly)	Value Line Publishing 711 3rd Avenue New York, NY 10017	$295.00 (one year)

SAMPLING OF VARIOUS RATING SERVICES—STOCKS

Name	Publisher	Cost
S&P Stock Market Encyclopedia (published quarterly)	Standard & Poor's Corporation 25 Broadway New York, NY 10004	$130.00 (one year)

The Value Line Investment Survey (published weekly)	Value Line Publishing 711 3rd Avenue New York, NY 10017	$525.00 (one year)
The Zweig Performance Ratings Report (published bimonthly)	Dr. Martin E. Zweig P.O. Box 360 Bellmore, NY 11710	$205.00 (one year)

SAMPLING OF VARIOUS RATING SERVICES—FINANCIAL NEWSLETTERS

Name	Publisher	Cost
Hulbert Financial Digest (published monthly)	Mark Hulbert 316 Commerce Street Alexandria, VA 22314	$135.00 (one year)

SAMPLING OF VARIOUS RATING SERVICES—MONEY MANAGERS

Name	Publisher	Cost
Money Manager Verified Ratings (published monthly)	Norman Zadeh P.O. Box 7634 Beverly Hills, CA 90212	$200.00 (one year)

SAMPLING OF FINANCIAL NEWLETTERS

Name	Publisher	Cost
Donoghue's Moneyletter (published bimonthly)	The Donoghue Organization, Inc. P.O. Box 8008 360 Woodland Street Holliston, MA 01746 (800) 343-5413	$109.00 (one year)
The Ehrenkrantz and King Report (published monthly)	Ladenburg, Thalmann and Company, Inc. 540 Madison Avenue New York, NY 10022 (800) 523-8425	$120.00 (one year)

Environmental Investing News (published monthly)	Robert Mitchell Associates 2 Cannon Street Newton, MA 02161 (617) 244-7819	$108.00 (one year)
Fidelity Profit Alert (published monthly)	Mutual Fund Investors Association 20 William Street, G-70 Wellesley Hills, MA 02181 (800) 638-1987	$149.00 (one year)
Growth Fund Guide (published monthly)	Growth Fund Research, Inc. Box 6600 Rapid City, SD 57709 (800) 621-8322	$89.00 (one year)
Individual Investor Special Situations Report (published monthly)	Financial Data Systems, Inc. 38 East 29th Street, 4th Floor New York, NY 10016 (800) 321-5200	$150.00 (one year)
Investor's Digest (published monthly)	Norman King Fosback, Editor The Institute for Econometric Research 3471 North Federal Highway Ft. Lauderdale, FL 33306 (800) 327-6720	$58.00 (one year)
The Kiplinger Washington Letter (published weekly)	Austin Kiplinger 1729 H Street, N.W. Washington, DC 20077 (800) 544-0155	$63.00 (one year)
The Low Priced Stock Survey (published biweekly)	Dow Theory Forecasts, Inc. 7412 Calumet Avenue Hammond, IN 46324 (219) 931-6480	$48.00 (one year)
Merrill Lynch Market Letter (published bimonthly)	Merrill Lynch World Financial Center–North Tower New York, NY 10281 (212) 236-1000	$195.00 (one year)
Mutual Fund Forecaster (published monthly)	The Institute for Econometric Research 3471 North Federal Highway Ft. Lauderdale, FL 33306 (800) 327-6720	$100.00 (one year)

The No Load Fund Investor (published monthly)	Sheldon Jacobs P.O. Box 283 Hastings-on-Hudson, NY 10706 (800) 252-2042	$95.00 (one year)
Bob Nurock's Advisory (published every 3 weeks)	Bob Nurock Box 988-B Paoli, PA 19301 (800) 227-8883	$247.00 (one year)
OTC Growth Stock Watch (published monthly)	OTC Research Group P.O. Box 305 Brookline, MA 02146 (617) 327-8420	$75.00–$125.00 (one year)
Personal Finance (published bimonthly)	Stephen Leeb, Editor KCI Communications, Inc. 1101 King Street, Suite 400 Alexandria, VA 22314 (800) 832-2330	$78.00 (one year)
Portfolio Selector (published monthly)	Argus Research Corporation 17 Battery Place New York, NY 10004 (212) 425-7500	$390.00 (one year)
Retirement Letter (published monthly)	Phillips Publishing 7811 Montrose Road Potomac, MD 20854 (800) 722-9000	$49.00 (one year)
The Ruff Times (published bimonthly)	Main Street Alliance 4457 Willon Road Pleasanton, CA 94566 (415) 463-2200	$149.00 (one year)
Standard & Poor's The Edge (published bimonthly)	Hank Riehl P.O. Box 7588 San Francisco, CA 94120 (800) 845-3498	$360.00 (one year)
United Mutual Fund Selector (published bimonthly)	Babson United Investment Advisors, Inc. 101 Prescott Street Wellesley Hills, CA 02181 (617) 235-0900	$130.00 (one year)
Value Line Investment Survey (published weekly)	Value Line, Inc. 711 3rd Avenue New York, NY 10017 (800) 833-0046	$525.00 (one year)

Name	Publisher	Cost
The Zweig Forecast (published every 3 weeks)	Dr. Martin E. Zweig P.O. Box 360 Bellmore, NY 11710 (800) 633-2252	$265.00 (one year)

SAMPLING OF STOCK RESEARCH REPORTS

Name	Publisher	Cost
Moody's Dividend Record (published quarterly)	Moody's Investor Service 99 Church Street New York, NY 10007 (800) 342-5647	$460.00 (one year)
Moody's Handbook of Common and OTC Stocks (published quarterly)	Moody's Investor Service 99 Church Street New York, NY 10007 (800) 342-5647	$299.00 (one year)

*Standard & Poor's
  Dividend Record*
(published weekly and quarterly)
	Standard & Poor's
	25 Broadway
	New York, NY 10004
	(212) 208-8369
		$145.00 (one year)
		  (quarterly reports)
		$370.00 (one year)
		  (weekly reports)

The Value Line Investment Survey (published weekly)	Value Line Publishing 711 3rd Avenue New York, NY 10017 (800) 833-0046	$525.00 (one year)
The Value Line OTC Special Situations Service (published bimonthly)	Value Line Publishing 711 3rd Avenue New York, NY 10017 (800) 535-9645	$390.00 (one year)

BROKERAGE COMPANIES OFFERING RESEARCH PUBLICATIONS

Brokerage Company	Publications
Dean Witter Reynolds, Inc. 530 Providence Tower East 5001 Spring Valley Road Dallas, TX 75244 (800) 827-2211	*Bond Market Comments* *Market View* *Market Watch* *Monthly Investment Strategy* *Monthly Statistical Review* *Weekly Technical Perspective*

Fidelity Investments, Inc.
Fidelity Brokerage Services
P.O. Box 9015
Boston, MA 02109
(800) 544-8666

Standard & Poor's Investor's Monthly

Merrill Lynch
2000 Premier Place
5910 North Central Expressway
Dallas, TX 75206
(800) 999-3056

Merrill Lynch Market Letter
Monthly Research Review
Research Highlights

PaineWebber
5151 Beltline, Suite 101
Dallas, TX 75248
(800) 288-1515

Asset Allocation/Equity Valuation
Focus List
Investment Strategy Pyramid
Portfolio Manager's Spotlight
Statistical Summary

Prudential Securities
10440 North Central
  Expressway
Suite 1600
Dallas, TX 75231
(214) 373-2700

Futures Monthly Report
Quantitative Monthly
Research Weekly
Strategy Weekly

Smith Barney Shearson, Inc.
140 58th Street
Brooklyn, NY 11220
Call your local branch office

Closed-End Country Funds
Convertibles
Credit Market Comment
Futures Market Analysis/A Technical Overview
Portfolio Strategist
Research Week
Statistical Summary

PUBLICATIONS SPECIFICALLY RELATED TO DRIPS

Name	Publisher	Cost
Buying Stocks Without a Broker Charles B. Carlson	McGraw-Hill, Inc. 11 West 19th Street New York, NY 10011 (800) 722-4726	$16.95 (paperback)
The Moneypaper Guide to *Dividend Reinvestment Plans*	The Moneypaper 1010 Mamaroneck Avenue Mamaroneck, NY 10543 (914) 381-5400	$25.00

Standard & Poor's Directory of *Dividend Reinvestment Plans*	Standard & Poor's Corporation 25 Broadway New York, NY 10004 (800) 289-8000	$39.95

A SAMPLING OF RELATED BOOKS

Name	Publisher	Cost

Barron's Finance
    and Investment Handbook
John Downes and
    Jordan Elliot Goodman
	Barron's
	250 Wireless Boulevard
	Hauppauge, NY 11788
	(916) 677-7562
		$26.25

Best Ways to Make Money Editors of *Money* *Magazine*	Money Books P.O. Box 2463 Birmingham, AL 35201 (800) 765-6400	$19.95
Business Week's Guide *to Mutual Funds* J. Laderman	McGraw-Hill, Inc. 11 West 19th Street New York, NY 10011 (800) 722-4726	$24.95
Buying Stocks Without a Broker Charles B. Carlson	McGraw-Hill, Inc. 11 West 19th Street New York, NY 10011 (800) 722-4726	$16.95 (paperback)
The Handbook for No-Load *Fund Investors, 10th Ed.* Sheldon Jacobs, Editor	Business One Irwin 1818 Ridge Road Homewood, IL 60430 (708) 206-2700	$34.95 (paperback)

Up on the Market with Carter Randall:
    Wisdom, Insights and Advice
    from a Lifetime on Wall Street
Carter Randall and
    William Gianopulos
	Probus Publishing Co.
	1925 North Clybourn Avenue
	Chicago, IL 60614
	(800) 776-2871
		$21.95

The Individual Investor's Guide
    to No-Load Mutual Funds
    12th Ed., 1993
	The American Association
	    of Individual Investors
	625 North Michigan Avenue
	Chicago, IL 60611
	(312) 280-0170
		$19.00 (paperback)

AN ALL-IN-ONE REFERENCE BOOK

The Do-It-Yourself Guide
to Investment Information,
Where to Find What You
Need To Know
Spencer McGowan

Probus Publishing Co.
1925 North Clybourn Avenue
Chicago, IL 60614
(800) 776-2871

$29.95

NETWORK AND CABLE TELEVISION FINANCIAL PROGRAMS*

Program	Host(s)	Station**
Network Television		
Adam Smith's Money World	Adam Smith	PBS
Nightly Business Report	Paul Kangas Cassie Seifert	PBS
Wall Street Week	Louis Rukeyser	PBS
The Wall Street Journal Report	Consuela Mack	NBC
Cable Television		
Business Day	Stuart Varney	CNN
Business Morning	Stuart Varney Deborah Marchini	CNN
CNBC/FNN	Variety of hosts and daily programs	CNBC
MoneyLine	Lou Dobbs	CNN
Money Week	Lou Dobbs	CNN
This Morning's Business	Doug Ramsey Felicia Taylor	CNBC
Your Money	Stuart Varne	CNN

*Check your local programming for dates and times.
**CNN = Cable News Network; CNBC = Cable News Business Channel; PBS = Public Broadcasting System; NBC = National Broadcasting System.

COMPANIES WITH DIVIDEND REINVESTMENT PROGRAMS (DRIPs)

Company	Stock Symbol	Where Traded	Min. OCP*	Transfer Agent	Phone Number
A					
AAR Corporation	AIR	NYSE	$10	First Chicago Trust Co. of NY	(800) 446-2617
Abbott Laboratories	ABT	NYSE	$10	Bank of Boston	(800) 442-2001
Acme-Cleveland Corporation	AMT	NYSE	$10	Society National Bank	(800) 321-1355
Adams Express	ADX	NYSE	$25	Bank of New York	(800) 524-4458
Advest Group	ADV	NYSE	None	Fleet Bank	(800) 456-9853
Aetna Life and Casualty Co.	AET	NYSE	$50	First Chicago Trust Co. of NY	(800) 446-2617
AFLAC, Inc.	AFL	NYSE	$20	Call company directly	(800) 235-2667
Air Products & Chemicals, Inc.	APD	NYSE	$25	Mellon Bank	(800) 526-0801
Albany International Corporation	AIN	NYSE	$10	Harris Trust & Savings Bank	(312) 461-6830
Alcan Aluminium Ltd.	AL	NYSE	$100	Chemical Bank	(800) 647-4273
Alco Standard Corporation	ASN	NYSE	$25	National City Bank	(216) 575-2532
Allegheny Ludlum Corporation	ALS	NYSE	$25	Mellon Bank	(800) 756-3353
Allegheny Power System, Inc.	AYP	NYSE	$50	Chemical Bank	(800) 647-4273

Members of the **Dow Jones Industrial Average (DJIA)** appear in bold typeface

Company	Stock Symbol	Where Traded	Min. OCP*	Transfer Agent	Phone Number
Allied Group, Inc.	ALGR	NASDAQ	$25	Harris Trust & Savings Bank	(312) 461-3121
Allied-Signal, Inc.	ALD	NYSE	$25	Bank of New York	(800) 524-4458
Aluminium Co. of America ("Alcoa")	AA	NYSE	$25	First Chicago Trust Co. of NY	(800) 446-2617
AMAX, Inc.	AMX	NYSE	$100	Chemical Bank	(800) 851-9677
Amcast Industrial Corporation	AIZ	NYSE	$25	Bank One, Indianapolis	(800) 753-7107
AMCORE Financial, Inc.	AMFI	NASDAQ	$10	Firstar Trust Co.	(800) 637-7549
Amerada Hess Corporation	AHC	NYSE	$50	Chemical Bank	(800) 647-4273
American Brands, Inc.	AMB	NYSE	$100	Call company directly	(203) 698-5000
American Business Products, Inc.	ABP	NYSE	$10	Wachovia Bank & Trust	(800) 633-4236
American Colloid Company	ACOL	NASDAQ	$25	Harris Trust & Savings Bank	(312) 461-7510
American Cyanamid Company	ACY	NYSE	$10	Call company directly	(201) 831-2774
American Electric Power Co., Inc.	AEP	NYSE	$25	First Chicago Trust Co. of NY	(212) 791-6422
American Express Company	AXP	NYSE	$50	Chemical Bank	(800) 647-4273
American Filtrona Corporation	AFIL	NASDAQ	$25	Wachovia Bank & Trust	(800) 633-4236
American General Corporation	AGC	NYSE	$25	First Chicago Trust Co. of NY	(800) 446-2617
American Greetings Corporation	AGREA	NASDAQ	NA	AmeriTrust Co. Nat'l Assoc.	(216) 687-5742
American Health Properties, Inc.	AHE	NYSE	$50	Chemical Bank	(800) 647-4273
American Heritage Life Investment	AHL	NYSE	NA	Trust Company Bank	(800) 568-3476
American Home Products Corp.	AHP	NYSE	$50	Chemical Bank	(800) 647-4273
American Real Estate Partners, LP	ACP	NYSE	NA	Registrar and Transfer Co.	(800) 866-1340

Company	Stock Symbol	Where Traded	Min. OCP*	Transfer Agent	Phone Number
American Recreation Centers, Inc.	AMRC	NASDAQ	$25	First Interstate Bank	(800) 522-6645
American Southwest Mortgage	ASR	ASE	$250	Chemical Trust Co. of CA	(213) 621-8253
American Telephone & Telegraph Co.	T	NYSE	$100	First Chicago Trust Co. of NY	(800) 348-8288
American Water Works Co., Inc.	AWK	NYSE	NA	Bank of Boston	(800) 442-2001
Ameritech	AIT	NYSE	$50	First Chicago Trust Co. of NY	(800) 233-1342
Amoco Corporation	AN	NYSE	$10	First Chicago Trust Co. of NY	(800) 446-2617
AMP, Inc.	AMP	NYSE	$50	Chemical Bank	(800) 647-4273
AmSouth Bancorp.	ASO	NYSE	$10	First Chicago Trust Co. of NY	(800) 446-2617
AmVestors Financial Corporation	AVFC	NASDAQ	$25	Commerce Bank & Trust	(913) 267-8457
Angeles Mortgage Investment Trust	ANM	ASE	$25	Mellon Bank	(800) 526-0801
Angeles Participating Mortgage	APT	ASE	$25	Mellon Bank	(800) 526-0801
Anheuser-Busch Companies, Inc.	BUD	NYSE	$25	Boatmen's Trust Co.	(800) 456-9852
Aon Corporation	AOC	NYSE	$20	First Chicago Trust Co. of NY	(800) 446-2617
Apache Corporation	APA	NYSE	$50	Norwest Bank Minnesota	(800) 551-6161
Aquarion Company	WTR	NYSE	$10	Mellon Bank	(800) 526-0801
ARCO Chemical Company	RCM	NYSE	$10	First Chicago Trust Co. of NY	(800) 446-2617
Arizona Public	ARP	NYSE	$10	Call company directly	(800) 457-2983
Arkla, Inc.	ALG	NYSE	$10	Norwest Bank Minnesota	(800) 551-6161
Armstrong World Industries, Inc.	ACK	NYSE	$50	Call company directly	(717) 396-2029
Arrow Financial Corporation	AROW	NASDAQ	$25	Call company directly	(518) 745-1000
Arvin Industries, Inc.	ARV	NYSE	$25	Harris Trust & Savings Bank	(312) 461-7715
ASARCO, Inc.	AR	NYSE	$25	Bank of New York	(800) 524-4458
Ashland Oil, Inc.	ASH	NYSE	$10	Call company directly	(606) 264-7162
Asset Investors Corporation	AIC	NYSE	NA	Society National Bank	(800) 542-7792
Associated Banc-Corporation	ASBC	NASDAQ	NA	Harris Trust & Savings Bank	(800) 236-2722

Companies with Dividend Reinvestment Programs (DRIPs)   209

Company	Stock Symbol	Where Traded	Min. OCP*	Transfer Agent	Phone Number
Atlanta Gas Light Company	ATG	NYSE	$25	Wachovia Bank & Trust	(800) 633-4236
Atlantic Energy, Inc.	ATE	NYSE	None	Call company directly	(609) 645-4506
Atlantic Richfield Company	ARC	NYSE	$10	First Chicago Trust Co. of NY	(800) 446-2617
Atmos Energy Corporation	ATO	NYS	$25	First Chicago Trust Co. of NY	(800) 446-2617
Avery Dennison Corporation	AVY	NYSE	$25	First Interstate Bank	(800) 522-6645
Avnet, Inc.	AVT	NYSE	$10	Bank of New York	(800) 524-4458
Avon Products, Inc.	AVP	NYSE	$10	First Chicago Trust Co. of NY	(212) 791-6422

B

Company	Stock Symbol	Where Traded	Min. OCP*	Transfer Agent	Phone Number
Baker Hughes, Inc.	BHI	NYSE	$10	First Chicago Trust Co. of NY	(800) 446-2617
Ball Corporation	BLL	NYSE	$25	First Chicago Trust Co. of NY	(800) 446-2617
Baltimore Bancorp	BBB	NYSE	$100§	Security Trust Co., NA	(800) 435-7016
Baltimore Gas and Electric Company	BGE	NYSE	$10	Call company directly	(800) 258-0499
Banc One Corporation	ONE	NYSE	$10	Bank One, Indianapolis	(800) 753-7107
Bancorp Hawaii	BOH	NYSE	$25	Bank of New York	(800) 524-4458
Bangor Hydro-Electric Company	BGR	NYSE	$25	Call company directly	(207) 945-5621
Bank of Boston Corporation	BKB	NYSE	$25	Bank of Boston	(800) 442-2001
Bank of Granite Corporation	GRAN	NASDAQ	NA	Call company directly	(704) 396-3141
Bank of New York Company, Inc.	BK	NYSE	$25	Bank of New York	(800) 524-4458
Bank South Corporation	BKSO	NASDAQ	$25	Mellon Bank	(800) 526-0801
BankAmerica Corporation	BAC	NYSE	$100	Chemical Bank	(800) 647-4273
Bankers First Corporation	BNKF	NASDAQ	$50	First Chicago Trust Co. of NY	(800) 446-2617
Bankers Trust New York Corporation	BT	NYSE	$25	Harris Trust and Savings Bank	(800) 547-9794
Banponce Corporation	BPOP	NASDAQ	$25	Call company directly	(809) 765-9800
Banta Corporation	BNTA	NASDAQ	$10	Firstar Trust Co.	(800) 637-7549
Banyan Short Term Income Trust	VST	ASE	NA	First Chicago Trust Co. of NY	(800) 446-2617

Company	Stock Symbol	Where Traded	Min. OCP*	Transfer Agent	Phone Number
Bard, C.R., Inc.	BCR	NYSE	$10	First Chicago Trust Co. of NY	(800) 446-2617
Barnes Group, Inc.	B	NYSE	$10	Mellon Bank	(800) 288-9541
Barnett Banks, Inc.	BBI	NYSE	$25	Bank of New York	(800) 524-4458
Bausch & Lomb, Inc.	BOL	NYSE	$25	Bank of Boston	(800) 442-2001
Baxter International, Inc.	BAX	NYSE	$25	First Chicago Trust Co. of NY	(800) 446-2617
Bay State Gas Company	BGC	NYSE	$10	Bank of Boston	(800) 442-2001
BayBanks, Inc.	BBNK	NASDAQ	$10	Bank of Boston	(800) 442-2001
BB&T Financial Corporation	BBTF	NASDAQ	$25	Call company directly	(919) 399-4606
BCE, Inc.	BCE	NYSE	None	Montreal Trust Co.	(514) 982-7555
Becton, Dickinson & Company	BDX	NYSE	$25	First Chicago Trust Co. of NY	(800) 446-2617
Bell Atlantic Corporation	BEL	NYSE	$100	American Transtech Inc	(800) 631-2355
Bell South Corporation	BLS	NYSE	$50	Chemical Bank	(800) 631-6001
Bemis Company, Inc.	BMS	NYSE	$25	Norwest Bank Minnesota	(800) 551-6161
Beneficial Corporation	BNL	NYSE	$10	First Chicago Trust Co. of NY	(800) 446-2617
Berkshire Gas Company	BGAS	NASDAQ	$15	Boston Fin. Data Services	(800) 426-5523
Bethlehem Steel Corporation	BS	NYSE	$10	First Chicago Trust Co. of NY	(800) 446-2617
Black & Decker Corporation	BDK	NYSE	$25	First Chicago Trust Co. of NY	(800) 446-2617
Black Hills Corporation	BKH	NYSE	$100	Chemical Bank	(800) 647-4273
H & R Block, Inc.	HRB	NYSE	$25	Boatman's Trust Co.	(800) 456-9852
Blount, Inc.	BLT.A	ASE	$10	Bank of Boston	(800) 442-2001
BMJ Financial Corporation	BMJF	NASDAQ	$100	Registrar & Transfer Co.	(800) 368-5948
Boatman's Bancshares, Inc.	BOAT	NASDAQ	$100	Boatmen's Trust Co.	(800) 456-9852
Bob Evans Farms, Inc.	BOBE	NASDAQ	$10	Call company directly	(614) 492-4952
Boddie-Noell Restaurant Properties	BNP	ASE	$25	First Union Nat'l Bank of NC	(800) 829-8432
Boise Cascade Corporation	BCC	NYSE	$10	Call company directly	(208) 384-7590
Borden, Inc.	BN	NYSE	$10	Bank of New York	(800) 524-4458

Company	Stock Symbol	Where Traded	Min. OCP*	Transfer Agent	Phone Number
Boston Bancorp	SBOS	NASDAQ	$100	Bank of New York	(800) 524-4458
Boston Edison Company	BSE	NYSE	None	Bank of Boston	(800) 442-2001
Bowater, Inc.	BOW	NYSE	$100	Bank of New York	(800) 524-4458
Braintree Savings Bank	BTSB	NASDAQ	$100	Bank of Boston	(800) 442-2001
Briggs & Stratton Corporation	BGG	NYSE	$25	Firstar Trust Co.	(800) 637-7549
Bristol-Myers Squibb Company	BMY	NYSE	$100	Chemical Bank	(800) 356-2026
British Airways PLC	BAB	NYSE	$10	Morgan Guaranty Trust	(800) 428-4237
British Petroleum Co. PLC	BP	NYSE	$10	Morgan Guaranty Trust	(800) 428-4237
Brooklyn Union Gas Company	BU	NYSE	$10	First Chicago Trust Co. of NY	(212) 792-6422
Brown-Forman Corporation	BF.B	ASE	$50	First Chicago Trust Co. of NY	(800) 446-2617
Brown Group, Inc.	BG	NYSE	$25	Boatmen's Trust Co.	(800) 456-9852
Browning-Ferris Industries, Inc.	BFI	NYSE	$25	First Chicago Trust Co. of NY	(800) 446-2617
Brunswick Corporation	BC	NYSE	$10	Call company directly	(708) 735-4294
Brush Wellman, Inc.	BW	NYSE	$10	Society National Bank	(800) 542-7792
Burnham Pacific Properties, Inc.	BPP	NYSE	$100	Call company directly	(800) 568-2722
C					
Cabot Corporation	CBT	NYSE	$10	Bank of Boston	(800) 442-2001
Cadmus Com. Corp	CDMS	NASDAQ	$25	First Union Nat'l Bank of NC	(800) 829-8432
CalFed, Inc.	CAL	NYSE	$100	Chemical Bank	(800) 647-4273
California Real Estate Investment	CT	NYSE	NA	Chemical Bank	(800) 356-2017
California Water Service Company	CWTR	NASDAQ	NA	Bank of Boston	(800) 442-2001
Campbell Soup Company	CPB	NYSE	$25	First Chicago Trust Co. of NY	(800) 446-2617
Canadian Pacific Ltd.	CP	NYSE	None	Montreal Trust Co.	(514) 982-7555
Capital Holding Corporation	CPH	NYSE	$10	First Chicago Trust Co. of NY	(800) 446-2617
Capital Southwest	CSWC	NASDAQ	$25	Society National Bank	(800) 527-7844
Capstead Mortgage	CMO	NYSE	NA	Society National Bank	(800) 527-7844

Company	Stock Symbol	Where Traded	Min. OCP*	Transfer Agent	Phone Number
Carlisle Companies Inc.	CSL	NYSE	$10	Harris Trust and Savings Bank	(312) 461-3324
Carolina Freight Corporation	CAO	NYSE	None	First Union Nat'l Bank of NC	(800) 829-8432
Carolina Power & Light Company	CPL	NYSE	$20	Wachovia Bank & Trust	(800) 633-4236
Carpenter Technology Corporation	CRS	NYSE	$10	First Chicago Trust Co. of NY	(800) 446-2617
Cascade National Gas Corporation	CGC	NYSE	$25	Bank of New York	(800) 524-4458
Caterpillar, Inc.	CAT	NYSE	$10	First Chicago Trust Co. of NY	(800) 446-2617
CBI Industries, Inc.	CBH	NYSE	$25	First Chicago Trust Co. of NY	(800) 446-2617
CBS, Inc.	CBS	NYSE	$25	First Chicago Trust Co. of NY	(800) 446-2617
CCB Financial Corporation	CCBF	NASDAQ	$25	First Union Nat'l Bank of NC	(800) 829-8432
Centel Corporation	CNT	NYSE	$25	First Chicago Trust Co. of NY	(800) 446-2617
Centerbank	CTBX	NASDAQ	$25	Mellon Bank	(800) 288-9541
Centerior Energy Corporation	CX	NYSE	$10	Call company directly	(800) 433-7794
Central Bankshares	CBSS	NASDAQ	None	Bank of Boston	(800) 442-2001
Central & South West Corporation	CSR	NYSE	$10	Call company directly	(800) 527-5797
Central Fidelity Banks, Inc.	CFBS	NASDAQ	$25	Call company directly	(804) 697-6942
Central Holding Company	CHOL	NASDAQ	$25	National Bank of Detroit	(800) 257-1770
Central Hudson Gas & Electric	CNH	NYSE	$25	First Chicago Trust Co. of NY	(800) 446-2617
Central Jersey Bancorp	CJER	NASDAQ	$10	Mellon Bank	(800) 526-0801
Central Louisiana Electric Co., Inc.	CNL	NYSE	$25	First Chicago Trust Co. of NY	(800) 446-2617
Central Maine Power Company	CTP	NYSE	$10	Call company directly	(800) 695-4267
Central Vermont Public Service	CV	NYSE	$50	Call company directly	(802) 747-5406
Centura Bank Inc.	CBC	NYSE	$25	Wachovia Bank & Trust	(800) 633-4236
Century Telephone Enterprises, Inc.	CTL	NYSE	$25	Society National Bank	(800) 527-7844
Champion International Corporation	CHA	NYSE	$10	Chemical Bank	(800) 647-4273
Charter One Financial, Inc.	COFI	NASDAQ	$10	Bank of Boston	(800) 442-2001
Chase Manhattan Corporation	CMB	NYSE	$100	Mellon Bank	(800) 284-4262
Chemed Corporation	CHE	NYSE	$10	Mellon Bank	(800) 756-3353

Company	Stock Symbol	Where Traded	Min. OCP*	Transfer Agent	Phone Number
Chemical Banking Corporation	CHL	NYSE	NA	Call company directly	(800) 647-4273
Chemical Financial Corporation	CHFC	NASDAQ	$10	Society National Bank	(800) 542-7792
Chemical Waste Management, Inc.	CHW	NYSE	$25	Harris Trust and Savings Bank	(312) 461-3309
Chesapeake Corporation	CSK	NYSE	$10	Harris Trust and Savings Bank	(312) 481-6834
Chesapeake Utilities	CPK	NYSE	$50	Amer. Stock Trans & Trust	(800) 937-5449
Chevron Corporation	CHV	NYSE	$25	Harris Trust and Savings Bank	(800) 547-9794
Chrysler Corporation	C	NYSE	$25	First Chicago Trust Co. of NY	(800) 446-2617
Chubb Corporation	CB	NYSE	$10	First Chicago Trust Co. of NY	(800) 446-2617
Church & Dwight Co., Inc.	CHD	NYSE	$250	Chemical Bank	(800) 647-4273
CIGNA Corporation	CI	NYSE	$10	First Chicago Trust Co. of NY	(800) 446-2617
CILCORP	CER	NYSE	$25	Call company directly	(800) 622-5514
Cincinnati Bell, Inc.	CSN	NYSE	$25	Society National Bank	(800) 542-7792
Cincinnati Financial Corporation	CINF	NASDAQ	$25	Fifth Third Bank	(800) 336-6782
Cincinnati Gas & Electric Company	CIN	NYSE	$25	Call company directly	(800) 325-2945
Cincinnati Milacron, Inc.	CMZ	NYSE	$25	Mellon Bank	(800) 756-3353
CIPSCO, Inc.	CIP	NYSE	$10	Illinois Stock Transfer Co.	(312) 427-2953
Citicorp	CCI	NYSE	$100	Citibank, N.A.	(800) 422-2066
Citizens Bancorp	CIBC	NASDAQ	$100	Call company directly	(301) 206-6468
Citizens Banking	CBCF	NASDAQ	$25	Mellon Bank	(800) 756-3353
Citizens First Bancorp, Inc.	CFB	ASE	$10	Call company directly	(201) 445-3400
Clarcor, Inc.	CLC	NYSE	$25	First Chicago Trust Co. of NY	(800) 446-2617
Cleveland-Cliffs, Inc.	CLF	NYSE	$10	Society National Bank	(800) 321-1355
Clorox Company	CLX	NYSE	$10	First Chicago Trust Co. of NY	(800) 446-2617
CML Group	CML	NYSE	$25	Bank of Boston	(800) 442-2001
CMS Energy Corporation	CMS	NYSE	$25	Call company directly	(517) 788-1867
CNA Income Shares	CNN	NYSE	$25	Bank of New York	(800) 524-4458
CNB Bancshares, Inc.	CNBE	NASDAQ	$25	Citizens Nat. Bank of Evansville	(800) 777-3949

Company	Stock Symbol	Where Traded	Min. OCP*	Transfer Agent	Phone Number
Coca-Cola Bottling Co. Consolidated	COKE	NASDAQ	$10	First Union Nat'l Bank of NC	(800) 829-8432
The Coca-Cola Company	KO	NYSE	$10	First Chicago Trust Co. of NY	(800) 446-2617
Coca-Cola Enterprises, Inc.	CCE	NYSE	$10	First Chicago Trust Co. of NY	(800) 446-2617
Colgate-Palmolive Company	CL	NYSE	$20	First Chicago Trust Co. of NY	(800) 446-2617
Colonial BancGroup, Inc.	CLBGA	NASDAQ	$10	Trust Company Bank	(800) 568-3476
Colonial Gas Company	CGES	NASDAQ	$10	Bank of Boston	(800) 442-2001
Colorado National Bankshares, Inc.	COLC	NASDAQ	$50	First Chicago Trust Co. of NY	(800) 446-2617
Columbia Gas System, Inc.	CG	NYSE	$10	Harris Trust and Savings Bank	(312) 461-4075
Columbia Real Estate Investments, Inc.	CIV	ASE	NA	First National Bank, Maryland	(410) 613-3071
Comerica, Inc.	CMA	NYSE	$10	Norwest Bank Minnesota	(800) 551-6161
Commercial Intertech Corporation	TEC	NYSE	$30	Mahoning National Bank	(216) 742-7000
Commonwealth Edison Company	CWE	NYSE	$25	First Chicago Trust Co. of NY	(800) 950-2377
Commonwealth Energy System	CES	NYSE	$10	Call company directly	(800) 447-1183
Communications Satellite Corporation	CQ	NYSE	$25	Bank of New York	(800) 524-4458
Community Bank System, Inc.	CBSI	NASDAQ	$25	Chemical Bank	(800) 647-4273
ConAgra, Inc.	CAG	NYSE	$25	Chemical Bank	(800) 647-4273
Connecticut Energy Corporation	CNE	NYSE	$50	Bank of Boston	(800) 442-2001
Connecticut Natural Gas Corporation	CTG	NYSE	$25	Chemical Bank	(800) 647-4273
Connecticut Water Services, Inc.	CTWS	NASDAQ	$100	State Street Bank & Trust	(800) 426-5523
Consolidated Edison Co. of New York	ED	NYSE	$20	Call company directly	(800) 522-5522
Consolidated Natural Gas Company	CNG	NYSE	$25	Society National Bank	(800) 542-7792
Consolidated Rail Corporation	CRR	NYSE	None	First Chicago Trust Co. of NY	(800) 446-2617
Consumers Water Company	CONW	NASDAQ	$10	Call company directly	(800) 292-2925
Continental Bank Corporation	CBK	NYSE	$25	Mellon Bank	(800) 526-0801
Cooper Industries, Inc.	CBE	NYSE	$25	First Chicago Trust Co. of NY	(800) 446-2617
Copley Properties, Inc.	COP	ASE	$100	Boston Fin. Data Services	(800) 426-5523

Company	Stock Symbol	Where Traded	Min. OCP*	Transfer Agent	Phone Number
CoreStates Financial Corporation	CSFN	NASDAQ	$50	First Chicago Trust Co. of NY	(800) 446-2617
Corning, Inc.	GLW	NYSE	$10	Harris Trust and Savings Bank	(800) 255-0461
Countrywide Mortgage Investments	CWM	NYSE	$10	Chemical Bank	(800) 647-4273
CPC International, Inc.	CPC	NYSE	$10	First Chicago Trust Co. of NY	(800) 446-2617
Crane Company	CR	NYSE	$10	First Chicago Trust Co. of NY	(800) 446-2617
Crestar Financial Corporation	CRFC	NASDAQ	$10	Mellon Bank	(800) 526-0801
Crompton & Knowles Corporation	CNK	NYSE	$30	Mellon Bank	(800) 526-0801
CRSS, Inc.	CRX	NYSE	$10	Society National Bank	(800) 542-7792
CSX Corporation	CSX	NYSE	$25	Harris Trust and Savings Bank	(800) 521-5571
CT Energy Corp.	CNE	NYSE	$50	Bank of Boston	(800) 442-2001
CT Water Service	CTWS	NASDAQ	$100	Boston Fin. Data Services	(800) 426-5523
Cummins Engine Company, Inc.	CUM	NYSE	$10	First Chicago Trust Co. of NY	(800) 446-2617
Curtice Burns Foods, Inc.	CBI	ASE	$25	First Union Bank of NC	(800) 829-8432
Cyprus Minerals Company	CYM	NYSE	$50	Society National Bank	(800) 643-4296

D

Company	Stock Symbol	Where Traded	Min. OCP*	Transfer Agent	Phone Number
Dana Corporation	DCN	NYSE	$25	Chemical Bank	(800) 647-4273
Dauphin Deposit Corporation	DAPN	NASDAQ	$50	Mellon Bank	(800) 526-0801
Dayton Hudson Corporation	DH	NYSE	$10	First Chicago Trust Co. of NY	(800) 446-2617
Dean Foods Company	DF	NYSE	$25	Harris Trust and Savings Bank	(312) 461-3324
Deere & Company	DE	NYSE	$50	Chemical Bank	(800) 647-4273
Delmarva Power & Light Company	DEW	NYSE	None	Call company directly	(800) 365-6495
Delta Air Lines, Inc.	DAL	NYSE	$25	First Chicago Trust Co. of NY	(212) 791-6422
Delta National Gas Company	DGAS	NASDAQ	$25	Liberty National Bank	(800) 395-2662
Deposit Guaranty Corporation	DEPS	NASDAQ	$50	Bank of New York	(800) 524-4458
Detroit Edison Company	DTE	NYSE	$20	Call company directly	(800) 551-5009
Dexter Corporation	DEX	NYSE	$25	Mellon Bank	(800) 288-9541

Company	Stock Symbol	Where Traded	Min. OCP*	Transfer Agent	Phone Number
Dial Corporation	DL	NYSE	$10	Call company directly	(800) 453-2235
Dial REIT, Inc.	DR	NYSE	$25	Harris Trust and Savings Bank	(312) 461-7715
Diebold, Inc.	DBD	NYSE	$10	Society National Bank	(800) 321-1355
Dominion Resources, Inc.	D	NYSE	None	Call company directly	(800) 552-4034
Donaldson Company, Inc.	DCI	NYSE	$10	Norwest Bank Minnesota	(800) 551-6161
R.R. Donnelley & Sons Company	DNY	NYSE	$10	First Chicago Trust Co. of NY	(800) 446-2617
Dow Chemical Company	DOW	NYSE	$10	Society National Bank	(800) 542-7792
Dow Jones & Company, Inc.	DJ	NYSE	$25	First Chicago Trust Co. of NY	(800) 446-2617
DPL, Inc.	DPL	NYSE	$25	Bank of Boston	(800) 442-2001
DQE, Inc.	DQE	NYSE	$10	Call company directly	(800) 247-0400
Dresser Industries, Inc.	DI	NYSE	$25	Call company directly	(214) 740-6708
Dreyfus Corporation	DRY	NYSE	NA	Bank of New York	(800) 524-4458
Duff & Phelps	DNP	NYSE	$100	Bank of New York	(800) 524-4458
Du Pont, E.I. de Nemours & Company	DD	NYSE	$20	Mellon Bank	(800) 526-0801
Duke Power Company	DUK	NYSE	$25	Call company directly	(800) 488-3853
Duriron Company, Inc.	DURI	NASDAQ	$25	Bank One, Indianapolis	(800) 753-7107
E					
E-Systems, Inc.	ESY	NYSE	$25	Society National Bank	(800) 527-7844
E'Town Corporation	EWAT	NASDAQ	$100	Bank of New York	(800) 524-4458
Eagle-Picher Industries, Inc.	EPI	NYSE	$10	Society National Bank	(800) 321-1355
Eastern Company	EML	ASE	$25	Bank of Boston	(800) 442-2001
Eastern Enterprises	EFU	NYSE	$10	Bank of New York	(800) 524-4458
Eastern Utilities Associates	EUA	NYSE	None	Bank of Boston	(800) 442-2001
Eastman Kodak Company	EK	NYSE	$10	First Chicago Trust Co. of NY	(800) 253-6057
Eaton Corporation	ETN	NYSE	$10	Society National Bank	(800) 321-1355
Ecolab, Inc.	ECL	NYSE	$10	First Chicago Trust Co. of NY	(212) 791-6422

Company	Stock Symbol	Where Traded	Min. OCP*	Transfer Agent	Phone Number
EG&G, Inc.	EGG	NYSE	$10	Bank of Boston	(800) 442-2001
Elco Industries, Inc.	ELCN	NASDAQ	$25	First Chicago Trust Co. of NY	(800) 446-2617
EMC Insurance	EMCI	NASDAQ	$100	Harris Trust and Savings Bank	(312) 461-2731
Emerson Electric Company	EMR	NYSE	$25	Boatmen's Trust Co.	(800) 456-9852
Empire District Electric Company	EDE	NYSE	$50	Chemical Bank	(800) 647-4273
Energen Corporation	EGN	NYSE	$25	Harris Trust and Savings Bank	(312) 461-5139
EnergyNorth, Inc.	ENNI	NASDAQ	$50	Boston Fin. Data Services	(800) 426-5523
Engelhard Corporation	EC	NYSE	$10	Mellon Bank	(800) 526-0801
Engraph, Inc.	ENGH	NASDAQ	$25	First Union Nat'l Bank of NC	(800) 829-8432
Enron Corporation	ENE	NYSE	$10	First Chicago Trust Co. of NY	(800) 446-2617
Enserch Corporation	ENS	NYSE	$10	First Chicago Trust Co. of NY	(800) 446-2617
Enserch Exploration Partners, Ltd.	EP	NYSE	$100	Call company directly	(214) 670-2885
Equifax, Inc.	EFX	NYSE	$10	Call company directly	(404) 885-8000
Equitable Resources	EQT	NYSE	$10	Mellon Bank	(800) 526-0801
Essex County Gas	ECGC	NASDAQ	None	Boston Fin. Data Services	(800) 426-5523
Ethyl Corporation	EY	NYSE	$25	Harris Trust and Savings Bank	(312) 461-6834
Exxon Corporation	XON	NYSE	$10	Bank of Boston	(800) 252-1800
F					
F&M National Corporation	FMNT	NASDAQ	$25	Nations Bank	(800) 772-5564
Fay's, Inc.	FAY	NYSE	$25	Amer. Stock Trans & Trust	(800) 937-5449
Federal-Mogul Corporation	FMO	NYSE	$10	Bank of New York	(800) 524-4458
Federal National Mortgage Association	FNM	NYSE	$10	Chemical Bank	(800) 647-4273
Federal Paper Board Company	FBO	NYSE	$10	Amer. Stock Trans & Trust	(800) 937-5449
Federal Realty Investment Trust	FRT	NYSE	$50	Amer. Stock Trans & Trust	(800) 937-5449
Federal Signal Corporation	FSS	NYSE	$25	Harris Trust & Savings Bank	(312) 461-6879

Company	Stock Symbol	Where Traded	Min. OCP*	Transfer Agent	Phone Number
Ferro Corporation	FOE	NYSE	$10	National City Bank	(216) 575-2532
Fifth Third Bancorp	FITB	NASDAQ	$25	Call company directly	(800) 336-6782
Figgie International, Inc.	FIGI	NASDAQ	$10	Bank of Boston	(800) 442-2001
Fina, Inc.	FI	ASE	$10	First Chicago Trust Co. of NY	(800) 446-2617
First Alabama Bancshares, Inc.	FABC	NASDAQ	$20	Call company directly	(205) 832-8450
First American Corporation	FATN	NASDAQ	$25	Call company directly	(615) 748-2441
First Bancorp of Ohio	FBOH	NASDAQ	$30	First National Bank of Ohio	(216) 384-7347
First Bank of Illinois	FBIC	NASDAQ	$25	Firstar Trust Co.	(800) 637-7549
First Bank System, Inc.	FBS	NYSE	$25	First Chicago Trust Co. of NY	(800) 446-2617
First Chicago Corporation	FNB	NYSE	$25	First Chicago Trust Co. of NY	(800) 446-2617
First Colonial Bankshares Corporation	FCOLA	NASDAQ	$25	First Chicago Trust Co. of NY	(800) 446-2617
First Commerce Corporation	FCOM	NASDAQ	$50	First Chicago Trust Co. of NY	(212) 791-6422
First Empire State Corporation	FES	ASE	$10	Bank of Boston	(800) 442-2001
First Fidelity Bancorp.	FFB	NYSE	$50	Bank of New York	(800) 524-4458
First Financial Holdings, Inc.	FFCH	NASDAQ	$25	Norwest Bank Minnesota	(800) 551-6161
First Harrisburg Bancor, Inc.	FFHP	NASDAQ	$25	Registrar and Trans. Co.	(800) 368-5948
First Interstate Bancorp	I	NYSE	NA	First Interstate Bank	(800) 522-6645
First Michigan Bank Corporation	FMBC	NASDAQ	$100	FMB Financial Group	(800) 441-3622
First Midwest Bancorp, Inc.	FMBI	NASDAQ	$100	Illinois Stock Transfer	(312) 427-2953
First Mississippi Corporation	FRM	NYSE	$25	Society National Bank	(800) 321-1355
First National Bank Corporation	MTCL	NASDAQ	$50	National Bank of Detroit	(800) 257-1770
First of America Bank Corporation	FOA	NYSE	$25	Norwest Bank	(800) 782-4040
First Security Corporation	FSCO	NASDAQ	$50	Call company directly	(801) 246-5289
First Tennessee National Corporation	FTEN	NASDAQ	$25	Bank of Boston	(800) 442-2001

Company	Stock Symbol	Where Traded	Min. OCP*	Transfer Agent	Phone Number
First Union Corporation	FTU	NYSE	$25	Call company directly	(704) 374-6782
First Union Real Estate Investments	FUR	NYSE	$20	National City Bank	(216) 575-2532
First Virginia Banks, Inc.	FVB	NYSE	$25	Security Trust Co, NA	(800) 435-7016
First Western Bancorp	FWBI	NYSE	$25	Call company directly	(412) 652-8550
Firstar Corporation	FSR	NYSE	$50	Firstar Trust Co.	(800) 637-7549
Fleet Financial Group, Inc.	FLT	NYSE	$10	Fleet National Bank	(800) 538-1516
Fleming Companies, Inc.	FLM	NYSE	$25	Liberty National Bank	(800) 395-2662
Florida Progress Corporation	FPC	NYSE	$10	Call company directly	(800) 352-1121
Florida Public Utilities Company	FPU	ASE	$25	Bank of New York	(800) 524-4458
Flowers Industries, Inc.	FLO	NYSE	$25	Wachovia Bank & Trust	(800) 633-4236
Food Lion	FDLNB	NASDAQ	$10	Wachovia Bank & Trust	(800) 633-4236
Foote, Cone & Belding	FCB	NYSE	$25	First Chicago Trust Co. of NY	(800) 446-2617
Ford Motor Company	F	NYSE	$10	Chemical Bank	(800) 647-4273
Foster Wheeler Corporation	FWC	NYSE	$10	Mellon Bank	(800) 526-0801
Fourth Financial Corporation	FRTH	NASDAQ	NA	Bank IV Kansas	(800) 444-4400
FPL Group, Inc.	FPL	NYSE	$100	Bank of Boston	(800) 442-2001
Freeport-McMoRan, Inc.	FTX	NYSE	$10	Mellon Bank	(800) 526-0801
H.B. Fuller Company	FULL	NASDAQ	$10	Norwest Bank Minnesota	(800) 551-6161
Fulton Financial Corporation	FULT	NASDAQ	$25	Call company directly	(800) 626-0255
G					
Gannett Company, Inc.	GCI	NYSE	$10	First Chicago Trust Co. of NY	(800) 446-2617
GATX Corporation	GMT	NYSE	$25	Chemical Bank	(800) 647-4273
GenCorp, Inc.	GYT	NYSE	$10	Call company directly	(216) 869-4453
General Cinema Corporation	GCN	NYSE	$25	Bank of Boston	(800) 442-2001
General Electric Company	GE	NYSE	$10	Call company directly	(800) 242-0134

Company	Stock Symbol	Where Traded	Min. OCP*	Transfer Agent	Phone Number
General Mills, Inc.	GIS	NYSE	$10	Harris Trust and Savings Bank	(800) 445-4802
General Motors Corporation	GM	NYSE	$25	First Chicago Trust Co. of NY	(212) 791-3909
General Public Utilities Corporation	GPU	NYSE	$50	Chemical Bank	(800) 647-4273
General Re Corporation	GRN	NYSE	$10	Amer. Stock Trans & Tr	(800) 937-5449
General Signal Corporation	GSX	NYSE	$25	Bank of New York	(800) 524-4458
Genuine Parts Company	GPC	NYSE	$10	Trust Company Bank	(800) 568-3476
Georgia-Pacific Corporation	GP	NYSE	$25	First Chicago Trust Co. of NY	(800) 446-2617
Gerber Products Company	GEB	NYSE	$25	Harris Trust and Savings Bank	(800) 824-6309
Giant Food, Inc.	GFS.A	ASE	$10	Amer. Stock Trans & Trust	(800) 937-5449
Giddings & Lewis, Inc.	GIDL	NASDAQ	NA	Firstar Trust	(800) 637-7549
Gillette Company	GS	NYSE	$10	Bank of Boston	(800) 442-2001
Glaxo Holdings	GLX	NYSE	$50	Bank of New York	(800) 524-4458
B.F. Goodrich Company	GR	NYSE	$25	Bank of New York	(800) 524-4458
Goodyear Tire & Rubber Company	GT	NYSE	$10	First Chicago Trust Co. of NY	(800) 446-2617
Gorman-Rupp Company	GRC	ASE	$20	National City Bank	(216) 575-2532
Goulds Pumps, Inc.	GULD	NASDAQ	$10	Amer. Stock Trans & Trust	(800) 937-5449
W.R. Grace & Company	GRA	NYSE	$1	Chemical Bank	(800) 647-4273
Graco, Inc.	GGG	NYSE	$25	Norwest Bank Minnesota	(800) 551-6161
Grand Metropolitan Pub. Ltd Co.	GRM	NYSE	$10	Morgan Guaranty Trust	(800) 428-4237
Great Lakes Bancorp, FSB	GLBC	NASDAQ	$100	Bank of New York	(800) 524-4458
Great Western Financial Corporation	GWF	NYSE	$100	First Interstate Bank	(800) 522-2645
Green Mountain Power Corporation	GMP	NYSE	$50	Chemical Bank	(800) 647-4273
Grumman Corporation	GQ	NYSE	$25	Bank of New York	(800) 524-4458
GTE Corporation	GTE	NYSE	$25	Call company directly	(800) 225-5160
Guardsman Products, Inc.	GPI	NYSE	$200	Chemical Bank	(800) 647-4273
Gulf States Utilities Company	GSU	NYSE	$25§	Call company directly	(800) 231-9266

Company	Stock Symbol	Where Traded	Min. OCP*	Transfer Agent	Phone Number
H					
Handleman Company	HDL	NYSE	$10	National Bank of Detroit	(800) 257-1770
Handy & Harman	HNH	NYSE	$10	First Chicago Trust Co. of NY	(800) 446-2617
M.A. Hanna Company	MAH	NYSE	$25	Society National Bank	(800) 542-7792
Hannaford Brothers Company	HRD	NYSE	$25	Continental Stock Transfer	(212) 509-4000
Harcourt General, Inc.	H	NYSE	$25	Bank of Boston	(800) 442-2001
Harley-Davidson, Inc.	HDI	NYSE	$30	Firstar Trust Company	(800) 637-7549
Harleysville Group	HGIC	NASDAQ	$100	Mellon Bank	(800) 526-0801
Harris Corporation	HRS	NYSE	$10	Society National Bank	(800) 542-7792
Harsco Corporation	HSC	NYSE	$10	Mellon Bank	(800) 526-0801
Hartford Steam Boiler Inspection & Ins. Co.	HSB	NYSE	$10	Bank of Boston	(800) 442-2001
Hartmarx Corporation	HMX	NYSE	$25	First Chicago Trust Co. of NY	(800) 446-2617
Haverfield Corporation	HVFD	NASDAQ	$20	Call company directly	(216) 226-0510
Hawaiian Electric Industries, Inc.	HE	NYSE	$25	Call company directly	(808) 532-5841
Hawkins Chemical	HWKN	NASDAQ	None	Norwest Bank Minnesota	(800) 551-6161
Health & Rehabilitation Properties	HRP	NYSE	None	Boston Fin. Data Services	(800) 426-5523
Health Care REIT, Inc.	HCN	ASE	$10	Chemical Bank	(800) 647-4273
Health Equity Properties, Inc.	EQP	NYSE	$100	Amer. Stock Trans & Trust	(800) 937-5449
HealthVest	HVT	ASE	$50	First Union Nat'l Bank of NC	(800) 829-8432
H.J. Heinz Company	HNZ	NYSE	$25	Mellon Bank	(800) 253-3399
Hercules, Inc.	HPC	NYSE	$10	Chemical Bank	(800) 647-4273
Hershey Foods Corporation	HSY	NYSE	$50	Chemical Bank	(800) 647-4273
Hibernia Corporation	HIB	NYSE	$100	Chemical Bank	(800) 647-4273
Home Depot	HD	NYSE	$10	Bank of Boston	(800) 442-2001
Homestake Mining Company	HM	NYSE	$25	Bank of Boston	(800) 442-2001
Honeywell, Inc.	HON	NYSE	$25	Chemical Bank	(800) 647-4273

Company	Stock Symbol	Where Traded	Min. OCP*	Transfer Agent	Phone Number
Geo. A. Hormel & Company	HRL	NYSE	$25	Norwest Bank Minnesota	(800) 551-6161
Hotel Investors Trust Corporation	HOT	NYSE	$25§	First Interstate Bank	(800) 522-6645
Houghton Mifflin	HTN	NYSE	$25	Bank of Boston	(800) 442-2001
Household International, Inc.	HI	NYSE	$100	Harris Trust and Savings Bank	(800) 926-2335
Houston Industries, Inc.	HOU	NYSE	$50	Call company directly	(800) 231-6406
HRE Properties	HRE	NYSE	NA	Bank of New York	(800) 524-4458
Hubbell, Inc.	HUBB	NYSE	$100	Chemical Bank	(800) 647-4273
Hubco, Inc.	HCO	ASE	$10	Amer. Stock Trans & Trust	(800) 937-5449
Huffy Corporation	HUF	NYSE	$10	Bank One, Indianapolis	(800) 753-7107
Huntington Bancshares, Inc.	HBAN	NASDAQ	$50	Call company directly	(800) 255-1342
I					
IBP, Inc.	IBP	NYSE	$10	Mellon Bank	(800) 526-0801
ICM Property Investors, Inc.	ICM	NYSE	$25	Mellon Bank	(800) 526-0801
Idaho Power Company	IDA	NYSE	$10	Call company directly	(800) 635-5406
IES Industries, Inc.	IEL	NYSE	$25	Call company directly	(800) 247-9785
Illinois Power Company	IPC	NYSE	$25	Call company directly	(800) 800-8220
IMCERA Group, Inc.	IMA	NYSE	$25	First Chicago Trust Co. of NY	(800) 446-2617
Imperial Oil Ltd.	IMO	ASE	$50	Montreal Trust	(514) 981-9533
Inco Ltd.	N	NYSE	$30	Call company directly	(212) 612-5846
Independence Bancorp	INBC	NASDAQ	$50	Mellon Bank	(800) 526-0801
Independent Bank Corporation (MI)	IBCP	NASDAQ	$15	National Bank of Detroit	(800) 257-1770
Indiana Energy, Inc.	IEI	NYSE	$25	First Chicago Trust Co. of NY	(800) 446-2617
Ingersoll-Rand Company	IR	NYSE	$10	Bank of New York	(800) 524-4458
Inland Steel Industries, Inc.	IAD	NYSE	$25§	Harris Trust and Savings Bank	(312) 461-4075
Insteel Industries Inc.	III	NYSE	$10	First Union Nat'l Bank of NC	(800) 829-8432
Integra Financial Corporation	ITG	NYSE	$100	Call company directly	(412) 644-8664

Company	Stock Symbol	Where Traded	Min. OCP*	Transfer Agent	Phone Number
Intel Corporation	INTL	NASDAQ	$25	Bank of Boston	(800) 442-2001
Intermark, Inc	IMI	ASE	$10§	First Interstate Bank	(800) 522-6645
International Business Machines	IBM	NYSE	$10	First Chicago Trust Co. of NY	(212) 735-7000
International Multifoods Corporation	IMC	NYSE	$10	Norwest Bank Minnesota	(800) 551-6161
International Paper Company	IP	NYSE	$25	Chemical Bank	(800) 647-4273
Interpublic Group of Companies, Inc.	IPG	NYSE	$10	First Chicago Trust Co. of NY	(800) 446-2617
Interstate Power Company	IPW	NYSE	$25	Call company directly	(319) 557-2230
Iowa-Illinois Gas & Electric Company	IWG	NYSE	$25	Call company directly	(800) 373-4443
IPALCO Enterprises, Inc.	IPL	NYSE	$25	Call company directly	(800) 877-0153
IRT Property Company	IRT	NYSE	NA	Trust Company Bank	(404) 588-7822
ITT Corporation	ITT	NYSE	$50	Call company directly	(800) 342-5488
IWC Resources Corporation	IWCR	NASDAQ	$25	Bank One, Indianapolis	(800) 753-7107
J					
Jefferson Bankshares, Inc.	JBNK	NASDAQ	$30	Call company directly	(800) 468-6604
Jefferson-Pilot Corporation	JP	NYSE	$20	First Union Nat'l Bank of NC	(800) 829-8432
Johnson & Johnson	JNJ	NYSE	$25	First Chicago Trust Co. of NY	(800) 446-2617
Johnson Controls, Inc.	JCI	NYSE	$50	Firstar Trust Co.	(800) 637-7549
Jostens, Inc.	JOS	NYSE	$25	Norwest Bank Minnesota	(800) 551-6161
Justin Industries, Inc.	JSTN	NASDAQ	$25	Society National Bank	(800) 527-7844
K					
Kaman Corporation	KAMNA	NASDAQ	$25	Chemical Bank	(800) 647-4273
Kelley Oil & Gas Partners, Ltd.	KLY	ASE	$25	Mellon Bank	(800) 526-0801
Kellogg Company	K	NYSE	$25	Harris Trust and Savings Bank	(800) 323-6138
Kemper Corporation	KEM	NYSE	$25	Harris Trust and Savings Bank	(800) 526-8762
Kennametal, Inc.	KMT	NYSE	$25	Mellon Bank	(800) 756-3353

Company	Stock Symbol	Where Traded	Min. OCP*	Transfer Agent	Phone Number
Kerr-McGee Corporation	KMG	NYSE	$10	Liberty National Bank	(800) 395-2662
Key Centurion Bancshares, Inc.	KEYC	NASDAQ	$25	Wachovia Bank & Trust	(800) 633-4236
Key Corporation	KEY	NYSE	$10	Mellon Bank	(800) 526-0801
Keystone Heritage Group, Inc.	KHGI	NASDAQ	$10	Call company directly	(717) 274-6845
Keystone International, Inc.	KII	NYSE	None	Continental Stock Transfer	(212) 509-4000
Kimberly-Clark Corporation	KMB	NYSE	$25	Bank of Boston	(800) 442-2001
Kmart Corporation	KM	NYSE	$25	National Bank of Detroit	(800) 257-1770
Knape & Vogt	KNAP	NASDAQ	$100	Harris Trust and Savings Bank	(312) 461-3121
KN Energy, Inc.	KNE	NYSE	$5	Call company directly	(303) 989-1740
Knight-Ridder, Inc.	KRI	NYSE	$25	Chemical Bank	(800) 982-7648
Kollmorgen Corp.	KOL	NYSE	$25	Bank of Boston	(800) 442-2001
KU Energy Corporation	KU	NYSE	$20	Illinois Stock Trans Co.	(312) 427-2953
Kuhlman Corporation	KUH	NYSE	$10	National Bank of Detroit	(800) 257-1770
Kysor Ind. Corporation	KZ	NYSE	$10	National Bank of Detroit	(800) 257-1770
L					
La-Z-Boy Chair Company	LZB	NYSE	$25	Amer. Stock Trans & Trust	(800) 937-5449
Laclede Gas Company	LG	NYSE	NA	Boatmen's Trust Co.	(800) 456-9852
Lafarge Corporation	LAF	NYSE	NA	Montreal Trust Co.	(514) 982-7555
Lakeland First Financial Group, Inc.	LLSL	NASDAQ	$100	Amer. Stock Trans & Tr	(800) 937-5449
Lance, Inc.	LNCE	NASDAQ	$10	Wachovia Bank & Trust	(800) 633-4236
LG&E Energy Corporation	LGE	NYSE	$25	Call company directly	(800) 235-9705
Liberty National Bancorp, Inc.	LNBC	NASDAQ	$25	Call company directly	(502) 566-2000
Eli Lilly & Company	LLY	NYSE	$25	Call company directly	(800) 833-8699
The Limited, Inc.	LTD	NYSE	$30	First Chicago Trust Co. of NY	(800) 446-2617
Lincoln National Corporation	LNC	NYSE	$25	Bank of Boston	(800) 442-2001
Lincoln Telecommunications Co.	LTEC	NASDAQ	$100	Mellon Bank	(800) 756-3353

Company	Stock Symbol	Where Traded	Min. OCP*	Transfer Agent	Phone Number
Liz Claiborne	LIZ	NYSE	$25	First Chicago Trust Co. of NY	(800) 446-2617
Loctite Corporation	LOC	NYSE	$25	Bank of Boston	(800) 442-2001
Louisiana-Pacific Corporation	LPX	NYSE	$25	First Chicago Trust Co. of NY	(800) 446-2617
Lowe's Companies, Inc.	LOW	NYSE	$10	Wachovia Bank & Trust	(800) 633-4236
Luby's Cafeterias, Inc.	LUB	NYSE	$20	Society National Bank	(800) 527-7844
Lukens, Inc.	LUC	NYSE	$50	Mellon Bank	(800) 756-3353
Lyondell Petrochemical Company	LYO	NYSE	$25	Bank of New York	(800) 524-4458

M

Company	Stock Symbol	Where Traded	Min. OCP*	Transfer Agent	Phone Number
MacDermid, Inc.	MACD	NASDAQ	$50	Harris Trust and Savings Bank	(312) 461-7369
Madison Gas & Electric Company	MDSN	NASDAQ	$10	Call company directly	(800) 356-6423
Magna Group, Inc.	MAGI	NASDAQ	$25	Magna Trust Co.	(618) 233-2120
MAPCO, Inc.	MDA	NYSE	$10	Harris Trust and Savings Bank	(312) 461-7763
Marion Merrell Dow, Inc.	MKC	NYSE	None	First Chicago Trust Co. of NY	(212) 791-6422
Maritime Telegraph & Telephone	MTT	TSE	None	RM Trust	(902) 420-3221
Mark Twain Bancshares, Inc.	MTWN	NASDAQ	$10	Society National Bank	(800) 321-1355
Marsh & McLennan Companies	MMC	NSYE	$10	Harris Trust and Savings Bank	(800) 457-8968
Marsh Supermarkets, Inc.	MARS	NASDAQ	$100	National City Bank	(216) 575-2532
Marshall & Ilsley Corporation	MRIS	NASDAQ	$25	Bank of New York	(800) 524-4458
Martin Marietta Corporation	ML	NYSE	$50	First Chicago Trust Co. of NY	(800) 446-2617
MASSBANK Corporation	MASB	NASDAQ	$50	Bank of Boston	(800) 442-2001
May Department Stores Co.	MA	NYSE	$25	Bank of New York	(800) 524-4458
Maytag Corporation	MYG	NYSE	$25	Bank of Boston	(800) 442-2001
McCormick & Company, Inc.	MCCRK	NASDAQ	$100	Call company directly	(800) 424-5855
McDermott International, Inc.	MDR	NYSE	$25	First Chicago Trust Co. of NY	(800) 446-2617
McDonald's Corporation	MCD	NYSE	$50	First Chicago Trust Co. of NY	(800) 621-7825
McGraw-Hill, Inc.	MHP	NYSE	$10	Chemical Bank	(800) 647-4273

Company	Stock Symbol	Where Traded	Min. OCP*	Transfer Agent	Phone Number
McKesson Corporation	MCK	NYSE	$10	First Chicago Trust Co. of NY	(800) 446-2617
MCN Corporation	MCN	NYSE	$25	National Bank of Detroit	(800) 257-1770
MDU Resources Group, Inc.	MDU	NYSE	$50	Norwest Bank Minnesota	(800) 551-6161
Mead Corporation	MEA	NYSE	$25	Bank of Boston	(800) 442-2001
Media General, Inc.	MEG.A	ASE	$25	Wachovia Bank & Trust	(800) 633-4236
Meditrust SBI	MT	NYSE	$100	Fleet National Bank	(800) 538-1516
Medtronic, Inc.	MDT	NYSE	$25	Norwest Bank Minnesota	(800) 551-6161
Mellon Bank Corporation	MEL	NYSE	$100	Mellon Bank	(800) 756-3353
Mercantile Bancorp, Inc.	MTRC	NASDAQ	$10	Society National Bank	(800) 321-1355
Mercantile Bankshares Corporation	MRBK	NASDAQ	$25	Mercantile–Safe Deposit & Trust	(410) 237-5211
Merck & Company, Inc.	MRK	NYSE	$25	Norwest Bank Minnesota	(800) 551-6161
Meridian Bancorp, Inc.	MRDN	NASDAQ	$10	Call company directly	(215) 655-2775
Merrill Lynch & Company, Inc.	MER	NYSE	NA	Call company directly	(212) 637-7455
Merry Land & Investment Company, Inc.	MRY	NYSE	$25	First Union Nat'l Bank of NC	(800) 829-8432
Metropolitan Financial Corporation	MFC	NYSE	$50	American Stock Trans & Tr	(800) 937-5449
Michigan National Corporation	MNCO	NASDAQ	$25	First Chicago Trust Co. of NY	(800) 446-2617
Middlesex Water Company	MSEX	NASDAQ	$25	Registrar and Trans. Comp	(800) 365-6063
Midlantic Corporation	MIDL	NASDAQ	$10	First Chicago Trust Co. of NY	(800) 446-2617
Midwest Resources	MWR	NYSE	$100	Call company directly	(800) 247-5211
Millipore Corporation	MIL	NYSE	$25	Bank of Boston	(800) 442-2001
Minnesota Mining & Manufacturing	MMM	NYSE	$10	Norwest Bank Minn.	(800) 551-6161
Minnesota Power & Light Company	MPL	NYSE	$10	Call company directly	(800) 535-3056
Mobil Corporation	MOB	NYSE	$10	Mellon Bank	(800) 648-9291
Mobile Gas Service Corporation	MBLE	NASDAQ	NA	AmSouth Bank	(800) 284-4100
Modine Manufacturing Company	MODI	NASDAQ	$10	American Stock Trans & Tr	(800) 937-5449
Monmouth Real	MNRT	NASDAQ	$500	Mellon Bank	(800) 288-9541

Company	Stock Symbol	Where Traded	Min. OCP*	Transfer Agent	Phone Number
Monsanto Company	MTC	NYSE	$10	Call company directly	(314) 694-5514
Montana Power Company	MTP	NYSE	$10	Call company directly	(800) 245-6767
J.P. Morgan & Company, Inc.	JPM	NYSE	$50	First Chicago Trust Co. of NY	(800) 446-2617
Morrison Knudsen Corporation	MRN	NYSE	$25	Chemical Bank	(800) 356-2017
Motorola, Inc.	MOT	NYSE	$25	Harris Trust and Savings Bank	(312) 461-2549
Multibank Financial Corporation	MLTF	NASDAQ	$25	Bank of Boston	(800) 442-2001
N					
Nalco Chemical Company	NLC	NYSE	$50	First Chicago Trust Co. of NY	(800) 446-2617
Nash-Finch Company	NAFC	NASDAQ	$10	Norwest Bank Minnesota	(800) 551-6161
Nashua Corporation	NSH	NYSE	$100	Bank of Boston	(800) 442-2001
National City Corporation	NCC	NYSE	$20	National City Bank	(800) 622-6757
National Commerce Bancorp	NCBC	NASDAQ	$100	Trust Company Bank	(800) 568-3476
National Data Corporation	NDTA	NASDAQ	$25	Wachovia Bank & Trust	(800) 633-4236
National Fuel Gas Company	NFG	NYSE	$25	Chemical Bank	(800) 647-4273
National Medical Enterprises, Inc.	NME	NYSE	$10	Bank of New York	(800) 524-4458
National Service Industries, Inc.	NSI	NYSE	$10	Wachovia Bank & Trust	(800) 633-4236
National Standard Company	NSD	NYSE	$10§	National Bank of Detroit	(800) 257-1770
NationsBank Corporation	NB	NYSE	$20	Chemical Bank	(800) 647-4273
NBD Bancorp, Inc.	NBD	NYSE	$10	Security Trans Services	(800) 257-1770
NBSC Corporation	NSCB	NASDAQ	$25	Call company directly	(803) 778-8213
Neiman-Marcus Group, Inc.	NMG	NYSE	$25	Bank of Boston	(800) 442-2001
Nevada Power Company	NVP	NYSE	$25	Call company directly	(800) 344-9239
New England Electric System	NES	NYSE	$25	Call company directly	(508) 366-9011
New Jersey Resources Corporation	NJR	NYSE	$25	Bank of Boston	(800) 442-2001
New Plan Realty Trust	NPR	NYSE	$100	Bank of Boston	(800) 442-2001
New York State Electric & Gas	NGE	NYSE	$25	Call company directly	(800) 225-5643

Company	Stock Symbol	Where Traded	Min. OCP*	Transfer Agent	Phone Number
New York Times Company	NYT.A	ASE	$10	First Chicago Trust Co. of NY	(800) 446-2617
Niagara Mohawk Power Corporation	NMK	NYSE	$25	Call company directly	(800) 962-3236
NICOR, Inc.	GAS	NYSE	$25	Call company directly	(708) 305-9500
NIPSCO Industries, Inc.	NI	NYSE	$25	Harris Trust and Savings Bank	(312) 461-4093
Nooney Realty Trust, Inc.	NRTI	NASDAQ	$50	Boatmen's Trust Co.	(800) 456-9852
Nordson Corporation	NDSN	NASDAQ	$10	Society National Bank	(800) 321-1355
Norfolk Southern Corporation	NSC	NYSE	$10	Bank of New York	(800) 524-4458
North Carolina Natural Gas Corporation	NCNG	NASDAQ	$25	Wachovia Bank & Trust	(800) 633-4236
North Fork Bancorp, Inc.	NFB	NYSE	$200	First Chicago Trust Co. of New York	(800) 446-2617
Northeast Utilities Service Company	NU	NYSE	$100	Call company directly	(800) 999-7269
Northern States Power Company	NSP	NYSE	$10	Call company directly	(800) 527-4677
Northern Telecom Ltd.	NT	NYSE	$40	Montreal Trust Co.	(416) 981-9633
Northrop Corporation	NOC	NYSE	$100	Chemical Bank	(800) 647-4273
Northwest Illinois Bancorp, Inc.	NWIB	NASDAQ	NA	Mellon Bank	(800) 288-9541
Northwest Natural Gas Co	NWNG	NASDAQ	$25	Call company directly	(503) 220-2591
Northwestern Public Service Company	NPS	NYSE	$10	Call company directly	(800) 245-6977
Norwest Corporation	NOB	NYSE	$25	Norwest Bank Minnesota	(800) 551-6161
NOVA Corporation of Alberta	NVA	NYSE	$50	RM Trust	(403) 232-2437
NOVO-Nordisk A/S	NVO	NYSE	NA	Morgan Guaranty Trust	(617) 774-4237
Nucor Corporation	NUE	NYSE	$10	First Union Nat'l Bank of NC	(800) 829-9432
NUI Corporation	NUI	NYSE	$25	Mellon Bank	(800) 526-0801
NYNEX Corporation	NYN	NYSE	None	Bank of Boston	(800) 358-1133
O					
Occidental Petroleum Corporation	OXY	NYSE	$50	Chemical Bank	(800) 647-4273

Company	Stock Symbol	Where Traded	Min. OCP*	Transfer Agent	Phone Number
Ohio Casualty Corporation	OCAS	NASDAQ	$10	Mellon Bank	(800) 756-3353
Ohio Edison Company	OEC	NYSE	$10	Call company directly	(800) 736-3403
Oklahoma Gas & Electric Company	OGE	NYSE	$10	Liberty National Bank	(800) 395-2662
Old National Bancorp	OLDB	NASDAQ	$100	Call company directly	(800) 264-6621
Old Republic International Corporation	ORI	NYSE	$100	First Chicago Trust Co. of NY	(800) 446-2617
Old Stone Corporation	OSTN	NASDAQ	None	Chemical Bank	(800) 647-4273
Olin Corporation	OLN	NYSE	$50	Chemical Bank	(800) 647-4273
Omnicare, Inc.	OCR	NYSE	$10	Mellon Bank	(800) 756-3353
Oneida Ltd.	OCQ	NYSE	NA	Harris Trust and Savings Bank	(312) 461-7763
Oneok, Inc.	OKE	NYSE	$25	Liberty National Bank	(800) 395-2662
Orange & Rockland Utilities, Inc.	ORU	NYSE	$25	Chemical Bank	(800) 647-4273
Otter Tail Power Company	OTTR	NASDAQ	$10	Call company directly	(218) 739-8479
Outboard Marine	OM	NYSE	$10	Bank of Boston	(800) 442-2001

P

Company	Stock Symbol	Where Traded	Min. OCP*	Transfer Agent	Phone Number
Pacific Enterprises	PET	NYSE	$25	Chemical Bank	(800) 356-2017
Pacific Gas & Electric	PCG	NYSE	NA	Call company directly	(800) 367-7731
Pacific Telesis Group	PAC	NYSE	$100	American Transtech	(800) 637-6373
Pacific Western Bancshares	PWB	ASE	$25§	First Interstate Bank	(800) 522-6645
PacifiCorp	PPW	NYSE	$25	Call company directly	(800) 233-5453
Paine Webber Group, Inc.	PWJ	NYSE	$10	Mellon Bank	(800) 526-0801
Pall Corporation	PLL	ASE	$10	Wachovia Bank & Trust	(800) 633-4236
Panhandle Eastern Corporation	PEL	NYSE	$25	Call company directly	(800) 225-5838
Paramount Communications, Inc.	PCI	NYSE	$100	Chemical Bank	(800) 647-4273
Parker-Hannifin Corporation	PH	NYSE	$10	Society National Bank	(800) 321-1355
J. C. Penney Company, Inc.	JCP	NYSE	$20	Chemical Bank	(800) 647-4273

Company	Stock Symbol	Where Traded	Min. OCP*	Transfer Agent	Phone Number
Pennsylvania Enterprises	PENT	NASDAQ	$10	Chemical Bank	(800) 647-4273
Pennsylvania Power & Light Company	PPL	NYSE	None	Call company directly	(800) 345-3085
Pennzoil Company	PZL	NYSE	$40	Call company directly	(713) 546-4000
Pentair, Inc.	PNTA	NASDAQ	$10	Norwest Bank Minnesota	(800) 551-6161
Peoples Bancorp of Worchester	PEBW	NASDAQ	$100	Amer. Stock Trans & Tr	(800) 937-5449
Peoples Energy Corporation	PGL	NYSE	$25	Harris Trust and Savings Bank	(312) 461-3157
Pep Boys	PBY	NYSE	$100	Amer. Stock Trans & Tr	(800) 937-5449
PepsiCo, Inc.	PEP	NYSE	$10	Bank of Boston	(800) 226-0083
Perkin-Elmer Corporation	PKN	NYSE	NA	Bank of Boston	(800) 442-2001
Petro & Res Corp.	PEO	NYSE	$50	Bank of New York	(800) 524-4458
Pfizer, Inc.	PFE	NYSE	$10	Call company directly	(212) 573-3704
Phelps Dodge Corporation	PD	NYSE	$10	Chemical Bank	(800) 647-4273
Philadelphia Electric Company	PE	NYSE	$25	First Chicago Trust Co. of NY	(800) 626-8729
Philadelphia Suburban Corporation	PSC	NYSE	$25	Mellon Bank	(800) 756-3353
Philip Morris Companies, Inc.	MO	NYSE	$10	First Chicago Trust Co. of NY	(800) 446-2617
Phillips Petroleum Company	P	NYSE	$10	Chemical Bank	(800) 647-4273
Piccadilly Cafeterias, Inc.	PICC	NASDAQ	$100	Wachovia Bank & Trust	(800) 633-4236
Piedmont Natural Gas Company	PNY	NYSE	$25	Wachovia Bank & Trust	(800) 633-4236
Pinnacle West Capital Corporation	PNW	NYSE	$10	Call company directly	(800) 457-2983
Pioneer Hi-Bred	PHYB	NASDAQ	$25	Bank of Boston	(800) 442-2001
Pitney Bowes	PBI	NYSE	$100	Chemical Bank	(800) 647-4273
PNC Financial Corporation	PNC	NYSE	$50	Chemical Bank	(800) 982-7652
Polaroid Corporation	PRD	NYSE	$10	First Chicago Trust Co. of NY	(800) 446-2617
Portland General Corporation	PGN	NYSE	$25	First Chicago Trust Co. of NY	(212) 791-6422
Portsmouth Bank Shares, Inc.	POBS	NASDAQ	NA	Bank of Boston	(800) 442-2001
Potlatch Corporation	PCH	NYSE	$25	Harris Trust and Savings Bank	(312) 461-3324
Potomac Electric Power Company	POM	NYSE	$25	Riggs National Bank	(202) 835-4082

Company	Stock Symbol	Where Traded	Min. OCP*	Transfer Agent	Phone Number
PPG Industries, Inc.	PPG	NYSE	$10	Chemical Bank	(800) 647-4273
Praxair, Inc.	PX	NYSE	$250	Bank of New York	(800) 524-4458
Premier Bancorp, Inc.	PRBC	NASDAQ	$10	National City Bank	(216) 575-2532
Premier Industrial Corporation	PRE	NYSE	$10	National City Bank	(216) 575-2532
Presidential Realty Corporation	PDLB	ASE	$100	Amer. Stock Trans & Tr	(800) 937-5449
Preston Corporation	PTRK	NASDAQ	None	Chemical Bank	(800) 647-4273
Procter & Gamble Company	PG	NYSE	NA*	Call company directly	(800) 742-6253
Providence Energy Corporation	PVY	ASE	$25	Mellon Bank	(800) 288-9541
PSI Resources, Inc.	PIN	NYSE	$25	First Chicago Trust Co. of NY	(800) 446-2617
Public Service Co. of Colorado	PSR	NYSE	$25	Call company directly	(800) 635-0566
Public Service Co. of North Carolina	PSNC	NASDAQ	$25	Call company directly	(704) 864-6731
Public Service Enterprise Group, Inc.	PEG	NYSE	$25	Call company directly	(800) 242-0813
Puget Sound Power & Light Company	PSD	NYSE	$25	Call company directly	(206) 462-3719

Q

Company	Stock Symbol	Where Traded	Min. OCP*	Transfer Agent	Phone Number
Quaker Oats & Company	OAT	NYSE	$10	Harris Trust and Savings Bank	(800) 344-1198
Quaker State Corporation	KSF	NYSE	$10	Mellon Bank	(800) 756-3353
Quanex Corporation	NX	NYSE	$10	Chemical Bank	(800) 647-4273
Quantum Chemical Corporation	CUE	NYSE	$25	Chemical Bank	(800) 647-4273
Questar Corporation	STR	NYSE	$50	Call company directly	(801) 534-5885
Quincy Savings	QUIN	NASDAQ	$50	Bank of Boston	(800) 442-2001

R

Company	Stock Symbol	Where Traded	Min. OCP*	Transfer Agent	Phone Number
Ralston Purina Company	RAL	NYSE	$10	Call company directly	(314) 982-3000
Raymond Corporation	RAYM	NASDAQ	$10	Amer. Stock Trans & Tr	(800) 937-5449
Raytheon Company	RTN	NYSE	$10	Bank of Boston	(800) 442-2001
Real Estate Investment Trust of CA	RCT	NYSE	$500	Call company directly	(310) 476-7793

Company	Stock Symbol	Where Traded	Min. OCP*	Transfer Agent	Phone Number
Regional Bancorp, Inc.	REGB	NASDAQ	$100	Boston Fin. Data Services	(800) 426-5523
Resort Income Investors, Inc.	RII	ASE	NA	Midlantic National Bank	(908) 205-4537
Resource Mortgage	RMR	NYSE	$50	Security Trust Co., NA	(800) 435-7016
Reynolds & Reynolds Company	REY	NYSE	$100	Bank One, Indianapolis	(800) 753-7107
Reynolds Metals Company	RLM	NYSE	$25	Mellon Bank	(800) 526-0801
Rhone-Poulenc Rorer, Inc.	RPR	NYSE	$25	Bank of New York	(800) 524-4458
Rite Aid Corporation	RAD	NYSE	$25	Harris Trust and Savings Bank	(312) 461-7369
Roadway Services, Inc.	ROAD	NASDAQ	$10	Society National Bank	(800) 321-1355
Rochester Gas & Electric Corporation	RGS	NYSE	$10	Bank of Boston	(800) 442-2001
Rochester Telephone Corporation	RTC	NYSE	$25	First Chicago Trust Co. of NY	(800) 446-2617
Rockefeller Center Properties, Inc.	RCP	NYSE	$100	Chemical Bank	(800) 647-4273
Rockwell International Corporation	ROK	NYSE	$10	Mellon Bank	(800) 756-3353
Rollins, Inc.	ROL	NYSE	NA	Trust Company Bank	(800) 568-3476
Rollins Environment	REN	NYSE	$25	Registrar and Trans. Comp	(800) 368-5948
Rollins Truck Leasing Corporation	RLC	NYSE	$25	Registrar and Trans. Comp	(800) 368-5948
Roosevelt Financial	RFED	NASDAQ	$25	Harris Trust and Savings Bank	(312) 461-6833
Rose's Stores, Inc.	RSTO	NASDAQ	$10	Wachovia Bank & Trust	(800) 633-4236
Rouse Company	ROUS	NASDAQ	$50	Security Trust Co., NA	(800) 435-7016
RPM, Inc.	RPOW	NASDAQ	$25	Society National Bank	(800) 321-1355
Rubbermaid, Inc.	RBD	NYSE	$10	Society National Bank	(216) 737-5745
Russell Corporation	RML	NYSE	$10	Call company directly	(205) 329-4832
Ryder System, Inc.	R	NYSE	$25	First Chicago Trust Co. of NY	(800) 446-2617
Rykoff-Sexton, Inc.	RYK	NYSE	NA	Chemical Bank	(800) 647-4273
Rymac-Mortgage, Invest	RM	ASE	$50	Security Trust Co., NA	(800) 435-7016

S

Company	Stock Symbol	Where Traded	Min. OCP*	Transfer Agent	Phone Number
St. Joseph Light & Power Company	SAJ	NYSE	$100	Harris Trust and Savings Bank	(800) 643-8517

Company	Stock Symbol	Where Traded	Min. OCP*	Transfer Agent	Phone Number
St. Paul Bancorp, Inc.	SPBC	NASDAQ	$50	Bank of Boston	(800) 442-2001
St. Paul Companies, Inc.	SPC	NYSE	$10	First Chicago Trust Co. of NY	(800) 446-2617
Safety Kleen Corporation	SK	NYSE	$25	First Chicago Trust Co. of NY	(800) 446-2617
Salomon, Inc.	SB	NYSE	$10	First Chicago Trust Co. of NY	(800) 446-2617
Samson Energy Co.L.P.	SAM	ASE	$150	Chemical Bank	(800) 647-4273
San Diego Gas & Electric	SDO	NYSE	$25	First Interstate Bank	(800) 522-6645
Santa Fe Pacific Corporation	SFX	NYSE	$10	First Chicago Trust Co. of NY	(800) 526-5678
Sara Lee Corporation	SLE	NYSE	$10	Harris Trust and Savings Bank	(312) 461-3932
Savannah Foods & Industries, Inc.	SVAN	NASDAQ	$10	Wachovia Bank & Trust	(800) 633-4236
SCANA Corporation	SCG	NYSE	$25	Call company directly	(800) 763-5891
SCE Corporation	SCE	NYSE	None	Call company directly	(800) 347-8625
Schering-Plough Corporation	SGP	NYSE	$25	Bank of New York	(800) 524-4458
Scott Paper Company	SPP	NYSE	$10	First Chicago Trust Co. of NY	(800) 752-0771
Seafield Capital Corporation	SFLD	NASDAQ	$25	Amer. Stock Trans & Tr	(800) 937-5449
Sears, Roebuck & Company	S	NYSE	$25	First Chicago Trust Co. of NY	(212) 791-3357
Second National	SNLB	NASDAQ	$100	Mellon Bank	(800) 756-3353
Selective Insurance Group, Inc.	SIGI	NASDAQ	$100	First Chicago Trust Co. of NY	(800) 446-2617
ServiceMaster Limited Partnership	SVM	NYSE	$25	Harris Trust & Savings Bank	(800) 858-0840
Shawmut National Corporation	SNC	NYSE	$25	Chemical Bank	(800) 647-4273
The Sherwin-Williams Company	SHW	NYSE	$10	Society National Bank	(800) 321-1355
Sierra Pacific Resources	SRP	NYSE	$25	Call company directly	(800) 662-7575
SIFCO Industries, Inc.	SIF	ASE	$20	National City Bank	(216) 575-2532
Signet Banking Corporation	SBK	NYSE	$10	Mellon Bank	(800) 451-7392
Simpson Industries, Inc.	SMPS	NASDAQ	$10	National Bank of Detroit	(800) 257-1770
A.O. Smith Corporation	SMC.A	ASE	None	Firstar Trust Co.	(800) 637-7549
SmithKline Beecham plc	SBE	NYSE	$10	Morgan Guaranty Trust	(800) 428-4237
J. M. Smucker Company	SJM	NYSE	$20	National City Bank	(216) 575-2532

Company	Stock Symbol	Where Traded	Min. OCP*	Transfer Agent	Phone Number
Snap-On Tools Corporation	SNA	ASE	$100	Harris Trust & Savings Bank	(800) 524-0687
Society Corporation	SOCI	NYSE	$25	Society National Bank	(800) 542-7792
Society for Savings Bancorp	SOCS	NASDAQ	$100	Bank of Boston	(800) 442-2001
Sonat, Inc.	SNT	NYSE	$25	Chemical Bank	(800) 647-4273
Sonoco Products Company	SONO	NASDAQ	$10	Wachovia Bank & Trust	(800) 633-4236
Southeastern Michigan Gas	SMGS	NASDAQ	$25	Call company directly	(800) 255-7647
Southern California Edison	SCE	NYSE	None	Call company directly	(800) 347-8625
Southern California Water Company	SWTR	NASDAQ	$50	First Interstate Bank	(800) 522-6645
Southern Company	SO	NYSE	$25	Call company directly	(404) 668-2774
Southern Indiana Gas & Electric Co.	SIG	NYSE	$25	Harris Trust and Savings Bank	(312) 461-2549
Southern National	SNAT	NASDAQ	$25	Call company directly	(919) 671-2273
Southern New England Telecomm	SNG	NYSE	None	Call company directly	(800) 245-1110
South Jersey Industries, Inc.	SJI	NYSE	$25	Call company directly	(609) 561-9000
SouthTrust Corporation	SOTR	NASDAQ	$25	Call company directly	(205) 254-6764
Southwest Gas Corporation	SWX	NYSE	$25	Call company directly	(702) 876-7280
Southwest Water Company	SWWC	NASDAQ	$25	Chemical Bank	(800) 647-4273
Southwestern Bell Corporation	SBC	NYSE	$50	Bank of New York	(800) 531-7221
Southwestern Electric Service Company	SWEL	NASDAQ	$25	Ameritrust Texas	(800) 527-7844
Southwestern Energy Company	SWN	NYSE	$25	First Chicago Trust Co. of NY	(800) 446-2617
Southwestern Public Service Company	SPS	NYSE	$25	Society National Bank	(800) 527-7844
Sprint Corporation	FON	NYSE	$25	United Missouri Bank	(816) 860-7787
SPX Corporation	SPW	NYSE	$25	Bank of New York	(800) 524-4458
Standard Commercial Corporation	STW	NYSE	$25	First Union Nat'l Bank of NC	(800) 329-8432
Standard Federal	SFB	NYSE	$25	Registrar and Transfer Co.	(800) 368-5948
Standard Products Company	SPD	NYSE	$50	National City Bank	(216) 575-2532
Standex International Corporation	SXI	NYSE	NA	Bank of Boston	(800) 442-2001

Company	Stock Symbol	Where Traded	Min. OCP*	Transfer Agent	Phone Number
Stanhome, Inc.	STH	NYSE	$10	Mellon Bank	(800) 288-9541
Standley Works	SWK	NYSE	$25	Mellon Bank	(800) 288-9541
Star Banc Corporation	STRZ	NASDAQ	$50	Mellon Bank	(800) 756-3353
State Street Boston Corporation	STBK	NASDAQ	None	Call company directly	(800) 426-5523
Stone & Webster, Inc.	SW	NYSE	$50	Chemical Bank	(800) 647-4273
Stride Rite Corporation	SRR	NYSE	$10	Bank of Boston	(800) 442-2001
Suffolk Bancorp	SUBK	NASDAQ	$300	Amer. Stock Trans & Tr	(800) 937-5449
Summit Bancorp	SUBN	NASDAQ	$50	Chemical Bank	(800) 647-4273
Sun Company, Inc.	SUN	NYSE	None	Call company directly	(800) 323-3025
Sundstrand Corporation	SNS	NYSE	$25	First Chicago Trust Co. of NY	(800) 446-2617
SunTrust Banks, Inc.	STI	NYSE	$10	Trust Company Bank	(800) 568-3476
SuperValu Stores, Inc.	SVU	NYSE	$10	Norwest Bank Minnesota	(800) 551-6161
Susquehanna Bancshares, Inc.	SUSQ	NASDAQ	$100	Chemical Bank	(800) 647-4273
Synovus Financial Corporation	SNV	NYSE	$25	Columbus Bank Trust	(706) 649-2034
T					
Talley Industries, Inc.	TAL	NYSE	$10	Chemical Trust Co of CA	(213) 621-8253
Tambrands, Inc.	TMB	NYSE	$25	First Chicago Trust Co. of NY	(800) 446-2617
TCF Financial Corporation	TCB	NYSE	$25	Chemical Bank	(800) 647-4273
TECO Energy	TE	NYSE	$25	Bank of Boston	(800) 442-2001
Telephone & Data Systems, Inc.	TDS	ASE	$10	Harris Trust & Savings Bank	(312) 461-2339
Temple-Inland, Inc.	TIN	NYSE	$25	First Chicago Trust Co. of NY	(800) 446-2617
Tenneco, Inc.	TGT	NYSE	$50	First Chicago Trust Co. of NY	(800) 446-2617
Texaco, Inc.	TX	NYSE	$50	Call company directly	(800) 283-9785
Texas Utilities Company	TXU	NYSE	$25	Call company directly	(800) 828-0812
Textron, Inc.	TXT	NYSE	$25	First Chicago Trust Co. of NY	(800) 446-2617

Company	Stock Symbol	Where Traded	Min. OCP*	Transfer Agent	Phone Number
Thomas & Betts Corporation	TNB	NYSE	$10	First Chicago Trust Co. of NY	(212) 791-6422
Thomas Industries	TH	NYSE	$25	Wachovia Bank & Trust	(800) 633-4236
Tidewater, Inc.	TDW	NYSE	$25	Chemical Bank	(800) 647-4273
Time Warner, Inc.	TWX	NYSE	$25	First Chicago Trust Co. of NY	(800) 446-2617
Times Mirror 'A'	TMC	NYSE	$250	First Interstate Bank	(800) 522-6645
Timken Company	TKR	NYSE	NA	Call company directly	(216) 471-3376
TNP Enterprises, Inc.	TNP	NYSE	$25	Society National Bank	(800) 527-7844
Toro Company	TTC	NYSE	$10	Norwest Bank Minnesota	(800) 551-6161
Total Petroleum (preferred stock only)	TPN	ASE	NA	R & M Trust	(403) 263-1460
Trammel Crow Real Estate	TCR	NYSE	NA	Society National Bank	(800) 527-7844
TransAlta Utilities	TAU	TSE	None	Montreal Trust Co.	(514) 982-7555
Transamerica Corporation	TA	NYSE	$10	First Chicago Trust Co. of NY	(800) 446-2617
TransCanada Pipelines Ltd.	TRP	NYSE	$50	Montreal Trust Co.	(514) 982-7555
Travelers Corporation	TIC	NYSE	$5	Bank of Boston	(800) 442-2001
Tribune Company	TRB	NYSE	$50	First Chicago Trust Co. of NY	(800) 446-2617
Trinova Corporation	TNV	NYSE	$10	First Chicago Trust Co. of NY	(800) 446-2617
TRW, Inc.	TRW	NYSE	$10	Bank of Boston	(800) 442-2001
Twin Disc, Inc.	TDI	NYSE	$10	Firstar Trust Co.	(800) 637-7549
Tyco Laboratories, Inc.	TYC	NYSE	$25	Mellon Bank	(800) 756-3353
U					
UGI Corporation	UGI	NYSE	$25	Mellon Bank	(800) 756-3353
UJB Financial Corporation	UJB	NYSE	$10	First Chicago Trust Co. of NY	(800) 446-2617
Union Bank	UBNK	NASDAQ	$25	Harris Trust & Savings Bank	(800) 554-3406
Union Camp Corporation	UC	NYSE	$25	Bank of New York	(800) 524-4458
Union Carbide Corporation	UK	NYSE	$25	Call company directly	(203) 794-2212
Union Electric Company	UEP	NYSE	None	Call company directly	(800) 255-2237

Company	Stock Symbol	Where Traded	Min. OCP*	Transfer Agent	Phone Number
Union Pacific Corporation	UNP	NYSE	$10	First Chicago Trust Co. of NY	(800) 446-2617
Union Planters Corporation	UPC	NYSE	$100	Union Planters National Bank	(901) 523-6980
United Carolina Bancshares Corporation	UCAR	NASDAQ	$25	Call company directly	(800) 822-7862
United Cities Gas Company	UCIT	NASDAQ	$25	Harris Trust and Savings Bank	(312) 461-2302
United Dominion Realty	UDR	NYSE	$50	Mellon Bank	(800) 756-3353
United Illuminating Company	UIL	NYSE	$10	Call company directly	(203) 499-2270
United States Bancorp	USBC	NASDAQ	$25	First Chicago Trust Co. of NY	(800) 446-2617
United States Shoe Corporation	USR	NYSE	$25	First Chicago Trust Co. of NY	(800) 446-2617
United States Trust Corporation	USTC	NASDAQ	$30	Call company directly	(800) 548-6565
United Water Resources, Inc.	UWR	NYSE	$25	First Interstate Bank	(800) 522-6645
UNITIL Corporation	UTL	ASE	$25	Bank of Boston	(800) 442-2001
Universal Corporation	UVV	NYSE	$10	Wachovia Bank & Trust	(800) 633-4236
Universal Foods Corporation	UFC	NYSE	$25	Firstar Trust Co.	(800) 637-7549
Universal Health Realty Income	UHT	NYSE	$25	Bank of Boston	(800) 442-2001
Unocal Corporation	UCL	NYSE	$25	Chemical Bank	(800) 647-4273
UNUM Corporation	UNM	NYSE	$100	First Chicago Trust Co. of NY	(800) 446-2617
Upjohn Company	UPJ	NYSE	$25	Harris Trust and Savings Bank	(800) 323-1849
Upper Peninsula Energy Corporation	UPEN	NASDAQ	$50	National Bank of Detroit	(800) 257-1770
USF&G Corporation	FG	NYSE	$50	First Chicago Trust Co. of NY	(800) 446-2617
USLICO Corporation	USC	NYSE	$100	American Stock Trans. Corp	(800) 937-5449
USLIFE Corporation	USH	NYSE	$10	Chemical Bank	(800) 647-4273
USP Real Estate Investment Trust	USPT	NASDAQ	None	Boston Fin. Data Services	(800) 426-5523
UST Corporation	USTB	NASDAQ	Varies	Call company directly	(617) 726-7262
UST, Incorporated	UST	NYSE	$10	Bank of Boston	(800) 442-2001
U.S. West, Inc.	USW	NYSE	None	Boston Fin. Data Services	(800) 537-0222
USX-Marathon	MRO	NYSE	$50	Call company directly	(412) 433-4801
USX-US Steel	X	NYSE	$50	Call company directly	(412) 443-4801

Company	Stock Symbol	Where Traded	Min. OCP*	Transfer Agent	Phone Number
UtiliCorp United, Inc.	UCU	NYSE	None	First Chicago Trust Co. of NY	(800) 446-2617
V					
Valley Bancorporation	VYBN	NASDAQ	$10	Bank of Boston	(800) 442-2001
Valley National Bancorp	VNBP	NASDAQ	$50	Amer. Stock Trans & Tr.	(800) 937-5449
Valley Resources, Inc.	VR	ASE	$25	Boston Fin. Data Services	(800) 426-5523
Varian Associates, Inc.	VAR	NYSE	$10	Bank of Boston	(800) 442-2001
Vermont Financial Services Corporation	VFSC	NASDAQ	None	Call company directly	(802) 257-7151
V.F. Corporation	VFC	NYSE	$10	First Chicago Trust Co. of NY	(800) 446-2617
Volvo (Class B)	VOLVY	NASDAQ	$25	Norwest Bank Minnesota	(800) 551-6161
Vulcan Materials Company	VMC	NYSE	$10	First Chicago Trust Co. of NY	(800) 446-2617
W					
Wachovia Corporation	WB	NYSE	$20	Wachovia Bank & Trust	(800) 633-4236
Walgreen Company	WAG	NYSE	$10	Harris Trust and Savings Bank	(312) 461-6830
Warner-Lambert Company	WLA	NYSE	$10	First Chicago Trust Co. of NY	(800) 446-2617
Washington Energy Company	WEG	NASDAQ	$25	Harris Trust and Savings Bank	(312) 461-2475
Washington Gas Light Company	WGL	NYSE	$25	Call company directly	(800) 221-9427
Washington Mutual Savings Bank	WAMU	NASDAQ	$100	First Interstate Bank	(800) 522-6645
Washington National Corporation	WNT	NYSE	$25	First Chicago Trust Co. of NY	(800) 446-2617
Washington Real Estate Investment	WRE	ASE	$100	Amer. Stock Trans & Tr.	(800) 937-5449
Washington Water Power Company	WWP	NYSE	None	Call company directly	(800) 727-9170
Weingarten Realty Investors	WRI	NYSE	$100	Society National Bank	(800) 321-1355
Weis Markets, Inc.	WMK	NYSE	$10	Amer. Stock Trans & Tr.	(800) 937-5449
Wells Fargo & Company	WFC	NYSE	$150	First Chicago Trust Co. of NY	(800) 446-2617
Wendy's International, Inc.	WEN	NYSE	$20	Amer. Stock Trans & Tr.	(800) 937-5449

Company	Stock Symbol	Where Traded	Min. OCP*	Transfer Agent	Phone Number
West One Bancorp	WEST	NASDAQ	$25	Call company directly	(208) 383-7179
WestAmerica Bancorp	WAB	ASE	None	Chemical Bank	(800) 647-4273
Westcoast Energy, Inc.	WE	NYSE	$50	Montreal Trust Co.	(514) 982-7555
Western Investment RE Trust	WIR	ASE	$500	Chemical Bank	(800) 647-4273
Western Resources	WR	NYSE	$25	Chemical Bank	(800) 647-4273
Westinghouse	WX	NYSE	$100	Call company directly	(412) 244-3654
Westvaco Corporation	W	NYSE	None	Chemical Bank	(800) 647-4273
Wetterau Properties	WTPR	NASDAQ	$10	Boatmen's Trust Co.	(314) 231-9300
Weyerhaeuser Company	WY	NYSE	$100	Chemical Bank	(800) 647-4273
Whirlpool Corporation	WHR	NYSE	$10	Harris Trust and Savings Bank	(312) 461-2543
Whitman Corporation	WH	NYSE	$10	First Chicago Trust Co. of NY	(800) 446-2617
WICOR, Inc.	WIC	NYSE	$100	Chemical Bank	(800) 647-4273
Willis Corroon Group, Inc.	WCG	NYSE	$10	Morgan Guaranty Trust	(800) 428-4237
Wilmington Trust Company	WILM	NASDAQ	$10	First Chicago Trust Co. of NY	(800) 446-2617
Winn–Dixie Stores, Inc.	WIN	NYSE	$10	Call company directly	(904) 783-5000
Wisconsin Energy Corporation	WEC	NYSE	$25	Call company directly	(800) 558-9663
Wisconsin Public Service Company	WPS	NYSE	$25	Call company directly	(800) 236-1551
Wisconsin Southern Gas Company, Inc.	WISC	NASDAQ	$50	Firstar Trust Co.	(800) 637-7549
Witco Corporation	WIT	NYSE	$10	First Chicago Trust Co. of NY	(800) 446-2617
Woolworth Corporation	Z	NYSE	$20	First Chicago Trust Co. of NY	(800) 446-2617
Worthington Industries, Inc.	WTHG	NASDAQ	$50	Bank of Boston	(800) 442-2001
WMX Technologies	WMX	NYSE	$25	Harris Trust and Savings Bank	(312) 461-2543
WPL Holdings, Inc.	WPH	NYSE	$20	Call company directly	(800) 356-5343
William Wrigley, Jr. Company	WWY	NYSE	$50	Call company directly	(800) 824-9681

X

Company	Stock Symbol	Where Traded	Min. OCP*	Transfer Agent	Phone Number
Xerox Corporation	XRX	NYSE	$10	Call company directly	(800) 828-6396

Company	Stock Symbol	Where Traded	Min. OCP*	Transfer Agent	Phone Number
Y					
York Financial Corporation	YFED	NASDAQ	$25	Harris Trust and Savings Bank	(312) 461-4075
Z					
Zero Corporation	ZRO	NYSE	$25	First Interstate Bank	(800) 522-6645
Zions Bancorporation	ZION	NASDAQ	$10	Call company directly	(801) 524-4696
Zurn Industries, Inc.	ZRN	NYSE	$10	Society National Bank	(800) 321-1355

§ Company does not pay a dividend, but may continue to permit optional cash payments.

* With most companies the stated minimum is per month; with others the minimum is per quarter.

NA = Not available (optional cash payments are not part of the dividend reinvestment program).

NA* = Procter & Gamble discontinued the direct purchase of shares and optional cash payments on July 1, 1993.

None = The company does not have a stated minimum amount for the optional cash payment.

AME = American Stock Exchange.

NASDAQ = National Association of Securities Dealers Automatic Quotations or over-the-counter market.

NYSE = New York Stock Exchange.

TSE = Toronto Stock Exchange.

Notes: 1. Twenty-six of the companies that make up the 30-member Dow Jones Industrials Average offer dividend reinvestment programs. Only Boeing, Walt Disney, United Technologies and Westinghouse do not. 2. Be advised that companies do revise their dividend policy, make changes to their dividend reinvestment plan and/or even change transfer agents. When changes do occur simply call the company directly to learn the nature of the changes or obtain the name of the new transfer agent.

Companies with Direct Purchase Programs*

American Recreation Centers, Inc.
Atlantic Energy, Inc.
Atmos Energy Corporation
Centerior Energy Corporation
Central Hudson Gas & Electric.
Central Maine Power Company
Central Vermont Public Service
Citizens First Bancorp, Inc.
Connecticut Energy
The Dial Corporation
Duke Power Company
Exxon Corporation
First Alabama Bancshares, Inc.
W.R. Grace & Company
Hawaiian Electric Industries, Inc.
Idaho Power Company

Johnson Controls, Inc.
Meridian Bancorp, Inc.
Minnesota Power & Light Company
Montana Power Company
Nevada Power Company
New Jersey Resources Corporation
New York State Electric & Gas
Oklahoma Gas & Electric Company
Puget Sound Power & Light Company
SCANA Corporation
Southwest Gas Corporation
Texaco, Inc.
Union Electric Company
United Water Resources, Inc.
WICOR, Inc.
Wisconsin Energy Corporation

* Some restrictions apply, so call the companies to determine if you are eligible to participate in these dividend reinvestment programs.

Members of the **Dow Jones Industrial Average (DJIA)** appear in bold typeface.

Major Discount and Full-Service Brokerage Firms*

Discount Brokers

Brown and Company Securities
 Corporation
20 Winthrop Square
Boston, MA 02109
(800) 343-4300
(617) 357-4410

Burke, Christensen & Lewis Securities, Inc.
303 West Madison Street
Chicago, IL 60606
(312) 346-8283
(800) 621-0392 (outside Chicago)

Discount Brokerage Corporation
 of America
67 Wall Street
New York, NY 10005
(800) 328-1268
(212) 806-2888

Fidelity Brokerage Services, Inc.**
161 Devonshire Street
Boston, MA 02110
(800) 544-8666
(617) 570-7000

* Check your local telephone listings for an office near you.
** These firms offer programs whereby certain no-load mutual funds can be purchased with no transactions fees. The amount of the minimum initial and subsequent investments does vary, so check with each brokerage house for details of their particular program.

Kennedy, Cabot & Co.
9470 Wilshire Blvd.
Beverly Hills, CA 90212
(800) 252-0090
(310) 550-0711

Olde Discount Stock Brokers
910 3rd Avenue
Seattle, WA 98104
(800) 521-1111

Ovest Financial Services, Inc.
90 Broad Street
New York, NY 10004
(800) 255-0700
(212) 668-0600

Pacific Brokerage Services
5757 Wilshire Blvd.
Beverly Hills, CA 90211
(800) 421-8395
(213) 939-1100

Quick & Reilly
120 Wall Street
New York, NY 10005
(800) 222-7290
(212) 943-8686

Rose & Co. Investment Brokers, Inc.
One Financial Place
Chicago, IL 60605
(800) 621-3700
(312) 663-8300

Charles Schwab and Company**
101 Montgomery Street
San Francisco, CA 94104
(800) 442-5111
(415) 398-1000

Muriel Siebert and Company**
444 Madison Avenue
New York, NY 10022
(800) 872-0711
(212) 644-2400

Spear Securities
626 Wilshire Blvd
Los Angeles, CA 90017
(800) 346-5522
(213) 627-8422

USAA Brokerage Services
USAA Building
San Antonio, TX 78284-9859
(800) 531-8000
(210) 498-8000 (in San Antonio)

Jack White & Company**
9191 Towne Centre Drive
Suite 2220
San Diego, CA 92122
(800) 233-3411

FULL-SERVICE BROKERS

Alex. Brown & Sons, Inc.
135 East Baltimore Street
Baltimore, MD 21202
(410) 727-1700

Bear, Stearns & Co.
55 Water Street
New York, NY 10041
(212) 272-1000

Cowen & Company
One Battery Park Plaza
New York, NY 10004
(212) 495-6000

Dean Witter Reynolds, Inc.
130 Liberty Street
New York, NY 10006
(800) 827-2211
(212) 524-2222

Dillon Read & Company, Inc.
535 Madison Avenue
New York, NY 10022
(212) 906-7000

Donaldson, Lufkin and Jenrette Inc.
140 Broadway
New York, NY 10005
(212) 504-3000

Drexel Burnham Lambert Group, Inc.
60 Broad Street
New York, NY 10004
(212) 480-6000

Edward D. Jones & Company
201 Progress Parkway
St. Louis, MO 63043
(314) 851-2000

A.G. Edwards & Sons, Inc.
One North Jefferson
St. Louis, MO 63103
(314) 289-3000

First Boston Inc.
Park Avenue Plaza
New York, NY 10055
(212) 909-2000

Goldman Sachs & Company
85 Broad Street
New York, NY 10004
(212) 902-1000

Gruntal & Company, Inc.
14 Wall Street
New York, NY 10005
(212) 267-8800

Kemper Financial Services
120 South LaSalle Street
Chicago, IL 60603
(312) 781-1121

Kidder, Peabody & Company
10 Hanover Square
New York, NY 10005
(212) 510-3000

Legg Mason Wood Walker, Inc.
7 East Redwood Street
Baltimore, MD 21202
(410) 539-3400

Merrill Lynch & Company
One Liberty Plaza
New York, NY 10080
(800) MERRILL (637-7455)
(212) 637-7455

Morgan Stanley & Co., Inc.
1251 Avenue of the Americas
New York, NY 10020
(212) 703-4000

Oppenheimer & Company
World Financial Center
New York, NY 10281
(212) 667-7000

Paine Webber
1285 Avenue of the Americas
New York, NY 10019
(800) 288-1515
(212) 713-2000

Prudential Securities
One Seaport Plaza
199 Water Street
New York, NY 10292
(800) 527-1320
(212) 214-1000

Salomon Brothers
One New York Plaza
New York, NY 10004
(212) 747-7000

Smith Barney Shearson, Inc.
140 58th Street
Brooklyn, NY 11220
Call a local branch office

BROKERAGE COMPANIES WITH OFFICES IN CANADA

Canadian investors who wish to establish brokerage accounts with American discount and full-service brokers may call or write the offices listed in the U.S. for account information, prospectuses and application forms. Or contact one of the following firms already operating in Canada.

MUTUAL FUNDS

As noted in Appendix A, you can call or write a U.S. mutual fund or fund family directly for more information. Since mutual funds may also be purchased through a broker, you may be able to obtain more information from one of the following brokerage companies in Canada.

Discount Brokers (Canada)

Fidelity Investments of Canada, Ltd.
Ernst & Young Tower
222 Bay Street, Suite 900
P.O. Box 90
Toronto, Ontario M5K 1P1
CANADA
(800) 263-4077

Full-Service Brokers (Canada)

Edward D. Jones & Company
90 Burnhamthorpe Road West, Suite 902
Mississauga, Ontario L5B 3C3
CANADA
(905) 273-8400

CS First Boston Corporation
121 King Street West
25th Floor
Toronto, Ontario M5H 3T9
CANADA
(416) 947-2600

Goldman Sachs Canada
600 Boul de Maissonneuve Ouest
Bureau 2350
Montreal, Quebec H3A 3J2
CANADA
(514) 499-1510

Goldman Sachs Canada
150 King Street West, Suite 1201
Toronto, Ontario M5H 1J9
CANADA
(416) 343-8900

Merrill Lynch Canada
Place Montreal Trust 25th Floor
1800 Avenue McGill College
Bureau 2500
Montreal, Quebec H3A 3J6
CANADA
(514) 982-2700

Merrill Lynch Canada
Park Place, Suite 600
666 Burrard Street
Vancouver, B.C. V6C 3A5
CANADA
(604) 664-7011

Morgan Stanley Canada Ltd.
40 King Street West, Suite 3010
Toronto, Ontario M5H 3Y2
CANADA
(416) 365-6250

Note: If you intend to invest directly with a firm located in the United States, be sure to ask about transacting business in U.S. rather than Canadian dollars.

GLOSSARY

American Depository Receipts (ADRs) Tradable receipts for the shares of foreign corporations that are in American banks. Owners of ADRs are entitled to any and all dividends and capital gains distributed by these non-U.S. corporations.

American Stock Exchange (AMEX) The stock exchange on which stocks and bonds of small to medium size companies and options on New York Stock Exchange and some Over-the-Counter Market stocks are traded. The AMEX is located in Manhattan.

Analyst A person who studies a certain area or areas of the financial industry for a brokerage firm, a mutual fund or other financial institution then makes specific buy-and-sell recommendations based on that research.

Appreciation The increase in value of an asset (stock, bond, mutual fund, home, etc.) over your cost.

Asked price The lowest price that a seller is willing to accept and an essential part of trading language in the OTC market. A buyer will present a "bid price" to reflect the price that buyer is willing to pay for the security.

Asset Anything having sufficient commercial value that it can be bought and sold.

Automatic reinvestment A plan for shareholders of mutual funds and DRIPs (dividend reinvestment programs) whereby dividends and capital gains are used to purchase additional shares automatically upon distribution.

Automatic transfer The movement of money by electronic means from one account to another.

Back-end load A charge levied by some mutual funds at the time shares are sold (as opposed to a "front-end" load which levies the charge when shares are purchased).

Bear market A period in the financial markets marked by declining share prices in the case of stocks. Bear markets appear cyclically and are followed by bull markets.

Beta or beta coefficient A measure of a stock's volatility compared to a market index (usually the Standard & Poor's or S&P Index and equaling 1.00). Thus the higher the beta, the greater a stock's volatility. So a stock with a beta of 1.3 is 30% more volatile than the S&P Index. Conversely, an equity with a 0.8 beta is more conservative, so its stock price will rise and fall much more slowly.

Bid price The highest price a potential buyer is willing to pay for a given security and an essential part of trading language in the OTC market. The opposite of the bid price is the "asked price," which is the lowest price the seller reportedly is willing to accept.

The Big Board A popular way to refer to the New York Stock Exchange.

"Blue Chip" stocks Common stocks in well-known companies that produce high-quality products or services with a track record of solid earnings and profits and consistent dividend distributions. These companies typically are also known for their superb management and leadership in their industry.

Broker In the financial world, an individual who enables buyers and sellers to get together and execute a transaction, or trade, of stocks, bonds, options, etc., for a fee (commission).

Bull Market A period during which share prices of mutual funds, stocks, bonds, etc., are increasing. A "bull market" is a time when investors can potentially see the value of their assets increasing if they have these holdings in their portfolio.

Capital gain The *positive* difference between the purchase price and the sale price of an asset.

Capital loss The *negative* difference between the purchase price and the sale price of an asset.

Certificate, stock A document that provides proof of ownership in a corporation. A stock certificate will not only bear the name of the shareholder and a par value, but the date issued, the number of shares and the certificate number. It is advisable to record all certificate numbers and store separately to facilitate replacement if the original is lost.

Common stock Tradable units of ownership in a publicly traded corporation that entitle the shareholder to cast a single vote in matters related to the company.

Confirmation A written or oral acknowledgment of a trade. For example, confirmation can be given over the phone and then sent to you in writing, verifying that a stock was bought or sold at your request. Or you may receive a written confirmation of receipt of funds when you send money, in the form of an optional cash payment, to a dividend reinvestment account.

Distribution In the case of mutual funds, the payout of dividends and capital gains by the fund or the payment of dividends by a company for shareholders of its stock.

Dividends The earnings that a mutual fund or stock pays to its shareholders for each share in the form of cash or, in some instances, additional shares of common stock. So there can be cash dividends as well as stock dividend.

Dividend reinvestment plan (or program) Often referred to as a DRIP or DRP for common stocks that offer such an option. These programs allow shareholders to have their dividend reinvested into more shares of common stock and are sometimes supplemented by optional cash payments (OCPs) for individuals wishing to accumulate shares more quickly. Many firms absorb the fees and brokerage costs associated with the plan to encourage wider shareholder participation.

Dollar cost averaging A strategy whereby a fixed amount of money is invested on a regular basis to buy more shares at low prices and fewer shares at high prices, but actually reduces the overall costs of those shares. This approach is a recommended way for beginner and seasoned investors to purchase mutual funds and common stocks (through DRIPs).

Equity A popular, alternative term used to refer to an individual stock and differentiate that investment from a mutual fund or money market account. So a reference to the "equity market" is a comment directed to the stock market and "equities" can refer to stocks.

Ex-dividend The time between the announcement of a dividend and the actual payment of that dividend. Since both mutual funds and stocks pay dividends, this term can be applied to both types of investments. Typically, you will see an "x" after the name of the stock or mutual fund in the newspaper listing.

Family of funds Refers to a group of mutual funds offered by the same investment advisory or management company. A "family" exists because that management company wants to offer an array of funds with different financial objectives to attract more investors.

Front-end load A sales charge added to an investment initially when shares are purchased. This is the opposite of a back-end load.

Growth stock The stock of a company that has a history of performing above other similar companies and which is expected to continue to outperform its peers. Growth stocks are attractive investments because they tend to provide appreciation (rising share price), but no current income (dividends). This is beneficial for investors seeking to minimize the accumulation of assets that generate taxable income.

Index A measure of the changes, both good and bad, in financial markets or in the economy in general. Examples include the Dow Jones Industrial Average (DJIA), the S&P 500 made up of more than 500 stocks, the American Stock Exchange Index (AMEX), the NASDAQ Index, the Value Line Index, the Wilshire 5000 and many others. New followers of the market can be misled if they look only at the DJIA and not the "broader" markets (S&P 500, NASDAQ, Wilshire 5000, etc.) because the DJIA is composed of only 30 stocks.

Investment strategy A plan to acquire and allocate assets to include mutual funds, stocks, bonds as well as cash.

Liquidate To sell an asset.

Load fund A mutual fund that assesses a sales charge, or *load*, to purchase shares as opposed to a *no-load* fund that does not impose such a charge. In effect, the *load* reduces the amount of your investment by the amount of the sales charge each time shares are purchased.

Mutual fund A fund that pools the money collected from a number of investors and then invests those assets according to a prescribed financial objective under the management of an investment company. Mutual funds offer investors instant diversification by investing in a variety of financial opportunities, so their strategy can range from conservative to aggressive and everything in between. See expanded definition on first page of Step 7.

NASDAQ The National Association of Securities Dealers Automatic Quotation system that is used to execute trades on the OTC, over-the-counter market. Investors use the terms "bid" and "asked" price when placing trades.

Net asset value (NAV) With mutual funds this term refers to the actual market value of each share and with *no-load* funds, the offering and sale prices are one and the same, the NAV. For *load* mutual funds the sales charge is added to the NAV to produce what is referred to as the Sale Price. Investors purchase shares at the higher Sale Price and sell at the lower NAV price.

New York Stock Exchange (NYSE) The largest and oldest exchange in the United States located in New York City where a variety of financial instruments are bought and sold. See expanded definition in Step 8.

"Odd-lot" A purchase or sale in which less than 100 shares are traded. Generally, brokers assess an added commission because the transaction did not involve a "round lot."

Offering price In the case of mutual funds, the same as the "asked price."

Par value Refers to the "par" or "face" value of a particular security. Stock certificates will normally have a "par value" printed on them, and it represents the value of each share for accounting purposes.

Preferred stock A class of corporate stock that not only has a specified dividend but is given preference when dividends are distributed. Although preferred stockholders do not have voting rights in the company, they are second only to corporate debt and ahead of shareholders of common stock when it comes to distributing assets in the event the corporation is ever liquidated.

Price/Earnings ratio (PE) Also known as "the multiple." It is the ratio of the prevailing price of a stock divided by its earnings per share and expressed as a whole number. If the P/E ratio is computed with the *previous* year's earnings it is a "trailing P/E," as opposed to a "forward P/E" that is calculated using *projected* earnings.

Principal This is the actual amount of money placed in an investment and does not include any earnings that might be produced.

Quotation, or quote The standard way to convey the "bid" and "asked" prices for a given security based on the sale or purchase of a "round lot" such as 100, 200, 300 or more shares.

Redemption The sale of mutual fund shares at their net asset value (NAV).

Risk The measurable possibility that you will lose all or part of your principal.

"Round Lot" Stock trades that involve the purchase or sale in units of 100 shares.

Sales charge As related to mutual funds, a fee paid by investors to either buy or sell a fund's shares.

Security and Exchange Commission (SEC) Rule 12b-1 Permits mutual funds to assess shareholders a fee to recoup the cost of advertising and promoting the funds rather than absorb this expense themselves. The charge can range up to 1% and is computed on a fund's assets. By law this 12b-1 charge is seen in no-load mutual funds and, when present, must be disclosed by the investment company in the fund's prospectus.

Settlement date A date, five business days after the trade date, when an executed buy or sell order must be settled (paid for, if the transaction is a purchase, and securities delivered in the case of a sale).

Shareholder The owner of one or more shares of common stock in a mutual fund or a company who receives voting rights because of that ownership.

Stock split The increase in the number of shares of stock without an accompanying increase in the actual value of those shares. For example, investors who owned 50 shares of a stock trading at $10 per share have holdings worth $500. If a 2 for 1 stock split were declared, each investor would receive an additional 50 shares bringing their total number of shares to 100. Although they now have 2 shares for every 1 they originally owned, the price per share dropped to $5 so there was no net change to the value of their holdings. Stockholders eventually benefit if the lower priced shares attract new investors and push share prices upward.

Trade A transaction involving the purchase or sale of a security.

Trade date The day on which a security was actually bought or sold.

Volatility The movement of financial markets characterized by cyclic rises and falls.

"Wall Street" A collective term used to describe the huge financial area in New York City where the NYSE and AMEX are located and the home of many brokerage firms.

"When issued" (WI) Used to identify both newly issued stocks and bonds as well as stocks that have approved a split but shares have not been "issued" yet. The "wi" price reflects the reduced price at which a stock will trade after the split.

X or XD The symbol displayed in financial publications to identify those stocks that are trading *ex-dividend*, or without a dividend.

Yield The return on an investment. In the case of stocks, the yield is presented as a percentage (%) of the stock prices, so a stock with a $1.00 dividend that is trading at $10 per share has a yield of 10%.

INDEX